Making the New Europe

European Unity and the Second World War

Edited by M.L. Smith and Peter M.R. Stirk

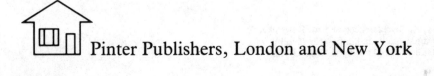 Pinter Publishers, London and New York

© M.L. Smith and Peter M.R. Stirk, 1990

First published in Great Britain in 1990 by
Pinter Publishers Limited
25 Floral Street, London WC2E 9DS and PO Box 197, Irvington, New York 10533

ISBN 0-86187-777-2

British Library Cataloguing in Publication Data

A CIP catalogue record for this book is available from the British Library

Library of Congress Cataloging-in-Publication Data

A CIP record for this book is available from the Library of Congress.

Typeset by Florencetype Ltd, Kewstoke, Avon
Printed and bound in Great Britain by
Biddles of Guildford and King's Lynn

Contents

List of contributors   vi

Acknowledgements   vii

1 Introduction: European unity and the Second World War
M.L. Smith   1

2 The prospects for the German domination of Europe
in the era of the world wars
W.H. Roobol   18

3 The Italian Fascist New Order in Europe
P.J. Morgan   27

4 The anti-Bolshevik crusade and Europe
M.L. Smith   46

5 Anti-Americanism in National Socialist propaganda
during the Second World War
Peter M.R. Stirk   66

6 The integration of Czechoslovakia in the economic
system of Nazi Germany
V. Průcha   87

7 Making the new Netherlands: ideas about renewal in Dutch
politics and society during the Second World War
J.C.H. Blom and W. ten Have   98

8 Shaping a new Belgium: the CEPAG—the Belgian Commission
for the Study of Post-War Problems, 1941–44
Brigitte Henau   112

9 Reality not rhetoric: Belgian-Dutch diplomacy in
Wartime London, 1940–44
Pierre-Henri Laurent   133

10 Political Catholicism, European unity and the rise
of Christian Democracy
Michael Burgess   142

11 British ideas of European unity and regional confederation
in the context of Anglo-Soviet relations, 1941–45
David Weigall   156

12 The wartime national fronts in eastern Europe: ideal
and reality
Ben Fowkes   169

13 The American challenge and the origins of the politics of growth
David Ellwood   184

Index   201

List of contributors

M.L. Smith—Head of the Department of European and Modern Dutch Studies, University of Hull.

W.H. Roobol—Professor of European Studies and History, Department of European Studies, University of Amsterdam.

P.J. Morgan—Lecturer in European Studies, Department of European and Modern Dutch Studies, University of Hull.

Peter M.R. Stirk—Lecturer, Department of Humanities, Teesside Polytechnic.

V. Průcha—Director of Research, Prague School of Economics.

J.C.H. Blom—Professor of Modern History and Dean of the Faculty, University of Amsterdam.

W. ten Have—Lecturer in Modern European History, Department of History, University of Amsterdam.

Brigitte Henau—Research Assistant, Catholic University of Leuven.

Pierre-Henri Laurent—Professor and Chair of History, Department of History, Tufts University.

Michael Burgess—Senior Lecturer in Politics, Faculty of Social Sciences, Plymouth Polytechnic.

David Weigall—Senior Lecturer, School of History, Anglia Higher Education College.

Ben Fowkes—Principal Lecturer, School of History, Polytechnic of North London.

David Ellwood—Professor of History, Department of History, University of Bologna.

Acknowledgements

It is a pleasant duty to record that the research project, *European Unity in Context* to which this volume of essays is one contribution, was funded by a substantial grant from the Leverhulme Trust. As well as providing for a full-time Research Fellow the grant enabled three conferences to be held at the University of Hull. Help towards the travelling expenses of some overseas delegates was also given by the British Council. The Editors wish to acknowledge the financial support of the European Educational Research Trust and the Ferens Education Trust in the preparation of the manuscript of this volume.

A particular recognition is due to Professor R.N. Berki of the Department of European and Modern Dutch Studies of the University of Hull for initially defining and then carrying through to fruition the idea of a project on the historical problematic of European unity. Finally, the work of Jacky Peters, Secretary of the Department in ensuring the smooth administration of the conferences not only contributed to the well-being of the delegates but helped make that environment in which creative and serious discussion could happily take place. Our thanks.

MLS
PMRS

1 Introduction: European unity and the Second World War

M.L. Smith

The essays collected in this book represent a selection of the papers given to a conference entitled *Making the New Europe? The Problem of European Unity and the Second World War*, held at the University of Hull in September 1988. This conference was the second of a three-part project—*European Unity in Context*—inquiring into the roots and historical development of European unity since the end of the First World War. It brought together scholars from eastern and western Europe, as well as North America, who were prepared to respond to the question: how far might our understanding of the possibilities and meaning of the unity of Europe be enlarged by identifying the nature of the integrative forces at work precisely during those years when the Continent was as violently divided as at any time in its modern history?

To ask such a question at all faced participants with a paradox. No one was, or could be, unaware that at that moment Europe was commemorating the Munich Agreement, under whose terms one of its peoples had been left to the predatory fury and destructive ideology of a neighbour. To consider the theme of unity at the time of such an anniversary risked seeming perverse, even indecent for, from the perspective of international collective action, the Munich Agreement surely stood as the low point of the inter-war period. It was at Munich that 'might' seemed to be recognised as the superior means to order European affairs. It was Munich which rendered it almost certain that Europeans would go to war or, if not, would inhabit a Continent surrendered to the dicatators.

Nor (or so it seemed in the autumn of 1988) were the prospects of the commemorations to come any less dismal in respect of what they would reveal about the foundations of the unity of Europe. Historians asked to respond to the public urge to invest anniversaries with significance are unlikely to find anything to say about unity as it was manifested in the 7 years following Munich except in negative terms. This is not necessarily because

1

the terms 'war' and 'unity' seem to be mutually exclusive as applied to the reality of the Second World War. In fact, this apparently obvious point is not self-evident: much has been made, after all, of the extent to which the roots of the European Community lie both in Franco-German reconciliation and in the integrative thinking that emerged in western Europe during and as a result of the experience of the war. The obstacles to positive evaluation have different origins. They are seated largely in the nature of the war, more distantly in its consequences. In relation to its nature the historian must assess a conflict whose features were, and remain, unprecedented in the recent European past. These were years in which Europe saw (to list only the salient features): the dismemberment of states and the subjection of their populations, often under conditions of extreme brutality and terror; the plunder and dissipation of much of the Continent's wealth and material resources; the destruction of its cities; above all, the murder of 50 million of its people, many as the result of the conscious application of a policy of genocide. In the face of this reality the years 1938–45, far from naturally encouraging visions of integration and unity, might most accurately be seen—in Michael Howard's phrase cited by one of the contributors to this volume—as the 'unmaking of Europe'.[1] So too, that phrase, insofar as it obliquely refers to the divisions and distrust that followed on the peace and most notably the emergence of oppositional superpowers with Europe as their field of conflict, would seem to confirm the difficulty for the historian of interpreting the war years in terms of their contribution to patterns of renewed unity. In short, it is not clear that they have anything to tell us on this theme unless it is to provide a negative and admonitory model of division, disorder and disunity.

Such a judgement would seem to be reinforced only from the more advantageous, and certainly more breathtaking, perspective of the events in Europe in the year following the conference. If the cold war really did 'end' in 1989 then so did the last threatening legacy of the Second World War. There is nothing new, of course, in acknowledging the war as a prelude to the patterns of European development in the half-century after 1945. (Although care is needed not to prejudge the rigidity of the arrangements in eastern and central Europe in the first 2 years of the peace). The point remains, nonetheless, that the end of the war is generally accepted as having provided the basic script for the subsequent unities, as much as the divisions, of Europe. It helped determine the form taken by western European integration as well as the nature of Soviet domination in the east. In this respect, therefore, the recent fall of dictators and dictatorial regimes, the loosening— even abandonment—of the Soviet Union's stranglehold over developments in eastern Europe and the waning attraction of communism as an integrative force in both east and west, the reassessment of America's role in Europe and, most central of all, the reopening of the question of a united Germany, prove the durability of the consequences of the war. A new chapter may have opened in the history of European integration and that demands that we recognise how much the war and its effects held this process back.

If this is the case, where does it leave the question of what we might learn that is new about the nature of European unity from the war itself? If we confine ourselves to what might seem an obvious starting position, namely the centrality of the history of the war years to the process of understanding how and why Europe came to be divided in precisely the way that it was, we remain to a degree prisoners of a teleology. From the perspective of European unity the risk of this conventional approach is that the significance of the history of the war lies in large part in what it brought, or prevented from being brought, into being. The approach has in many respects been a fruitful one. What it cannot and has not been able to do is give adequate weight to the patterns of the war years themselves, that is, to incorporate the negative and defeated visions into the whole European experience and to accept that the full post-war history of European unity is as much that of what was rejected and why as that of what was constructed.

Before examining this proposition further it is necessary to point out that any approach to the history of the war has two specific complications. First, there is the exceptional nature of the years 1939–45 to the generations who have followed. The history of all periods, especially violent ones, is in some sense exceptional, but these years are ones which are dominated by the particular phenomenon of Nazism and its policy of rationally applied mass murder. The recognition of this fact has been, and remains, inescapable for succeeding generations. It has fixed a tendency to treat the war years as standing apart, to be best understood in terms of a pathological growth within the body of Europe. Such a reaction is neither surprising nor illegitimate in view of the horrors perpetrated by the Nazis and their attempt to subjugate the whole of Europe. It has been further bolstered by the natural, even imperative, desire to establish a moral distance between the two worlds either side of 1945. In this respect the urge to define boundaries that are clearly marked good and bad as a basis on which to separate the Nazi and the post-war periods has encouraged the war years to be cordoned off, thus limiting and even pre-empting what can be said.

This is most obvious in respect of writing the history of those who to some extent agreed and collaborated with Nazism. It is no less so in the way that it has shaped judgements about the nature of the practice of European unity enforced during the war. What is at issue here is the moral requirement to preserve a sense of the particular and perverted character of the Third *Reich* and, consequently, of the enormity of what was done in its name. This introduces the second, related, complication in the approach to the war. For, above all, the aberrant behaviour of the Third *Reich* has meant that the starting point for evaluating modern German history has been one of responsibility for crimes. 'Fifty years after the outbreak of World War Two is it time to forgive the *Germans?*' is the rhetorical first sentence of the most recent attempt to summarise the arguments about the place of guilt in the interpretation of the German past.[2] At the heart of the matter lies the question of the relationship between Nazi history and the course of German history. That the two have been treated as inseparable since 1945 is, in the view of the present writer, inevitable and correct. Those historians who in the past few years have demanded that Nazism be relativised and who, like Michael Stürmer, have argued that the conflation of Nazi acts with more fundamental German necessities have hindered our proper understanding of deeper European problems, minimise—one might even say trivialise—the Europe-wide reality of the Third *Reich*.[3] What has driven the so-called *Historikerstreit* (Historians' Dispute) which has been so acrimoniously conducted in Germany since 1986 is precisely that the manner in which Germany attempted to create a unity of Europe is not finally separable from the question of the nature of its source.

The inescapability of the judgement that it was Nazi realities which were imposed during the course of the war returns us to the problem of how this experience might be incorporated in a wider view of European unity. If, as was suggested earlier, the patterns of European unity for the next half century were determined by the end of the war, it is plain that what was constructed was in large measure conceived in conscious opposition both to Nazism and to the recurrence of any alternative hegemonic aspiration of one state over the Continent. The form of reconstruction on which future unity was premised was motivated, therefore, by the need to express in new social and political arrangements the antithesis of the years that had just so violently disunited Europe. In part this came out, from the side of the western powers, as the determination to do away with the traditional basis of the authoritarian state. It is clear that this rejection served a number of immediately convenient purposes, not the least of which was the opposition to communist movements which were deemed to be supported and controlled by an expansionist Soviet Union. The alternative to both the attempted hegemony of the Third *Reich* and the putative one of the Stalinist Soviet state was, then, to seek the formation of a kind of new non-communist international.

Such an alternative construction, however, needed underpinnings. These eventually took a global shape with the articulation of the dual, American-led, strategy of Marshall Aid and the Truman 'Doctrine'. But in 1945 itself the urgent requirement was the more modest, if crucial, one of providing stable arrangements for, and in, European societies as the precondition for their positive and peaceful future relations. The shape of these rapidly became clear. Order and justice, it was agreed, would be restored through a managed and planned capitalism operating within the framework of pluralist democracy. Above all, these foundations were expected to provide stability. But as Charles Maier, one of the most acute commentators on this period of European reconstruction, has observed: 'Efforts at stabilisation have naturally followed periods in which the issues subject to politics . . . have tempestuously expanded. Stabilisation means closing an agenda.'[4] For Maier, part of this abandoned agenda was the acceptance that a radical and broadly-based political discourse could help in the construction of a new European society. This, in his analysis, was sacrificed to the social conditions conducive to achieving widespread material prosperity. Such a priority was rooted, of course, in American interests in and plans for Europe. Nonetheless, it was not necessarily inconsistent with the consensus that had emerged within Europe itself in the closing stages of the conflict. This consensus, articulated largely in terms of accepting Keynesean economic principles, supported by the application of neo-corporatist structures, formed the bedrock of post-war welfarism. As such it met the two goals of rejecting the social and economic forms which the Nazis had tried to impose and of defining the conditions from which stability must follow.

The agenda was 'closed' in another sense. If the war marked the start of a new chapter it also ended a period of argument in European history which stretched further back than the war years alone. Nazism had represented one solution to the search for order after 1918 or, more especially, 1929. That Europe eventually went to war testified not only to the Nazis' appropriation of German expansionist aims but equally to the depth of the division between the remedies for economic depression and social injustice advanced in the inter-war period. The war was the one decisive, perhaps inevitable, way of settling the argument, but precisely for this reason the vitality of the argument ended with it. In 1945, the last thing that those who were searching to create a new Europe were prepared to do was to look for historical patterns of social harmony in the ideas or practice of those they had just defeated. This is not to say that no correlation was made between mass unemployment in the 1930s and the rise to power of the Nazis. On the contrary, in 1945, and for many years thereafter, this was regarded as having been the main factor in creating their initial support. But there was no possibility of bringing back into public discussion any of the various proposals for a new economic order that had been advanced alongside Fascist solutions before the War. These, too, by the very fact of inhabiting a world of which Nazism was also a part, were discredited.[5] What the post-war definition of a stable Europe had to stress instead was the newness of its vision. It was argued that the defeat of Fascism opened the way to the permanent absence of the conditions which had given rise to it. The instrument of stability, therefore, would not be drawn from the past. Rather it would be the liberalism of abundance. Such a concept was the more attractive because abundance in the material sense so obviously contrasted with the misery and poverty both of the war years and of the decade before. The nature of the urge to set new conditions for European stability meant distancing the prescriptions offered in 1945 from their antecedent polemic in the 1930s. This also meant that it was equally hard to take account of the issues raised in the war and, in some respects, by the war. For if, as was suggested above, Nazism was itself one answer to the impasse of the liberal economic system, the form in which its answer was given was that of conquest and oppression. For this reason the experience of the war years, when these features had been most in evidence, could be seen only as a distorted one.

This returns us to the problem that motivates a collection of essays whose sub-title is the theme of European unity during the Second World War. That is, to identify the possibility of broadening the basis on which these years are approached, returning them fully to the mainstream of the European experience. This does not mean forgetting the moral dimension outlined earlier, nor does it entail, as one conservative German historian, Andreas Hillgruber, has demanded, that we 'empathise', for instance, with the soldiers of the *Wehrmacht* in their struggle in 1944–45 to hold back the Red Army from overrunning Western Europe, thereby making of Nazism a positive force in the battle for European unity.[6] One set of conventions does not need to be changed for another.

The task is at once more simple and more daunting. It is to recognise that the Nazi attempt to shape the destiny of Europe was, in however perverted and unstable a manifestation, a form of European unity. This was obviously so in the geopolitical sense, inasmuch as the Nazi imperium at its furthest reach in 1942, stretching from the Atlantic coast to the Russian steppe, took in the realm of ancient Christendom. It was no less so at the level of ideology. Under cover of the justification that the revived German nation had a right to impose its own new-found will on others, the idea—conceded in 1815 and consummated by the settlement of 1919—that the sovereign nation state must be the basic building block of the European house, was effectively, if brutally, dismantled. In its place Nazism offered itself to Europe as a paradigm of the shaping force of a society which had superseded conflict. Thus, the attack on the Soviet Union and the desire to drive communism from the Continent were proposed not as German strategic goals but as the necessary conditions for the creation of a European society: a 'New Order' within which the constituent parts of Europe, freed from the civil war within and between themselves, would find their true common interests.

The idea that such claims could provide elements of a common experience in Europe came largely from the context in which they were made. First, there was the physical fact of territorial conquest. By the summer of 1940,

Nazi domination of the Continent appeared likely to survive for a very long time, a judgement reinforced by the successes of the following year. This needs to be acknowledged, otherwise neither the nature of the response that occupation provoked nor the terms in which the Nazis presented their ideas of unity can be properly understood. Discussion about the future shape of Europe—by which is meant also its political and social form, as well as the economic links within it—had to take account of the obvious, if regrettable, fact of the probable long term influence of the Nazis on its development. This is not to say that the vast majority of people in each of the Nazi occupied areas of Europe welcomed their invaders (though this is less true in the case of some parts of Europe—the Ukraine or Croatia for example—where populations felt oppressed by other dominant states and for whom, therefore, the Nazi redrawing of European boundaries promised some opportunities). It was more that the accomplished fact of defeat produced a resigned expectation of a common future under Nazi direction. Thus, even those most hostile to the pretensions of Nazism were led to take its influence seriously, simply because it seemed that nothing could be done to counter this. The pressure to accept the inevitable was not lessened even though it was increasingly clear that the arguments initially put forward about a New European Order were at best a parodic statement of the contours of unity, at worst the cynical manipulation of the widespread desire for peace and the peaceful settlement of a conflict which the Nazis themselves had willed. In this respect, few illusions were possible, for the rhetoric of cooperation was daily contradicted by the openly expressed contempt with which the Nazis administered the occupied territories whose populations—even when some elements were sympathetic—were clearly subjects to be exploited rather than partners in Europe. It is not hard to agree with the view, therefore, that in practice the New Order was a sham. We should take care not to identify what was, in actuality, the administration of Europe backed by repressive force as a real expression of European unity.

Yet, at a different level of meaning it may be suggested that the New Order did offer a form of experience to which it is proper to apply the term unity. Both the concept and its partial and temporary realisation under Nazi enforcement opened a dialogue. Naturally, the mendacity of the conditions in which the New Order was said to be operating meant that this dialogue would be a hostile one. The clearest and most public expression of unity, then, was that of pure rejection. This is most easily to be seen in the articulation of resistance (and ultimately of a coherent and organised Resistance) throughout Europe. Resistance movements had as a primary objective the bringing about of the end of Nazi subjection but, increasingly, that aim demanded that they state the principles of an alternative base on which to construct a new Europe that would neither fall prey to such a force as Nazism again, nor allow those conditions to re-emerge which had given Fascism meaning in the first place. In the individual countries of Europe, resistance took on the specific forms and focus that enabled it best to build an effective counter to the claims and the presence of the occupier. Thus, in eastern Europe resistance movements in general gathered their strength from their defence of the idea that nation and national independence were the preconditions for a better society after the invader had gone; in the west, the emphasis of their opposition lay more along the axis of justice and the rights of the individual. In both cases resistance expressed a basic reaction to the effects of the occupation on particular societies. Yet, small in numbers as it was, the Resistance was a Europe-wide phenomenon, testifying to a common European rejection of Nazism—the stronger and more truly unified precisely because of its diversity of form.

To propose that the Resistance and Nazism were engaged in a dialogue might seem at first sight to be invalidated by the often violent and savage reality of their mutual relations. This would be to fail to take into account the nature of the terms in which the antagonists argued, as it were, their respective cases. These were that Europe could, and should, have a unity. It is true that the New Order was the device by means of which the Nazis presented the permanence of their dominance: the shape and nature of the new Europe exactly conformed to the manner of its construction and of how it was to be maintained in being. But this permanence was itself founded on promoting an interpretation that the New Order exemplified the lasting form of the unity of Europe. For the Resistance and for all those who would not accept the truth of this proposition (let alone the brutal context of its realisation) the starting point for rejection could not be couched in smaller terms than those claimed by the Nazis. Thus, the question of what constituted European unity became the fixed point in the discussion both of the current reality and of what was needed in future if Europe, once freed from Nazism, was to remain free. What was at issue during the war years, therefore, was not the validity of the concept of a European order as such, but the inevitability or otherwise of its application under the conditions that Nazism demanded.

For this reason the New Order not only presented one, physically imposed, formulation of unity that could not be ignored, but actually necessitated the statement of alternatives. That this was so was also due to the fact that the Nazi interpretation of unity gave particular answers to questions in the recognition of the importance of which Nazism did not have a monopoly. First, and preceding all else, was the concept of order itself. Reference has already been made to the Europe-wide (as well as transatlantic) search in the 1930s for forms of social, political and economic order within states that would control and help to modify what were perceived as serious disfunctions in the operation of liberal-democratic societies. 'Order', as one author in the Netherlands writing in 1939 put it, was the key word, 'the central concept of its time', around which Europe's survival would be built.[7] This critique did not stop with the outbreak of the war, not was the centrality of the search for order superseded by its partial appropriation by the Nazis. It would be truer to say that the very manner in which the notion was expressed during these years—namely the disorder of European war—made its re-expression and redefinition the more urgent. Second, within the common broad framework of the principle of order, was the question of the economic re-ordering of the Continent for, inherent in the idea of the New Order, was a recognition of the concept of the necessity for economic integration on a European scale. The New Order as it was applied derived its own shape from the wish of the Nazis to extend the practice of autarky—on which they considered their success to have been built—from the level of nation to that of Europe. Built into its application, then, was the unequal relationship between the *Reich* heartland of Europe and the areas designated as dependent or satellite. This, in itself, may be said to have offered a distorted and invalid model of integration. So too, did the requirements, imposed by the nature of its organisation, that the subject territories should serve primarily (and ultimately, exclusively) the demands of the German war effort. Nonetheless, even within these constraints and even more, because of them, the New Order at once continued ideas about European integration and presented a challenge to them. Its very operation opened for discussion the form and nature of economic interrelation, whether in terms of defining regional links and affinities (the boundaries of the *Reich* being the expression of one such grouping) or in respect of the question of the functional interdependence of individual economies within the European whole. Above all, by asserting that economic integration was achievable, the New Order pointed the way to the idea that Europe's problems would be solved once it regarded itself as a unified trading bloc, setting the terms of its own relations with the rest of the world.

The claims made for the New Order, first, that it brought order to Europe at the level of politics, society and economy and second, that it was the instrument of European integration and autonomy, provided a major conceptual challenge to its opponents during the war years. These claims, both in their detailed application and in the way in which they shaped alternative views, form the themes to which the essays collected in this book provide a commentary.

As their starting point it is perhaps not surprising that there should stand the presence and problem of Germany, for the experience of Europe during the war was unavoidably the experience of, and reaction to, a German question. The historic roots and continuities of the drive by Germany to domination in Europe are rehearsed in the opening essay by W. Roobol on Germany in the era of the World Wars. He asks us to consider the proposition that the Second World War was, in part, caused by the impatience of Hitler to pursue the risks of German expansion in Europe to their end; contrasting this with what the quieter methods of Stresemann might have achieved in search of the same goal. Behind the lightness of touch of Roobol's counter-factual history lie some fundamental points about the relation between Germany and European unity. First, there is the question of the inevitability of Germany's aspirations to dominate Europe. Second, his account asks whether, given the history and the weight of Germany, European unity in this period was only conceivable under her 'guidance' and, more, whether the integration of Europe to which many were drawn in the inter-war years, required accepting a hegemonic power for its realisation. To pose these questions (with their supplementary: 'if not Germany, then who?') ensures that we do not too narrowly associate the outbreak and development of the war (and in particular the attack on the Soviet Union) with goals that are exclusively Nazi, rather than with decisions which are capable of properly being regarded as such. Indeed, Roobol insists that the Nazis did not have a distinct idea of Europe beyond what can also be ascribed to their predecessors among German statesmen. Nonetheless, as we are reminded, the way in which Germany tried during the war and by means of war to achieve her goals is not finally separable from the ideology of her rulers of the time. The idea that Germany both could be, and might have been, the motor force of European unity and, further, that only under her hegemony could Europe achieve this unity takes us unto defining the nature of that unity. But it has always to be tempered by an understanding of the force of the ideological drive that mobilised German traditional and national aspirations after 1933. Because it was Hitler who set the timetable, any resulting unity of Europe would have had to be a coerced one.

The ways in which such coercion was justified provides the focus of the next four essays. If the Nazis' aim was to achieve unchallenged supremacy in Europe in the face of opposition they were, naturally, unwilling to proclaim this as their public position. As the war intensified its demands and dangers, it was crucial for stability at home and for the external cooperation necessary to help implement their hegemonic plans that the gap between the reality of disunity and the rhetoric of a European unity assured by German victory should be disguised. This gap, so central to the actual operation of Nazi domination, led to the need to articulate a number of what might be called 'shaping myths', within whose parameters the New Order was defined. Three such are identified by the essays in this volume. These were:

1. That a new Europe would come into being only by the defeat of communism.

2. That Europe must maintain and develop its own values and culture distinct from those of the United States.
3. That prosperity would be ensured by the realisation of a *Grossraumwirtschaft*, or large area of economic cooperation.

All three prescriptions set German control as the precondition for their achievement.

The apparently most obvious myth—that of the shaping power of Fascism itself—according to the argument of P.J. Morgan's essay, lay outside the scope of Nazism. That this should be so indicates the real distance that there was between the claims that some put forward in the inter-war years for a generic Fascism as the force of renewal in Europe and the reality of the exercise of Nazi power on the Continent. Mussolini's Italy, as the progenitor of its own Fascist 'New Order', had developed a neo-Mazzinian vision of a community of European nations based on the notion of a 'new man' and a changed consciousness. This ideal, created largely to cover up the bombastic fraud of the Italian corporatist state, had appealed widely in Europe before the war. Morgan makes clear, however, that the dream of counteracting German domination by offering the 'fascistisation' of European politics and society was never attainable: Nazi hegemonic demands were in fact not compatible with a collaboration at the level of ideology. As Nazi Germany's treatment of her closest ally shows, therefore, the myth of the triumph of Fascism did not extend to accepting Italy as anything other than a subordinate in the task of constructing European unity.

Anti-communism presented no such difficulties for the Nazis. Its use as a device to maintain the subordination necessary for Nazi success both in Germany and in occupied western Europe provides the argument for M.L. Smith's study. Anti-communism had already proved to be a strong rallying point across Europe in the inter-war period, not least because of the developing power of Stalinist Russia. The Nazis relied, then, on an existing current of opinion that saw the spread of communism as incompatible with European peace. How deeply embedded was this fear of the disintegrative force of communism into which the Nazis tapped, is shown by the fact that the association of the danger of Soviet expansion and of internal communist disorder in western Europe, did not disappear with the end of the war but was built into a new interpretation of the need for European unity. Smith demonstrates, however, the particular functional use to which the Nazis put this theme, presenting themselves as the guardians of European values and civilisation as an aid to their plunder and suppression of European societies.

That this kind of myth was indistinguishable from opportunistic propaganda is not in question, although we should not necessarily take this to mean that it failed to find a receptive audience. But, as Peter Stirk argues in his essay on the use of anti-Americanism during the war, its value is in deepening our understanding of the reality of Nazi occupation policies and, consequently, of the claims to be creating European unity that sustained them. The need to define unity in terms of what it was not, or of what most threatened its achievement, also tells us a great deal about the difficulty that the Nazis had in finding a positive image for their New Order. This 'vacuity' of vision had, in Stirk's view, an important effect both during the war and after its end, in shaping perceptions; most notably an ambivalence with regard to the construction of European unity that depended on American 'imperialism'. If the analysis of Nazi propaganda gives, as Stirk believes, an insight into the 'perceptual' world to which Europeans were exposed by Nazi manipulation, V. Průcha, by contrast, emphasises that, in the economic sphere at least, the propaganda for the New Order was backed by a harsh and evident reality of exploitation that the war only worsened rather than initiated. His case study of the subjugation of the Czech and Slovak lands confirms the view that the concept of *Grossraumwirtschaft* was, in practice, interpreted purely as servicing a process of Germanisation. Průcha's evidence is overwhelming: the New Order in this part of Europe, continuing as it did pre-war German capital infiltration and other forms of intimidatory economic action, could never have extended into the European economic community, based on mutual trust, which it claimed to be preparing for. He too, testifies to the influence (in this case wholly negative) of this myth of economic integration in holding back alternative forms of cooperation on a transnational scale after the war.

If the Nazis sought to utilise the power of these negative and repressive myths, their very sterility as props for the New Order encouraged the emergence of more positive alternative visions. Inevitably, given that the reality of the Nazi unity of Europe was, in practice, the ruthless separation of its constituent parts from one another, the first formulations of new thinking tended to be at the level of individual countries. In many countries the occupation, despite its obviously unwelcome nature, produced what J.C.H. Blom and W. ten Have identify in their essay as a surge of energy and the widely-felt need for reflection and taking stock. Nowhere were the questions about the future shape of European societies more closely examined than in the Low Countries. Tolerant, firmly European, yet at the same time riven with internal divisions through religious and linguistic conflict, the Low Countries offered a microcosm both of the range of problems and of the potential that had characterised pre-war Europe. For each of them in their different way the occupation was seen as providing an opportunity to develop structures—particularly those that might address problems of economic management—better than those which had operated before the war and which had, by their nature, shared in the general European failure to prevent the war. In the Netherlands the opportunity was perceived as that of a chance to make a decisive break with the discredited social, political and economic arrangements of the past decade. As Blom and ten Have reveal, this urge was expressed independently of the question of whether or not the Germans would win the war. In this respect the occupation acted as a catalyst for processes of thought that were already there. The war, therefore, was a starting point for changes that were in part delineated during the occupation and put forward at the Liberation, but which perhaps only bore fruit some 20 years later.

This determination to build a better world also motivated the Belgians and was equally a result of the meeting between pre-war tendencies of thought and the reality of Nazi invasion. If the shape of renewal in the Netherlands was primarily articulated by groups who had stayed in the country and who took advantage of the temporary political vacuum to press radical ideas of change, in Belgium the equivalent driving force came from those who were in exile in London. This difference partly reflected the fact that politics within Belgium itself were still active and distorted, first by the presence of the King and, second by the question of Flemish separatism with which the Germans were apparently in sympathy. In any case it was the government-in-exile which took the initiative for reform through the creation of a Commission for the Study of Post-War Problems, which was charged with preparing the most precise plans possible for new structures of social and economic life. As in the Netherlands, the starting point was an agreement that the war signalled the moment of decisive break with the legitimacy of the whole pre-war system. As a consequence the time was right to consider thoroughgoing reforms. What Brigitte Henau's examination of the archives of the Commission provides is detailed evidence about the shaping of the means by which reforms were to be realised. In one sense the consensus that the Commission arrived at, advocating a middle road between the extremes of liberalism and state intervention, continued a process (most notably that which had found expression in the Labour Plan of 1934) which the war may be seen as having interrupted. In this respect the Commission's conclusions were intensely inward in their preoccupation, but in another respect, as Henau's look into the period later in the 1940s suggests, the commitment of the Commission to the principles of social justice and of the right of the individual to work were also part of a wider and widely-shared European vision. This vision had its origins in the rejection of Nazism and the impetus of occupation. It also drew much of its strength from the forcing-house of discussion in London. The effect of this environment in fostering cooperation and forward thinking is the theme of Pierre-Henri Laurent's essay on the *rapprochement* between the Belgian and Dutch governments-in-exile. What Laurent provides is a commentary on the formation of the post-war Benelux arrangement. London provided a context in which traditional suspicions could be overcome and lessons about the weakness of those European relations that had helped create the defeats of 1940 could be learned. Each of the future partners agreed that the future of Europe depended on overcoming the economic separatism that had prevailed before the war. What the exile provided was a 'realist' perspective in which they agreed, on returning to their countries, to limit themselves to doing what together lay in their power and competence. In Laurent's argument, it was this decision not to await the construction of the more extensive arrangements on which European stability would depend in the future that was itself a decisive component in the emergence of successful post-war integration.

A different integrative focus is presented by the development during the war in many countries of western Europe of Christian Democracy which, as Michael Burgess emphasises, represented the broadest statement of the movement toward federalism. Of course, the Catholic Church had always played an interventionist role in Europe, although in the 1930s this had seemed increasingly equivocal in the face of Nazism and authoritarian tendencies. What provided the impetus for a renewed moral basis for politics was the obvious excesses of the Nazi occupations. Everywhere the experience of the Resistance breathed life into a practical, shared determination that European society as a whole must be reformed on the basis of democracy, justice and the value of the individual. In this respect the Resistance itself, in its very *modus operandi* of small, equal and self-governing units, provided not only a model for societies but, as was increasingly argued within Christian Democrat circles, the form of a new European order.

The rise of Christian Democracy received much of its initial impetus from its advocacy of a path that was opposed to Fascism but was also, emphatically, not communist. For those (predominantly Catholics) who made up the personal network in which federalist thinking developed, the Soviet Union began, from quite early in the war, to be seen as the greatest future threat to their goals. That this should be so, even while the Resistance was so implacably engaged in its fight against Nazism and the principles of the New Order, reveals how decisively the war was felt to have shifted the potential distribution of power in Europe toward the Soviet Union. This appreciation of the new status that her efforts in the war had conferred on the Soviet Union and her system, as well as the realisation of the inevitable power over eastern Europe that would follow her defeat of Germany, gave an urgency to plans for new forms of post-war European cooperation. It was Germany's eastward drive in search of hegemony that had brought the Soviet Union *volens nolens*, into the war; and, as the agreement to accept her as an ally proved, the West acknowledged that the Soviet contribution was vital to the final elimination of the German menace. But where did that leave Europe? For the advocacy of new federative structures in eastern and central Europe to counterbalance the effect of the removal of the German presence was, as David Weigall points out in his essay on regional confederation, as unacceptable to the newly confident Soviet Union as it had been to Stalin in 1930. So too, the exponents of European union were faced with the choice between placating a necessary ally by dropping all such proposals, and their belief that union in various forms was the only guarantee of Europe's independence and peaceful development after the war. The propensity of Churchill, in particular, to think in terms of regional confederation (albeit under British leadership) was sacrificed to the wishes of the two emergent superpowers (for on this issue the Soviets and Americans had a common view) who favoured instead a balance of power by means of defined spheres of interest. That such a concession was made when so much appeared to be running in favour of European unity opened the way to the inevitable denouement of subsequent division.

What the fate of the proposals for European federation revealed, then, was that the definition of Europe's destiny lay increasingly in hands other than her own. Moreover, by acceding to the influence of the Soviet Union over eastern Europe the West, *ipso facto*, determined the form of its own renewal and that of Europe as a whole. The price of victory over the German New Order was to be the incorporation of two new and competing hegemonic impetuses. Their nature is delineated in the final two essays by Ben Fowkes and David Ellwood. It was clear as early as the Teheran Conference in 1943 that the United States and the Soviet Union, while agreeing in effect to block the development of any type of continental union independent of themselves, had already begun to give shape to their own plans. In eastern Europe these manifested themselves in the increasingly overt influence of Moscow on national movements through the agency of its client Communist parties. At the moment of the invasion of the Soviet Union by Germany, Stalin had accepted the formation in eastern Europe of broad 'National Fronts' as the best means to coordinate a successful struggle against Nazism. For these Fronts, victory over Hitler was only a first stage. It would also lead to the re-establishment of their national identities on a democratic base. As Fowkes shows, however, by 1944 the decision had been made in Moscow systematically to narrow the political composition of the groups who would take power after the War and to place them under communist control. The articulation of this process in the idea of a new anti-bourgeois people's democracy sealed the fate of the national coalitions and, with them (until the recent events in eastern Europe), the hope of creating revitalised and integrated democratic and socialist societies. It was this march of 'Leftism' to which the United States reacted even though she had acceded to the Soviet Union's right to a preponderant influence over developments in eastern Europe. The form in which this influence was expressed made an American counter-involvement inevitable because, if the United States had agreed to spheres of influence as conducive to stability, there was no question, in her interpretation, of this resulting in the economic autarky of part of Europe. Communist expansion therefore threatened the achievement of prosperity and economic growth without which the peace would be fragile. The threat necessitated, and would be met by, a commitment to freedom of trade within Europe and, as importantly, between America and Europe. This stake on the economic base of reconstruction was made, as Ellwood argues in his essay on the origins of the idea of growth, almost without thought for how it might be applied, let alone accepted, by Europeans themselves. Although it was just this commitment to abundance that was eventually to prove such a durable rallying point in the West it could not disguise the fact that it also formed the dividing line in the post-war fate of European unity.

In 1936 a group of writers and intellectuals gathered at the Abbey of Pontigny near Paris to consider how Europe might survive and be transformed by the dangers that were now so evident on the horizon. One of the group, Georges Matisse, invited his colleagues to consider the idea of a single unifying force:

> Let us imagine the worst in the simplistic, even improbable, form of a *single* nation conquering all others. Let us imagine Europe conquered by Germany. Well, I suggest that a Germany extended thus over the whole of Europe would no longer be the Germany that we know and which we subconsciously represent to ourselves when we think of her in such a transformed world. *This would be Europe* under a different name; a unified Europe. Or rather, it would be neither the Europe of today, nor the Germany of today, but something else: the European confederation of the *future*.[8]

The essays collected in this volume would suggest that this hope was, in one respect, naïve. The Nazi New Order was incapable of providing any unity to Europe other than one based on force and nihilism. In another respect it points, however, to a profound lesson offered by the war. Europe's search for unity will only end when it ceases to be made under the idea of domination — of whatever form — and finds its roots in that pluralism and tolerance which Nazism failed to extinguish. The dialogue that the war called into being about Europe's future has been a long one. Now as it takes, perhaps, a new turn, our understanding of its origins and nature is more vital than ever.

Notes

1. Michael Howard, 'War in the Making and Unmaking of Europe', in *The Causes of War and Other Essays* (London, Temple Smith, 1983), pp. 151–68.

2. Richard J. Evans, *In Hitler's Shadow. West German Historians and the Attempt to Escape from the Nazi Past* (London, Tauris, 1989), p. vii (my italics). Evans provides an excellent critique of the *Historikerstreit*. See also Ian Kershaw, *The Nazi Dictatorship. Problems and Perspectives of Interpretation* (2nd ed., London, Arnold, 1989), pp. 150–191.
3. See Richard J. Evans, *In Hitler's Shadow*, op. cit., pp. 103–4.
4. Charles S. Maier, *In Search of Stability, Explorations in Historical Political Economy* (Cambridge, Cambridge University Press, 1987), p. 263.
5. M.L. Smith, 'Ideas for a New Order in France, Britain and the Low Countries in the 1930s', in Peter M.R. Stirk (ed.), *European Unity in Context. The Interwar Period* (London, Pinter, 1989), pp. 149–69.
6. Cited in Kershaw, *The Nazi Dictatorship*, op. cit., p. 179.
7. J.A.A. van Doorn, 'Anatomie van de interventiestaat', in J.W. de Beus (ed.), *De Interventiestaat. Tradities-ervaringen-reacties* (Meppel, Boom, 1984), pp. 16–17.
8. *Entretiens sur les Sciences de l'Homme. Un essai collectif de Coordination. Document No. 1* (Paris, Centre d'Etude des Problèmes Humains, 1937), p. 102.

2 The prospects for the German domination of Europe in the era of the world wars

W.H. Roobol

The trouble with historians is that they hardly ever seem able to agree on even the most basic assumptions of their craft. Take, for instance, two such eminent British historians as James Joll and Paul Kennedy. On the one hand Joll stresses that, 'the precise form in which changes occur is determined by the actions of individuals', while on the other hand Kennedy maintains 'that to understand the course of world politics, it is necessary to focus attention upon the material and long term elements rather than the vagaries of personality or the week by week shifts of diplomacy and politics'.[1] Although both historians are of course much too sophisticated not to mitigate their statements, which are at first sight rather apodictic, their perspectives remain so divergent that the conscientious reader is somewhat baffled. He is inclined to lament with one of Aldous Huxley's heroes that 'existence is always one damned thing after another . . . The criterion of reality is its intrinsic irrelevance'.[2] As an introduction to the following comments on the prospects of German domination in the interwar period, this indication of historiographical differences will have to suffice.

From whatever perspective one looks at European history in the nineteenth and twentieth centuries, whether one supposes it to be a broad stream on which the politics of the individual is nothing but volatile foam or whether one considers the acts of individuals as the essence of all history, one of the most striking features is that there has always been, and still is, a German question. It might be added that the historiography of the German problem has been most acutely marked by the contending claim of our two divergent perspectives. Yet the hard core of the German question is relatively simple to express: the assembling of all people speaking a German tongue in one state would have led, on the one hand, to the destruction of several political entities and, on the other hand, to the creation of such a strong power centre in the heart of continental Europe that, as a kind of natural force, it would

18

have acquired some form of dominance. Whether this dominance would have been purely economic or political and military was less certain. In either case while many a German liked the idea other Europeans were not particularly charmed by it.

The outward appearance of the question, however, has changed fundamentally over the years. Somewhat broadly summarising the development of the German question one could say that between 1815 and 1870 the problem consisted of how to fill the power vacuum in what is usually referred to as Central or East-Central Europe. From 1870 to 1945 the question was how to establish or how to avoid German domination, depending on the point of view of the observer. After 1945 the question, to reunite or not to reunite, soon appeared to be of purely symbolic importance or at most a sentimental residue which was of little significance to the practical issues of the day. Recent events of course have transformed abruptly the situation and placed the question firmly back on the political agenda. Underlying the different manifestations of the German question is the clash between *Gleichgewicht* and *Hegemonie*, balance of power and hegemony.[3] A third (idealistic) concept, the idea of European unification on a voluntary basis, which as an idea reaches back into the Middle Ages, only began to play a part in real politics in the late 1920s.

As an initial approach to the prospects of German domination I would like to suggest the viewpoint of a perspicacious individual who, on the eve of the First World War, had at his disposal all the relevant facts and figures which have now been compiled so diligently by Kennedy in his great study, *The Rise and Fall of the Great Powers*. Had such a person tried to conjure up the contours of the European political landscape for 50 or so years to come he might easily have jumped to the conclusion that German economic domination in continental Europe or perhaps even political domination and European unity under the guidance of Germany, was almost inevitable. The absolute and relative rise of Germany after the unification of the early 1870s was unmistakable. The increase in population, the accumulation of capital, the rise of industrial output and defence spending had been conspicuous. The quest for *Weltmacht* in one way or another, whether seen as a dream of world power or as an awareness that national unity and solidarity could only be attained by foreign ventures, became the pivot around which a great deal of German political thinking revolved.

It is true that the Germans were not entirely confident. Certain developments in Russia, especially after Stolypin had tried with some success to get the bear moving again, made German statesmen a bit nervous. Postponing an inevitable war, they argued, could be dangerous. Indeed this nervousness, if not one of the main causes of the First World War, had much to do with the timing of the first attempt at the 'unmaking of Europe by means of war', as Michael Howard has put it.[4]

The same perspicacious person in the mid-1920s, grown older and certainly sadder, would have felt some doubt about his own farsightedness a decade before. At that time Europe had not yet fully recovered from the ravages and dislocation of war and instead of Germany it was France who seemed to be calling the tune. Nevertheless there were already a few indications that the balance had tipped once again in Germany's favour. Germany had lost the war but, despite stubborn attempts by Poincaré and Clemenceau to keep her small, weak and toothless, she survived as a great power. At least one historian, S.A. Shuker, considers the adoption of the Dawes plan in 1924 as the end of French predominance in Europe.[5]

Two statesmen, the Frenchman Aristide Briand and the German Gustav Stresemann, were well aware of this fact. They drew conclusions which can be considered to be embedded in the traditions of their respective countries. Both were ardent nationalists who regarded Europe more or less as the playground for their peoples. At the same time they did not like the idea of turning this playground into a slaughterhouse again, if only because they feared the final destruction of their own countries. Whatever their motives may have been, with the treaties of Locarno a *modus vivendi* had been established which could have been the beginning of a lasting peace. In the euphoria of the spirit of Locarno, Briand was able to launch his plan to unify Europe. The plan itself was based upon Coudenhove-Kalergi's Pan-European idea, but not without significant and interesting differences. It seems that Briand initiated this new course in order to put a brake on the renewed trend towards German hegemony. It is probable that he picked up the idea of European and political unification not so much because of his intrinsic European mindedness, but because he felt that the rise of Germany could not be held in check by France alone. He also felt that the British connection, not to mention the American one, was not altogether reliable in this respect. France's new friends in East-Central Europe had enough problems of their own. Yet by entwining Germany in a broad European web she could perhaps be domesticated. Many Germans rejected his plan for precisely this reason. Stresemann did not. Stresemann was even less fired by pro-European feelings than Briand. Rather, he was inclined to embrace Briand's plan because he foresaw that in a not too distant future it might give Germany an outstanding opportunity to establish at least an economic predominance in East-Central Europe. He may also have calculated, as some German diplomats did, that the desired customs union with Austria, which had been forbidden by the Treaty of Versailles, could be attained under the cover of Briand's plan for European unity.

As we know, this first concrete proposal by a leading statesman to unite Europe on a voluntary basis, a proposal which was discussed and commented upon by all European governments, came to nothing. From the comfortable position of hindsight it is easy to ridicule the plan as wholly unrealistic and utopian, especially since there were several officials who were dismissive at the time, but this is not the way that history ought to be written. Certainly, the motives of Briand and Stresemann were not unequivocal. Despite a certain superficial general good-will the situation in the late 1920s can barely be characterised as ideal and, even in a much more favourable landscape, the road to unification often seems impassable. But perhaps a seed of understanding could have taken root. If it had the prospects for Briand's strategy might have been promising. After all, the eventual creation of the European Economic Community can be readily interpreted as a means of Franco-German reconciliation.

At least two factors, one general and one particular, prevented such an outcome. The depression after Black Thursday induced a social, economic and political climate that favoured the narrow-minded forces of nationalism in every European state. The principle of *sauve qui peut* destroyed the last vestiges of whatever European solidarity had existed, but was the particular cause the death of Stresemann in October 1929, not as fateful as the general deterioration? He had been able to recover some of the lost ground and had kept the volatile homefront in check, while at least establishing a working relationship with the French. It is worth recalling that Stresemann, born in 1878, was 2 years younger than Adenauer whose main achievements did not occur until after the Second World War. Had Stresemann lived as long as Adenauer history might have taken another course. It is perfectly plausible, if highly speculative and quite beyond proof, that a cunning statesman—and whatever else one thinks of Stresemann there is no doubt that he was cunning—might have steered Germany clear of Hitler.

However this may be, amidst ill health, old age, shortsightedness, narrow-mindedness and a host of other such factors which flourished in the morass of the Depression, the locomotive of European unity ran out of steam. Stresemann's successors managed to arrange a 'first class funeral' for Briand's plan, as they had always intended. This did not immediately enhance the international position of Germany. Where the Treaty of Versailles had failed, namely in the attempt to turn Germany into a second ranking power, the Depression nearly succeeded. Of all the European powers Germany was the hardest hit by the slump. By 1931 the prospects for German domination in Europe were slim. Even the Austro-German customs union could be blocked by not much more than a gesture from France. From the standpoint of 1931 it was difficult to conceive that within the space of 5 years France could do little other than stand by impotently in the Rhineland crisis.

Not for the last time Germany demonstrated a remarkable resilience, a resilience for which historians have yet to provide an adequate explanation. Herr Hitler has not earned his place in the history books by the sympathetic traits of his character nor by the brightness of his ideas, which have been aptly described by Golo Mann as bad literature, but for some years at least his ideology of force and hate gave the German people a sense of direction unparalleled elsewhere in Europe. Our perspicacious observer, a decade older again in 1934 and by then not only old and sad but a cynic as well, would have had some reason to think that German hegemony in Europe was again a foregone conclusion. The 'false hegemony' of Britain and France, as it has been called, had come to an end. Our observer would have found much confirmation in the behaviour of Hitler. Immediately after consolidating his power, Hitler embarked upon an elaborate armaments programme which was clearly intended to give Germany a free hand in international relations. The first goal, of course, was to sweep away the remnants of the despised Versailles Treaty. Whether or not Hitler had any clear ideas about the next step, domination over Europe, and beyond, it was not a vision alien to his megalomania.

At this point it is perhaps useful to return to a question broached so provocatively by A.J.P. Taylor in 1961, in his still deservedly famous book, *The Origins of the Second World War*.[6] Many scholars have since debated the various aspects of the book, sometimes not without displays of malice. Taylor did indeed err when he himself claimed that his views now belong to the body of conventional wisdom. Yet it is remarkable that some of his contentions have, after the initial furious rejections, been more or less accepted.[7]

The question I have in mind here is that of the continuity of Hitler's foreign policy objectives with those of Stresemann. Taylor, with all his inconsistencies, premeditated or otherwise, rightly stresses the continental outlook of both men. German hegemony in Europe had to be attained by way of dominance in Central and Eastern Europe. Taylor allows that there were differences of method, but does not see these as having the same significance as the fundamental agreement of goals and broad strategy. But is he right in making this assumption? The final result of a certain policy is determined not so much by the general outlook or the broad strategy of the politician as by the means employed. Herein lies the rub. What Germany could have attained in the long run by the quiet and seemingly conciliatory methods of Stresemann was spoiled by the hectic impatience of Hitler. In the words of one of the fiercest critics of Taylor's book, Norman Rich: 'It was the policy of a fanatic ideologue who ignored sober calculations of national interest in order to put his manic ideas into practice.'[8]

Initially, however, Hitler's methods too seemed to be characterised by patience: 'He never made a frontal attack on a prepared position', writes Taylor, 'at least never until his judgement had been corrupted by easy victories'.[9] The result was that in 1936 the prospects of German hegemony in Europe looked bright indeed. The Saarland had been incorporated into the

Reich. The remilitarisation of the Rhineland testified to the weakness of Germany and the continuing aloofness of Britain. Henceforth the Treaties of Versailles and Locarno were obsolete. Revision had turned into abolition. For a short while, many an aloof observer concluded that European domination would simply fall into Germany's lap. Gradual and peaceful penetration of East-Central Europe by German capital, followed first by economic and afterwards by more or less stringent political domination, seemed perfectly possible and to some extent even desirable. Had not Keynes, in 1919, underlined the necessity of a unified economic region in this part of Europe? Did not Neville Chamberlain consider Eastern European affairs from a position of aloofness bordering on indifference?

Farsighted politicians could even have used the idea of European unity in order to justify the strengthening of the German position. Some fascists and Nazis did play with the idea of Europe, partly as an esoteric myth, partly as a promising instrument for the attainment or consolidation of European unity under their aegis. Yet neither moderate statesmen like Briand and Stresemann nor radical fanatics like Goebbels and Hitler succeeded in mobilising this idea for their ends. Goebbels was a late convert to the idea of Europe and Hitler barred discussion of a European Charter even in 1943.

If we accept Taylor's suggestion that Hitler's judgement was corrupted by easy victories, the question remains, when exactly did this corruption take place and, more importantly, at what point had his actions become so bold that a general war could no longer be avoided? The latter point is crucial because, as Kennedy and other historians have shown, the Third *Reich* was not strong enough to fight a prolonged war against several great powers at the same time. The so-called Hossbach memorandum of November 1937 may not have been the blueprint for action that it is sometimes taken to be. Yet it is clear from this curious document that by that time Hitler had abandoned any interest in the gradual extension of German domination, if he had ever believed in this cautious approach: 'Germany's problem could only be solved by means of force and this was never without attendant risk.'[10] The remarkable thing is not that a man like Hitler could cherish such ideas but that a host of relatively sophisticated people chose to ignore them or shared them.

The year 1937 was the highpoint for the prospects of German domination, economic and political, of Europe. Subsequent events were double-edged, apparently confirming the onward march of German power but at the same time alerting potential opponents. The *Anschluss*, although a walk-over in one sense, may be seen as the first step on a slippery slope and the Munich agreement of September 1938 appears to be a point of no return on Germany's road to destruction. From then on the *Drang nach Osten* seems to have led inescapably to general war. Chamberlain may have been prepared to make further concessions, even after the final destruction of Czechoslovakia in the spring of 1939, but the British public had grown tired of appeasement. The euphoria surrounding 'peace in our time' proved to be of short duration. Yet metaphors like 'turning point' or 'point of no return' are of doubtful utility for the historian. The structure of reality is such that at any point in history many possibilities remain open. The suggestion of a 'point of no return' may be attractive as a narrative device, but as an element of reality it is a fiction.

Although historians have contended that a 'dreadful logic' drove Germany towards 'a war for the plunder of manpower and materials'[11], it is also arguable that after Munich, and perhaps even at several later stages of the war, a Germany with or without Hitler might have considered its appetite satisfied. Clio the muse, alas for the historian but perhaps fortunately for history, knows nothing of a dreadful logic. Nor indeed did many contemporaries in the spring of 1941 who witnessed Hitler's invasion of Bulgaria, Yugoslavia and Greece. At that point Hitler dominated a larger part of Europe than even Napoleon. Europe was united to an extent never matched before or after.

Under the Molotov-Ribbentrop agreement, Germany still had a fairly intimate relationship with the Soviet Union. To be sure, the green light for Operation Barbarossa had been given, but not all Germans were convinced of the wisdom of the attack on the Soviet Union. As shrewd a man as Stalin could not fathom the stupidity of an attack on his country while Germany was engaged in a war in the west. Paradoxically, this worked to Hitler's temporary advantage. Stalin, trusting that Hitler would be wise enough to respect the order created by the Molotov-Ribbentrop agreement, had left his country so badly prepared for war that Hitler almost succeeded. And what would have happened if Japan had decided to attack the Soviet Union in the rear while Hitler's tanks were engaged in the battle for Smolensk? Hillgruber has shown how fateful the delay at Smolensk was for the Germans, a delay that probably would not have taken place if Japan had attacked.[12]

Yet there are limits to arguments for the contingency of history. The attitude of the United States suggests a different assessment. It is true that Roosevelt left the declaration of war after Pearl Harbor to Hitler, a declaration that is even more incomprehensible than the decision to attack the Soviet Union, but it is inconceivable that the United States would not have intervened at some point. Despite all its aversion to entangling alliances and the stupidity of European wars Washington could not, for its own security, tolerate German political and military domination of Europe. Indeed, the decisive step towards involvement had already been taken with the December 1940 commitment to Lend Lease. From then on Britain could no longer be defeated. In the early months of 1941 Britain was the only power that still withstood the might of German arms. Could she have been appeased as Hitler thought and wished? Even Churchill may have had some doubts about this issue. In any case, he rejoiced when Hitler launched Barbarossa and even more so when the United States entered the war. From the vantage point of hindsight Churchill concluded that henceforth 'all the rest was merely the proper application of overwhelming force', though Kennedy soberly comments on this conclusion: 'If the fate of the Axis powers was sealed after December 1941, there was little indication that they knew it.'[13] However all this may be, from early 1938 the chances of a gradual and, therefore, relatively stable accumulation of German power were diminishing. By the same token the prospects for an enduring German domination of Europe were decreasing, although her actual power can be said to have continued to grow until the defeat at Stalingrad in the winter of 1942–43.

The noble art of counterfactual history, in which I have indulged above, readily appears frivolous but it is not. In order to analyse what actually happened it is necessary to assess as precisely as possible the alternative courses of action. Only then can we come to a judgement about the relative merits of our two historians. In the years before the First World War, as well as in the mid-1930s, the prospects of German domination in Europe are not easily dismissed by pointing to the fact that this domination never material-ised. On the contrary, as Michael Howard has remarked on the First World War in his essay 'War in the Making and Unmaking of Europe', 'Without that counterweight (of the United States) the European system would have reverted to a natural German hegemony, tested almost to destruction under the strains of war'. Concerning Hitler's policies he observed, 'if Hitler had not had such boundless ambition and had not been in such a hurry to achieve them, the sheer industrial and economic power of Germany, even suffering under the burdens of defeat, even under the direction of the most moderate and reasonable of statesmen, would have brought her the unquestioned hegemony of Europe within at most a decade'.[14] For those who did not relish the prospect of German hegemony in the first decade of the century or in the 1930s, it must be an ironic and melancholy conclusion that Europe was spared this fate by the deliberate acts of those statesmen they usually and so rightfully detested.

And thus, the 'irrelevance of reality' has been such that what seemed highly probable and at some times even inevitable for the perspicacious observer with his relevant facts and figures, did not occur. With this I have come full circle. The causes of these events are—*n'en déplaise à* Paul Kennedy—not to be found in the first place in 'the material and long term elements' but rather in the 'vagaries of personality and the week to week shifts of diplomacy and politics'. Although the facts and figures unquestion-ably remain indispensable, it is for someone who wishes to understand the course of world history at least as important to study those vagaries and week to week shifts. The history of the German prospects for the domination of Europe is a good case in point.

Notes

1. James Joll, *Europe since 1870* (Harmondsworth, Penguin, 1978), p. ix; Paul Kennedy, *The Rise and Fall of the Great Powers* (New York, Random House, 1987), p. 17. In his 'Introduction' (p. xxiv), however, Kennedy refers to Hitler's folly as a determining force.
2. Aldous Huxley, *The Genius and the Goddess* (New York, Bantam, 1955), p. 1.
3. L. Dehio, *Gleichgewicht oder Hegemonie* (Krefeld, Scherpe, 1948).
4. Michael Howard, 'War in the Making and Unmaking of Europe', in *The Causes of War and other Essays* (London, Temple Smith, 1983), pp. 151–68.
5. S.A. Shuker, *The End of French Predominance in Europe. The Financial Crisis of 1924 and the Adoption of the Dawes Plan* (Chapel Hill, North Carolina, University of North Carolina Press, 1976).
6. A.J.P. Taylor, *The Origins of the Second World War* (New York, Fawcet, 1961).
7. See Gordon Martell (ed.), *The Origins of the Second World War Reconsidered. The A.J.P. Taylor Debate after Twenty-Five Years* (Boston, Allen and Unwin, 1986).
8. Norman Rich, 'Hitler's Foreign Policy', in Martell (ed.), *Origins of the Second World War Reconsidered*, op. cit., p. 124.
9. Taylor, op. cit., 2nd ed., p. 73.
10. Ibid., p. 129.
11. Kennedy, *The Rise and Fall of the Great Powers*, op. cit., p. 309, quoting Tim Mason.
12. Andreas Hillgruber, *Die Zerstörung Europas* (Berlin, Propylaen, 1988), pp. 296–309.
13. Kennedy, *The Rise and Fall of the Great Powers*, op. cit., p. 347.
14. Howard, 'War in the Making and Unmaking of Europe', op. cit., pp. 164–5.

3 The Italian Fascist New Order in Europe

P.J. Morgan

Italy's parallel or 'separate' war, a war fought alongside Germany against the same enemies, but in different theatres and for specifically Italian aims, lasted barely from June 1940 until April 1941, by which time German arms had bailed out Italy in both North Africa and the Balkans.[1] Italy then became economically and militarily reliant on Germany and, with the German invasion of the Soviet Union in June 1941, the Axis was increasingly fighting Germany's war. Italy's ability to take political initiatives within the Axis framework was severely compromised by this confirmation of where power in the Axis lay.

But even in 1940–41 when Italy apparently enjoyed some independence within the Axis, Italian Fascist official thinking about Europe was galvanised by the German victories in western Europe in the summer of 1940. Questions of a new European economic order prevailed, perhaps inevitably, given the immediacy of the Axis powers' task of organising the economies of occupied or allied countries for the continued prosecution of the war. The public statements of German Economic Minister Funk on the shape of European economic reconstruction in the summer of 1940 were constant reference points in Fascist formulations of an economic New Order.[2] This emphasises the way in which Italian thinking about Europe was often framed in response to and in reaction against German plans and the fear of German hegemony in Europe.

The various projections of an Italian Fascist New Order which emerged from government and official circles and from the regime's political, cultural and economic periodicals and publications, were in part a shadow of, in part an alternative to a Nazi New Order, reflecting that mix of emulation, fear and rivalry which characterised Italian-German relations as a whole.[3] As a nominally equal but actually weaker and subordinate ally, Fascist Italy found that its hopes both of achieving territorial ambitions and of helping to form the new Europe were simultaneously dependent on and restricted by German military and political successes. Actual German domination of Europe between 1941 and 1943 and the prolongation of the war only increased the political need felt in Fascist Italy and among other smaller Axis-aligned states that Nazi Germany should not decide the fate of Europe alone. But such German hegemony made it unlikely that the Fascist concept of the European New Order could influence Axis policy in and towards Europe. With the notable exception of anti-Jewish measures, Italian policy in its own occupied territories and 'sphere of influence', especially in the Balkans, was progressively conditioned by the linked pressures of a lengthening war and German interference. Finally, Italy's timid attempts in early 1943 to relaunch the Axis' European image, in the form of a 'Charter for Europe' which would define the place of smaller states in the New Order, foundered on the irretrievably weak position of Italy in relation to Germany.

Fascist Italy's territorial war aims to secure control of the Adriatic, the Mediterranean and an African empire were a familiar replay of inter-war revisionism. The Versailles settlement had frustrated the completion of national unification in the Adriatic, created too many small, unviable states whose abstract equality masked and made possible an Anglo-French condominium of Europe and sanctified the unjust distribution of territory and resources both in Europe and overseas.[4]

But the war was never portrayed simply in terms of territorial *realpolitik*. Some young Fascists rejected altogether a 'materialist' conception of the war. They projected it almost as a religious conflict between two irreconcilable ideals, two differing views of life, in which winning the war would open up Europe as 'revolutionary living space' for the widespread implementation of Fascism's universal principles and the creation of a new European political, social and spiritual order.[5] This kind of New Order thinking was particularly prevalent among the regime's youth and in university journals during the war[6], but it also featured strongly in all official pronouncements on the meaning of the war. As Mussolini said in his speech announcing the declaration of war in June 1940, this was a conflict between 'young and prolific nations' and 'sterile and declining' ones, a struggle between 'two centuries, two ideas'.[7] The portrayal of the war as a 'revolutionary war for social relations between peoples and among peoples'[8] fused interests and ideology: the redistribution of territory and resources would narrow the gap between nations and simultaneously allow them to reduce the gap between social classes and to create internally, a regime of social peace and justice.

That Fascism was the resolution of the crisis of the European 'system', echoed and reiterated recurring motifs of Mussolini's and official Fascism's concept of Europe and its future organisation from the years of the Depression.[9] Europe's post-First World War decline as a continent in global terms, its loss of cultural as much as economic primacy in face of the growing challenge from the United States and Japan, matched and was attributed to the decline of capitalist liberal democracy as the unifying force of Europe. The war in progress was therefore the final and conclusive act of a European civil war.[10] As the bearer of a universal *nuova civiltà* founded on the antithesis of the principles of 1789, order, hierarchy and discipline, Fascism posed as the new, regenerative source of European strength and unity. It offered a spiritual and moral transformation of Europeans corrupted by the materialism and individualism of liberal-democratic and capitalist values, to which Bolshevism was no real alternative, because in carrying a materialist civilisation to its extreme it accentuated the vices of 'demo-plutocracy'. Even those primarily concerned with a new European economic order approached it in redemptive and ethical terms and premised its permanence and success on a changed consciousness, the implanting of Fascism's spiritual and moral values, 'a new type of civiltà'. [11]

In the 1930s, the concept of 'universal fascism' suggested Fascist Italy's 'moral primacy', a 'spiritual and political conquest'[12], rather fudging the question of force. In the early years of the war, Fascist literature was more explicit: the New Order would have an hierarchy of states, with pre-eminence going to Italy and Germany as the nations which embodied the principles of a *nuova civiltà*, whose universal applicability was now confirmed and validated by Axis victories.[13] As one writer put it, the ethnic and cultural identity of small European peoples would be respected in the New Order, but they must necessarily 'conform to the principle that it is more just that the strong are strong and the weak are subordinate'.[14]

The hierarchy of states sanctioned by conquest and a superior value system was cloaked in the rhetoric of empire, again a motif which was carried over from the 1930s and figured in almost all the Fascist propaganda on the New Order.[15] Self-consciously drawing on the inspirational myth of ancient Imperial Rome, which conquered and then civilised its subject peoples, the idea of the Fascist 'empire' was used to reconcile Italian hegemony with the interests and rights of subordinate nations. The empire could masquerade as a 'community' even though blatantly—in both theory and fact—control by one state organising itself and its empire on totalitarian lines was hardly compatible with the parity and harmonious development of member nations.

Put simply, the Fascist New Order meant the 'fascistisation' of European politics and society. However elusive the 'spiritual' content of Fascism, politically and institutionally this would involve a totalitarian state governed by Fascist élites and, above all, a corporative social and economic structure. Those publicising the new European economic order insisted on this harmonisation of internal political and social systems as a prerequisite for the economic reorganisation of Europe.[16] The rhetoric, at least, of corporativism ran through all Fascist literature on the New Order, and was highlighted as the distinctive contribution of Fascism's *nuova civiltà*.

For some, particularly Bottai and his journal, *Critica Fascista*, corporativism was at the heart of Fascist 'Europeanism', as it had always been the essence of their concept of Fascism. Some of Bottai's collaborators were quite candid that corporativism in a European New Order could only operate at the level of myth, as an ideal to aspire to, in recognition of the merely formal and bureaucratic way in which corporative structures worked within Italy itself before the war. Indeed, the war was seen as a vehicle for keeping the ideal alive, as if projecting corporativism on a European level could somehow relaunch the corporations in Italy. By 1943, with the prospects of victory receding fast, Bottai was fatalistically recommending the ideal of corporativism to post-war generations as the only worthwhile legacy which would survive the defeat of Fascism.[17]

Corporativism embodied the Fascist claim to be creating a new form of international solidarity, an order which would be supranational but not federal, since that implied a union of equals, and in which individual nations might preserve their identity but not their political and economic independence. The corporative reorganisation of internal socio-economic systems was ideally portrayed as state coordination in the collective interest of self-regulating associations of producers. A corporative economy would not only rationalise and stimulate production, but also through institutionalised cooperation between hitherto competing social classes, inaugurate a regime of prosperity and social justice for all. The new European economic order, described as the 'projection of the corporative regime onto relations between nations'[18], would harmonise the interests of member states, uniting both victors and vanquished in a collaborative European 'community' framework and hence ensuring justice and peace among nations.[19] The transfer of corporative organs from internal to international relations resembled a kind of Mazzinian argument by analogy: corporations would be the basis for social unity within nations and by extension, also for unity and reconciliation between nations; a system applied nationally to bring about inter-class harmony would, when applied internationally, make for collaboration among nations.

There was more, however, to the projection of corporativism as the panacea to internal and international disunity than a logical sleight of hand. Bottai called for the inclusion in any peace treaty of an international charter of labour, inspired by Fascism's own 1927 Charter, and the preparation of an international corporative plan which would tackle, *inter alia*, questions of autarky, international economic organisations, relations between agricultural and industrial economies, raw materials and relations between the European system and the outside world.[20] The technocratic vision of long term,

Europe-wide centralised planning of corporatively organised economies recurred in other writings of economists and propagandists.[21] Some speculated on the development of existing cartelisation and clearing arrangements characterising Italian-German economic relations and those of the Axis with other countries before and during the war, as the embryos of international corporations. These cartels would represent and organise entire branches of the economies of all states and include, on an equal basis, representatives of capital and labour.[22]

This Fascist-corporative 'Europeanism' was very much a response to what was seen as the potentially dangerous consequences of German military victories. By asserting that the economic principles of the European New Order had been anticipated in Italy's prewar corporative system, Bottai was claiming an Italian Fascist ideological primacy within the Axis and contesting the German monopoly of the theme of the new Europe.[23] In similar vein, the two lengthy articles by Pacces in *Critica Fascista*[24] argued against the view of Clodius, the plenipotentiary Minister responsible for economic relations with Italy and the Balkan countries at the German Foreign Ministry, that the Axis countries were becoming fully integrated, complementary economies, which quite clearly meant relegating Italy to the position of agrarian client state. To offset in the future the acknowledged present Italian economic dependence on Germany, international cartels-cum-corporations would be the mechanisms for economic cooperation between Italy and Germany and their areas of influence. These corporations would be the meeting-places for the hammering out of joint and binding agreements on access to and exploitation of Europe's economic resources.

Corporativism, in other words, should be the cornerstone of an Axis, that is, combined Italian-German approach to the postwar international order.[25] From this perspective followed Bottai's plea that Fascist Italy urgently embark on the study and formulation of the New Order, a task which he believed Germany already had well under way. His call was echoed in other parts of the Italian government and had apparently led to the decision to coordinate such studies under the Foreign Ministry.[26] Bottai's own contribution was the launching of his wartime journal, *Primato* as the rallying point for Italian intellectual effort.[27]

This view of Axis economic planning for Europe recognised that Italy and Germany would have different regional 'zones of attraction'. Nevertheless, it still envisaged that Italy could best influence the new Europe by treating the continent and its African and Asian hinterlands as a relatively unified economic bloc whose development would be shaped by collective Axis policies.

Critica Fascista also aired an alternative scenario, which was shared by most other writers and government ministers and officials, and no less inspired by fears of German hegemony in Europe.[28] They all wanted to see the emergence of a bi-polar European economic bloc: separate, if linked, autarkic regional 'economic zones' centring on and directed by each of the Axis powers. Fascist Italy's Mediterranean zone, including the African and Middle Eastern countries of the Mediterranean basin and the hinterland to the Indian Ocean[29], would be the counterpoint to Nazi Germany's northern and central zone. These economic combinations would be formed on the basis of 'hierarchy' and 'interest'. In other words, Italy and Germany would be respectively the 'central organising nucleus'[30] of these economic zones, which would become lira and mark currency areas. The zones would integrate countries and territories which were geographically contiguous and above all, economically complementary. Zonal self-sufficiency would therefore derive from a specialisation and division of labour among member countries, each doing what it did best. This, in effect, meant rigidifying the relationship between industrialised and agricultural economies. Italy and Germany, in organising the economies of their respective zones, would be restraining the national autarkic development of individual countries in the name of a 'continental solidarity', identified primarily with the need of the industrialised Axis powers to control supplies of foodstuffs and raw materials.[31]

Trading relations between territories in the 'economic zone' would be regulated by long term economic agreements aiming at *scambi bilanciati*, the equal exchange of goods for goods, and would be facilitated by multilateral clearing arrangements. Both mechanisms were already operating in Axis-occupied territories and other countries in the Axis orbit.[32] The leading states, Italy and Germany, would represent, and act as clearing agents for, countries in their zones in economic relations with the rest of the world.

As far as possible, trade would be an exchange of products and not oiled by the flow of gold reserves. It was recognised, however, that foreign trade, especially with the United States, was one of the residual areas where gold and currency movements would still have a role as a means of exchange. The abandonment or redundancy of gold was therefore almost absolute. In part, this made a virtue of necessity, reflecting the relative paucity of the Axis' gold and currency reserves and the net outflow of gold from Europe to the United States. But the rejection of gold also had an emblematic and ideological significance in Axis economic propaganda, since it marked the transformation from the materialist, liberal capitalist economy to the totalitarian, corporatively organised economy of the European New Order. Gold was irrelevant once prices were determined not by the free market but by governments which regulated all economic activity and once trade was managed through clearing arrangements. The underlying strength of the 'fascistised' European economy and of its dominant currencies, the lira and the mark, would correspond not to the arbitrary possession of gold but to the state's political will and to the capacity and potential for labour and production. An economic order founded on the restored dignity of labour, the right and duty of labour, 'moralised' economic activity and properly subordinated economics to human and moral values.[33]

It was self-evident that wartime exigencies lay behind these formulations of integrated, regional economic areas and this was nakedly exposed even in public pronouncements on the European economic order as the war dragged on.[34] But the wartime reorganisation of European economies, geared to achieve contintental autarky, was usually portrayed as the embryonic basis of a postwar settlement, often justified from a global, intercontinental perspective. Italian writers gave much, ultimately inconclusive, attention to the United States, both feared and despised as the successor 'demo-plutocratic' power to Britain in the western hemisphere, exploiting the war and the emerging economic unity of Europe under Axis auspices to create its own pan-American economic bloc.[35]

In any case, overseas competition from rival continental trading blocs, together with the rapid modernisation of production and communications, provided a conveniently neutral and technocratic rationale for the creation of larger political and economic units in an Axis-dominated Europe. It justified the subordinate relationship of small countries to the organising power in the 'economic zone' which eroded the boundaries of the nation-state.[36] The principle of nationality, said one commentator, directly paraphrasing an article in the German press, conflicted with the economic life of modern states.[37]

The official and semi-official syntheses of the Fascist economic New Order summarised above closely followed Funk's model of a European-Mediterranean economic bloc subdivided into two independent economic zones linked by Italian-German collaboration. Some were barely disguised summaries or reworkings of German material appearing in 1940, which adopted the language and phraseology of the German proponents of *Grossraumwirtschaft*. The proposed methods of integrating countries into the Italian economic 'space' and the relationship between the leading state as the dominant industrial power and the others—primarily agricultural and raw materials producers servicing the industrial nation and absorbing its manufactures and capital investment—almost exactly replicated those of the Germanic economic order.

The derivative Italian models were reactions to a perceived German dominance in the New Order. Two separate spheres of influence in Europe, two autarkic economic blocs, were to be the guarantee of Italian power and independence in the new Europe. Fear of Germany was coupled to the muffled recognition that Italy still needed to acquire the strong economic base which would enable her to act as the organising nation in her economic zone. This explains the importance attached to colonial redistribution and access to raw materials and, especially, to Italy's continued industrial development.[38] Also Italy's own Mediterranean zone, still undeveloped economically and barely at the formative stage, would not be able to compete with an already functioning German economic area and the Italian zone itself would indeed be in danger of falling within the German orbit. This fear was exactly what Bottai expressed in his report to Mussolini in July 1940, in which he also explained his insistence that Italy should evolve an Axis New Order in collaboration with and not in isolation from Germany, so as to influence the outcome.

Some Italian Fascist formulations of the New Order, especially those envisaging a revolutionary and totalitarian 'fascistised' Europe, seem to have value only as projections of an unreal and unrealisable future, anticipating what would or should be. They remained a matter of rather vapid academic and intellectual debate in, for instance, the wartime conferences on the New Order, with little apparent relevance to the experience of the war actually being fought.[39] In a very obvious way, this is a valid observation: an Axis military victory looked increasingly uncertain after Stalingrad, making hypothetical the Axis reorganisation of Europe which had appeared not only possible but imminent in 1940–41. Fascist Italy's control of the Mediterranean was never at any point during the war sufficient to allow a political and economic reshaping of the whole area according to notions of regional autarky or an 'imperial community'. In retrospect organising a conference on 'The Idea of Europe' in November 1942, when the Allies were landing in North Africa and effectively destroying Italian pretensions to Mediterranean hegemony, seems like blowing into the wind, a futile exercise.

Most Fascist commentators, including some government ministers, on the New Order recognised that wartime conditions might require some largely provisional and expediential changes, but they also stated that the bases or premises of the postwar Europe were being laid during the war itself, and that the wartime experience was an integral stage of the process of European reconstruction under Axis auspices. Bottai, for instance, attempted to argue that the Italian Fascist New Order could be judged on the basis of facts rather than intention or propaganda, by extrapolating from the experience of Fascist control in Libya, Ethiopia and Albania before the outbreak of war and the wartime occupation regimes installed in those areas of the Balkans either annexed to or otherwise controlled by Italy.[40] Riccardi also chillingly indicated how wartime economic mechanisms introduced by the occupying power to push the costs of occupation onto defeated populations could solidify into wider and more permanent relationships within the Italian 'economic living space'.[41] Projections of the new economic order, or at least components of it, like clearing systems, sprang from operational models being tried and experienced both before and during the war.

It should be possible, then, to attempt to compare the New Order in aspiration and intention with the reality of occupation, even in the admittedly compressed time-span and often extraordinary circumstances of the war. It might become clearer how the air of unreality and fantasy clinging to Italian Fascist projections of the European New Order derives not so much from their intrinsic lack of concreteness, but from inescapable power relations within the Axis.

The Germans recognised in general terms both before and during the war that the Mediterranean area, including the Adriatic and those Balkan states gravitating towards it, Yugoslavia and Greece, was Italy's exclusive sphere of influence.[42] At all levels the Italians were anxious to translate this general division of interests in the Axis into quite precise and formal *a priori* agreements which would clearly demarcate the Italian and German positions.[43] Such reliance on formal guarantees in itself reflected Italy's awareness of her actual inferiority in respect to Germany. The Germans evaded any clear-cut definition of inter-Axis relations. In practice, they constantly interfered in Italy's 'exclusive' zone, particularly in the condominium of the Balkans, which Funk had identified in conversations with his Italian counterparts as falling in both countries' 'economic zones'.[44] The Germans ruthlessly monopolised the Balkan economies, crucial suppliers for both Axis powers in war and peace, barely disguising the subordination of Italian interests to their own with the empty formula which distinguished between Italian 'political' influence in the area and German 'economic' influence.[45]

Italy's Mediterranean hegemony could only be achieved at the expense of metropolitan and colonial France and, throughout the war, Italy's attitude to France was intransigent and unconciliatory.[46] However, even here, Axis relations with France in the war were largely determined by Germany. Mussolini was persuaded in June 1940 to accept that there could be no full satisfaction of Italian territorial claims on France until a final peace settlement by Hitler's argument that permanently alienating France at this stage would prejudice the continuation of the war against Great Britain. This was only overturned in November 1942 when the Allied landings in North Africa precipitated the full military occupation of metropolitan France, Corsica and Tunisia—a partial and shortlived enactment of what Mussolini had wanted in 1940.[47]

But it was Italian policy in the Balkans which suffered most from German competition and rivalry. Italy's occupation methods were meaningfully contrasted with those of Nazi Germany in the region and held up as distinctive traits of the Italian Fascist New Order. The 'union' with Albania in 1939 was heralded as the working model of the Fascist New Order in the Balkans, representing exactly that relationship of subordinate but associative collaboration between the leading state and the members of Italy's 'imperial community'.[48] The variations in Italy's occupation regimes seemed to make a virtue of pragmatism, but this was just the rationale that the Italian government wanted to give to its reorganisation of the former Yugoslav territories. 'We want to associate, not incorporate', said Mussolini[49], and the methods employed ranged from the satellisation of the new state of Croatia and that probably intended for the restored state of Montenegro, through the annexation of Southern Slovenia as the 'autonomous' province of Ljubljana, to the straight annexation of Dalmatia as *terra irredenta* but with a special administrative organisation for mainly Slav areas. The apparent concession of a degree of autonomy, reflecting an alleged sensitivity to local needs, levels of development and ethnic mix, was fitted in with the idea of a 'community' which would be progressively civilised by and aligned to Italy. The supposedly moderate and benign treatment of Slav populations exposed by contrast the harsh 'Germanisation' policies pursued by her ally in northern Slovenia.[50]

The ideal of 'association' was scarcely credible in reality. The Italian-Albanian union was the Italian absorption of Albania, demonstrated in the way Italy would speak for Albania in economic, foreign and military affairs, control the Albanian government both internally and externally and monopolise Albanian political life through a Fascist movement responsible to the Italian Fascist Party.[51] The rapid 'Italianisation' through 'Fascistisation' envisaged in Dalmatia was also extended to Slovenia, where the introduction of Fascist and corporative institutions contradicted almost immediately the direction apparently set by the province's autonomy statute.

But it was arguable anyway whether Italian administration of these areas was ever effective or normal, as Slav resistance to Italian rule increasingly determined the nature of occupation policy from as early as the late summer and autumn of 1941. The notion of autonomy linked to the benevolent rule of Slav peoples was kept nominally alive during a period of friction and conflict between the Italian military and civilian authorities over the response to partisan activity, but it had disappeared altogether by the summer of 1942 when the civil administration fell into line with the harsh repressive strategy of the military command. 'A head for a tooth' reprisals policy was hardly compatible with an 'autonomous' status intended to reconcile non-Italian peoples to Italian rule.[52]

The increasing unruliness of those Balkan areas under Italian control, as the Italian authorities struggled to put down partisan rebellions, was also one of the wedges for German interference in Italian occupation policy. Hitler was always concerned that continuing unrest among the Slavs of the Balkans would both encourage and facilitate Allied landings there, which would dangerously expose the southern flank of the German campaign against the Soviet Union and put at risk the most important supply areas of the war on the eastern front. The Germans became increasingly impatient at the Italian failure to maintain order in their zones and there was growing pressure on them to synchronise their methods with the repressive methods of the German armed forces in the Balkans. This meant joint military operations against all partisan bands and, in particular, an end to the Italian military's divide and rule agreements with the nationalist-Cetnik bands who were armed and equipped to fight Tito's communist partisans. Conflicts over these tactics, which were intended to economise on Italian military resources and clearly therefore reflected Italian inadequacy, practically dominated Axis relations in late 1942 and early 1943. By the spring of 1943, Mussolini had apparently been forced to swing round to the German view.[53]

A similar cycle in Axis relations was also evident in Greece where there were shifting zones of Italian and German occupation in a country acknowledged to be within the Italian orbit. The Germans contested and then conceded the Italian claim that Greek economic relations should be conducted through the Italian central clearing system and refused Italian appeals for aid during the terrible winter of 1941/42 on the grounds that Greece was exclusively an Italian sphere.[54] They then used this and other demonstrations of Italy's inability to administer Greece adequately as a lever for greater interference in Greek affairs. Italy's failure to persuade Germany to reduce Greece's crippling occupation costs marked a more general lack of any alternative to German occupation methods.[55]

These episodes show how rapidly and conclusively the pressures of war and a stronger German ally shattered the Fascist illusion of a separate and distinctive political New Order in the Balkans, directed Axis control in the area to the priorities of the German campaign in Russia and effectively made Italian occupation methods indistinguishable from those of Germany. The one important exception to the *de facto* identification of the Italian with the German New Order was racial policy. Despite German political and diplomatic pressures to induce Italy to extend anti-semitic measures of persecution and deportation to their own areas of occupation in France and the Balkans, and Mussolini's formal assurances that this was being done, Italian occupation zones were real places of refuge for both Italian Jews and those fleeing from German-inspired campaigns elsewhere.[56]

Italy made serious and concrete efforts to step up its economic activity in the Balkans so as to make good its claim to 'economic space' and contain an already considerable and expanding German economic penetration. Significantly, Italian economic expectations were linked to and dependent on direct political and military control. So in Croatia, for instance, the satellite or protectorate status apparently guaranteed in May 1941 by personal dynastic union and Italian-Croat treaties, was to be the bridgehead for Italian-led economic expansion. In common with Italian economic activity throughout the Balkan region, this centred on agricultural modernisation, mining and forestry, public works and infrastructural development. Yet by 1942 even the Italian authorities were acknowledging the dominance of German economic interests in Croatia.[57] Elsewhere, the Italian-Bulgarian economic agreements of October 1942 could apparently justify the continued projection of Bulgaria as part of the Italian Mediterranean 'economic zone', when in fact it was a functioning component of the German *Grossraumwirtschaft*.[58] As von Hassell, head of the major organisation behind the German economic drive in the Danubian and Balkan countries, observed of an aspect of Italo-German economic relations in the area, '(their) external parity would be rendered innocuous by actual German superiority',[59] a comment which would be a fitting epitaph for the Axis.

Crudely, the widening gap between Italian economic aspirations and the reality of German economic hegemony reflected the very different relative powers of attraction and penetration of the Italian and German economies. The fears on the Italian side of the consequences of Italian economic weakness had become a self-fulfilling prophecy. The prolonging of the war progressively sapped Italy's own economic resources and undermined the country's capacity to pose as the directing state of her 'economic space', leaving the field open to her rival and ally. The case of A.M.M.I., the state-owned mining enterprise, was a microcosm of the balance of forces within the Balkan 'condominium'. The creation of special joint Italian-German holding companies for the exploitation of Yugoslav mineral deposits, was proposed in the hope that this would guarantee both German recognition of Italian mining rights and the necessary injection of German technical and managerial expertise without which the Italian business could not undertake the project.[60] This situation epitomised the Italian dilemma of being actually dependent on the ally with and against whom Italy was claiming parity and equality. As was equally clear from the Italian maladministration of Yugoslavia and Greece—which led to the Italian assimilation of German methods of occupation—the imbalance of power and resources in the Axis set insurmountable limits to Italy's hopes of forging an independent role in the New Order.

In early 1943, Italian-German conflict over repression in the Balkans coincided and meshed with a wider disagreement concerning the impact of Axis occupation policies on the waging of a long war and the future shape of the European New Order. There had so far been only one joint Axis statement on war aims and the New Order. At Mussolini's instigation, this had been inserted into the communiqué issued after the talks with Hitler on the Russian front in August 1941: 'in order to give the occupied countries definite grounds for hope regarding their fate and the future of Europe'.[61] The statement itself was vague and imprecise. It declared that the Axis aimed to remove the causes of previous wars (basically a reiteration of 'revisionism') and to eliminate the threats of Bolshevism and plutocratic exploitation which would be the basis for the collaboration of European peoples. It required a considerable gloss to make much of this. As *Critica Fascista* commented, extracting what it could from the communiqué, inter-state political relations in the new Europe had still to be defined, and it was to be hoped that integration in the New Order would occur on the basis of parity and equality between nations.[62]

The Germans were clearly reluctant to issue any such statement on war aims, and the declaration's blandness mirrored this. The German attitude had, if anything, hardened by February 1943, when the Italian side, largely through the efforts of Bastianini, Under-Secretary for Foreign Affairs, again insisted on the publication of a statement on war aims after Ribbentrop's meeting with Mussolini.[63] German coolness to the declaration, which they argued was incompatible with and dangerous to the continued and necessarily more severe prosecution of the war effort, was once more reflected in a pallid, generic statement. It contained nothing of a distinctively Italian Fascist imprint on the New Order. In fact, it seemed to confirm the German view of the war. Speaking of the common resistance to 'the mortal danger of the Bolshev-isation of Europe', the declaration repeated the joint Italian and German commitment to establishing a New Order after victory which 'guarantees a secure existence to all European peoples in an atmosphere of justice and collaboration, liberated from all Jewish-plutocratic dependence, encouraged and stimulated in their activity and in the safeguarding of their mutual interests within the safe boundaries of the great European living space'.[64]

By this stage, Mussolini had recognised that there was no future for Italian Fascism outside the Axis alliance. He had for some time certainly been urging Hitler to make a compromise peace with Russia, if only to concentrate Axis efforts on the struggle against Great Britain in the Mediterranean; an attempt, in other words, to give some priority to the Italian war. But he disappointed the hopes of Ciano, and then Bastianini, who together with certain Axis allies, Hungary and Romania, wanted Italy to initiate a disengagement from the Axis and the war. For them, an Axis declaration on Europe which emphasised equal rights and collaboration between nations would offer an alternative to a New Order founded on German racism and hegemony and help to create the premises for a negotiated peace.[65] It was, in other words, to be a bridge to the western allies. Mussolini knew that a negotiated peace was unrealistic and unacceptable on two counts. The allies would demand capitulation and the end of Fascism in Italy, while the Germans would occupy Italy if it demanded to leave the Axis.[66]

The 'European Charter' of February 1943 was a rather pathetic postscript to Italian-German relations since 1940. It indicated not only Fascist Italy's umbilical links to Nazi Germany in the Axis, but also the former's inability to influence the shape of the European New Order, which reflected the limits of Italy's power.

Notes

1. See G. Warner, 'Politique de l'Italie à l'égard de la Grèce et de la Yugoslavie (mars 1939-octobre 1940)', in *La guerre en Méditerranée 1939–1945. Actes du Colloque International tenu a Paris du 8 au 11 avril 1969* (Paris, CNRS, 1971), p. 534.
2. See Funk's speech of 25 July 1940, in documents following M. Salewski 'National Socialist Ideas on Europe', in W. Lipgens (ed.), *Documents on the History of European Integration*, Vol. 1, *Continental Plans for European Union 1939–1945* (Berlin and New York, de Gruyter, 1985), pp. 65–71.
3. See E. Collotti, 'L'alleanza italo-tedesca 1941–1943', in G. Cherubini et al. (eds), *Storia della società italiana*, Vol 22, *La dittatura fascista* (Milan, Teti, 1983), pp. 449–508.
4. See V. Gayda, *Che cosa vuole l'Italia?* (Rome, Il Giornale d'Italia, 1940); M. Gianturco, *Lineamenti della nuova Europa* (Milan, Fratelli Bocca, 1941), chapters 4–7; extracts from M. Appelius, *Vincere*, in R. De Felice, *Autobiografia del Fascismo. Antologia di testi fascisti 1919–1945* (Bergamo, Minerva Italia, 1978), pp. 489–96.
5. See contributions of E. Sulis, G. Calza, N. Guglielmi, in *Nuova civiltà per la Nuova Europa* (Rome, Unione Editoriale d'Italia, 1942). The book's preface is reproduced in De Felice, *Autobiografia*, op. cit., pp. 511–16.
6. See M. Addis Saba, *Gioventù italiana del Littorio. La stampa dei giovani nella guerra fascista* (Milan, Feltrinelli, 1973)
7. See E. and D. Susmel (eds), *B. Mussolini. Opera Omnia* (Florence, La Fenice, 1951–1963) (hereafter, *OO*), Vol. 29, pp. 404–05.
8. 'Il duplice problema', *Gerarchia*, July 1940. *Gerarchia* was the regime's 'official' journal of political comment, and Mussolini contributed to many of its unsigned editorials.
9. See for instance, Mussolini's speeches and articles of 27 October 1930, *OO*, Vol. 24, p. 283; 14 November 1933, *OO*, Vol. 26, pp. 86–96; 2 January 1934, *OO*, Vol. 26, pp. 133–36; 1st November 1936, *OO*, Vol. 28, pp. 67–71; 6 October 1937, *OO*, Vol. 29, pp. 1–2. For a general discussion, see R. De Felice, *Mussolini il Duce. Gli anni del consenso, 1929–1936* (Turin, Einaudi, 1974), chapters 4–5; D. Cofrancesco, 'Ideas of the Fascist Government and Party on Europe' in W. Lipgens (ed.), *Documents*, op. cit., pp. 179–80; D. Cofrancesco 'Il mito europeo del fascismo (1939–1945)', *Storia Contemporanea*, Vol. 14, (1983), pp. 5–10.
10. See G.A. Castellani, *L'Europa nel conflitto ideale* (Milan, Corbaccio, 1938), chapters 9–10; 'Guerra rivoluzionaria', *Gerarchia*, May 1940; 'Vincere la guerra per vincere la pace', *Critica Fascista*, 15 June 1940, in the anthology, G. De Rosa and F. Malgeri (eds), *Critica Fascista 1923–1943*, Vol. 3 (S. Giovanni Valdarno, n.p., 1980), pp.1351–52.
11. See, for example, the article 'L'economia alla base della nuova civiltà europea', November 1941, by Riccardi, the Minister for Exchange and Currency, in R. Riccardi, *La collaborazione economica europea* (Rome, Ed. Italiane, 1943), p. 125;

A. De Stefani, *Sopravvivenze e programmi nell'ordine economico* (Rome, Ed. Italiane, 1942), pp. xx–xxii. De Stefani was the Minister of Finance, 1922–1925.

12. 'Verso l'Europa', *Critica Fascista*, 15 August 1930, in *Critica Fascista 1923–43*, op. cit., Vol. 2, p. 602. For a general study see M.A. Ledeen, *Universal Fascism. The Theory and Practice of the Fascist International. 1928–1936* (New York, Howard Fertig, 1972).

13. See Gianturco, *Lineamenti*, op. cit., 94–95; 'Vittoria della Rivoluzione', *Critica Fascista*, 1 July 1940, in *Critica Fascista 1923–43*, op. cit., Vol. 3, pp. 1353–54; F. Orestano, 'Nuovo ordine europeo', *Gerarchia*, January 1942.

14. G. De Matteis, *Verso l'equilibrio della Nuova Europa* (Florence, Sansoni, 1941), p. 160.

15. For a general view of the content and utility of the myth of Empire, see D. Cofrancesco, 'Appunti per un analisi del mito romano nell'ideologia fascista', *Storia Contemporanea*, Vol. 11 (1980), pp. 383–411.

16. See A. De Stefani, 'Il riordinamento e la pacificazione dell'Europa', *Rivista Italiana di Scienze Economiche*, October 1941; also translated and reproduced following Cofrancesco 'Ideas', op. cit., pp. 187–90.

17. See A. Le Grand, *Bottai e la cultura fascista* (Bari, Laterza, 1978), pp. 226–27; 'Difendere la Rivoluzione per difendere l'Italia', 15 February 1943, and 'Noi, i responsabili', 15 July 1943, in *Critica Fascista 1923–1943*, op. cit., Vol. 3, pp. 1493–95 and pp. 1514–15.

18. V. Gayda, *Profili della nuova Europa. L'economia di domani* (Rome, Il Giornale d'Italia, 1941), p. 36.

19. See 'Vincere la guerra, affermare la rivoluzione', *Gerarchia*, September 1940; F.M. Pacces, 'Appunti per servire l'idea di una Nuova Europa', *Critica Fascista*, 15 August 1940 in *Critica Fascista 1923–1943*, op. cit., Vol. 3, pp. 1361–70.

20. See Bottai's reports to Ciano and Mussolini, in July 1940, reproduced in the appendix to R. De Felice, *Mussolini il Duce. Lo stato totalitario 1936–1940* (Turin, Einaudi, 1981), pp. 920–28.

21. See for example, L. Gangemi, *Europa Nuova* (Rome, Ed. Italiane, 1941), chapter 4; Gianturco, *Lineamenti*, op. cit., chapter 8. Both writers thought this made inevitable the establishment of a European supranational political authority.

22. See for instance, F.M. Pacces, 'Appunti per servire l'idea di una Nuova Europa' *Critica Fascista*, 1 September 1940 in *Critica Fascista 1923–1943*, op. cit., Vol. 3, pp. 1370–79.

23. G. Bottai, *Contributi dell'Italia fascista al 'Nuovo Ordine'* (Rome, INCF, 1941), pp. 8–9. Bottai's lecture was interpreted as being anti-German: see diary entry for 19th November 1941 in G.B. Guerri (ed.), *Guiseppe Bottai. Diario, 1935–1944* (Milan, Rizzoli, 1982), p. 289.

24. See notes 19 and 22.

25. See also S. Panunzio, 'Consonanze economiche italo-germaniche', *Gerarchia*, January 1942.

26. Bottai's report to Mussolini, 20th July 1940, in De Felice *Mussolini il Duce. Lo stato totalitario*, op. cit., p. 928; Alfieri, Ambassador in Berlin, to Ciano, 23rd July and 1st August 1940, documents 294 and 341, *I Documenti diplomatici*

italiani (Rome, Libreria dello stato, 1952–), 9th series *1939–1943*, Vol. 5 (Hereafter, *DDI*). For Mussolini's indifferent response to Bottai's report, see entries for 12th and 13th August 1940 in *Bottai. Diario*, op. cit., pp. 221–22.

27. See 'Interventismo della cultura', *Primato*, 1 June 1940, in L. Mangoni (ed.) *Antologia di 'Primato' 1940–1943* (Bari, Laterza, 1977), pp. 56–58. Also, Le Grand, *Bottai*, op. cit., pp. 273–75, and G.B. Guerri, *Guiseppe Bottai, un fascista critico* (Milan, Feltrinelli, 1976), chapter 8.

28. C. Arena, 'Nuova Europa', *Critica Fascista*, 1 September 1940, in *Critica Fascista 1923–1943*, op. cit., Vol. 3, pp. 1382–84. Cofrancesco 'Il mito europeo', gives an excellent summary of the debates and divisions among intellectuals and economists over the continental and bi-zonal approaches to the New Order.

29. See the grandiose Mediterranean blueprint prepared by the Foreign Ministry in January 1942, reproduced in R. De Felice, 'Arabi e Medio Oriente nella strategia politica di guerra di Mussolini (1940–1943)', *Storia Contemporanea*, Vol. 17 (1986), pp. 1302–04.

30. Gayda, *Profili*, op. cit., pp. 45–46.

31. See 'Verso una nuova economia', August 1940; 'Riorganizzazione economica europea', 10 October 1940; 'Solidarietà economica europea', 31 October 1941; 'L'economia alla base della nuova civiltà Europea', November 1941; in Riccardi, *La collaborazione*, op. cit., pp. 52–57, pp. 70–75, pp. 104–08, pp. 113–14. Also, summary of Italian economic journals in late 1940, including view of Greece's role in Italy's autarkic zone, in F. Catalano, *L'economia italiana di guerra. La politica economica-finanziaria del fascismo dalla guerra d'Etiopia alla caduta del regime, 1935–1943* (Milan, INSMLI, 1969), pp. 54–55, 76–77.

32. See 'Guerra economica', May 1940; 'Il terzo fronte', April 1942, in Riccardi, *La collaborazione*, op. cit., pp. 23–31, pp. 166–67.

33. See, for example, 'La moneta-lavoro e la scomparso dell'oro', August 1940, and 'Le prospettive economiche della nuova Europa', October 1940, De Stefani, *Sopravvivenze*, op. cit., pp. 271–73, pp. 302–06; 'Riorganizzazione economica europea', 10 October 1940, 'L'economia alla base della nuova civiltà europea', November 1941, Riccardi *La collaborazione*, op. cit., pp. 73–75, p. 124; Gayda, *Profili*, op. cit., pp. 208–18.

34. See 'Collaborazione economica europea', March 1942, Riccardi, *La collaborazione*, op. cit., pp. 134–46, for the marked change of tone compared to the pronouncements of 1940–41.

35. See Gayda, *Profili*, op. cit., pp. 145–97; Gianturco, *Lineamenti*, op. cit., pp. 121–52.

36. See C. Pellizzi, 'The Idea of Europa', *Civiltà Fascista*, December 1942, translated and reproduced in Cofrancesco 'Ideas', op. cit., pp. 191–93.

37. Gangemi, *Europea Nuova*, op. cit., pp 48–49.

38. See Gayda, *Profili*, op. cit., pp. 68–77; Gianturco, *Lineamenti* op. cit., pp. 91–92; 'Collaborazione economica nel quadro della politica dell'Asse', September 1940, 'l'Europa e la sua autosufficienza', July 1942, Riccardi, *La Collaborazione*, op. cit., pp. 60–61, p. 258; Alfieri to Ciano, 1 August 1940, *DDI*, 9th series, Vol. 5, document 341; Catalano, *L'economia*, op. cit., pp. 55–57, p. 80; articles in economic journals of summer 1942, reported in E. Collotti, 'Il ruolo di

Bulgaria nel conflitto tra Italia e Germania per il nuovo ordine europeo', *Movimento di Liberazione in Italia*, Vol. 24 (1972), p. 68.

39. See summary of debates in wartime conferences, in Cofrancesco 'Il mito europeo', op. cit., pp. 15–17, 23–27.

40. Bottai *Contributi*, op. cit., pp. 12–21.

41. 'Il terzo fronte', 23 April 1942, Riccardi, *La collaborazione*, op. cit., pp. 176–85.

42. See E. Collotti, 'La politica dell'Italia nel settore danubiano-balcanico dal patto di Monaco all'armistizio italiano', in various authors *L'Italia nell'Europa danubiana durante la seconda guerra mondiale* (Milan, INSMLI, 1967), p. 31; E. Collotti, 'Il ruolo della Bulgaria', op. cit., pp. 59–61; Ciano's version of his meeting with Hitler in July 1940, in G. Ciano, *L'Europa verso la catastrofe* (Verona, Mondadori, 1948), pp. 569–70; Hitler's letter to Mussolini, 29 December 1941, in *OO*, Vol. 30, p. 231.

43. See Alfieri's reports to Ciano, 23 July, 1 August and 13 August 1940, *DDI*, 9th series, Vol. 5, documents 294, 341 and 406; German documents on Riccardi's visit to Berlin in October 1940, *Documents on German Foreign Policy 1918–1945* (London, HMSO, 1950–), Series D *1937–1945*, Vol. 11, documents no. 115, 173, and 181 (Hereafter, *DGFP*); von Hassell's summary of autumn 1940 meetings between major Italian and German businessmen, in his January 1941 report on Italian-German economic relations in South Eastern Europe, in E. Collotti and T. Sala, *Le potenze dell'Asse e la Yugoslavia. Saggi e documenti 1941–43* (Milan, Feltrinelli, 1974), pp. 107–110.

44. As reported by Alfieri to Ciano, 1 August 1940, *DDI*, 9th series, Vol. 5, document 341.

45 See Collotti, 'L'alleanza italo-tedesca'. op. cit., p. 481.

46. See H. Michel, 'Les relations franco-italiennes (de l'armistice de juin 1940 à l'armistice de septembre 1943)', in *La guerre en Méditerranée*, op. cit., pp. 485–511.

47. See Macgregor Knox, *Mussolini Unleashed, 1939–1941. Politics and Strategy in Fascist Italy's Last War* (Cambridge, CUP, 1982), pp. 125–32; F.W. Deakin, *The Brutal Friendship, Mussolini, Hitler and the Fall of Italian Fascism* (London, Weidenfeld & Nicolson, 1962), p. 72.

48. See Bottai *Contributi*, op. cit., p. 21; Ciano's January 1942 article in *Giornale d'Italia*, reported in F. Jacomini di San Savino, *La politica dell'Italia in Albania* (Bologna, Capelli, 1965), pp. 283–86.

49. Quoted in Bottai's diary for 14 May 1941, after the agreement of the Italian-Croatian treaties, in G. Bottai, *Vent'anni e un giorno* (Milan, Garzanti, 2nd ed., 1949), p. 203.

50. See T. Sala, 'Occupazione militaire e amministrazione civile nella "provincia" di Lubiana (1941–43)', in various authors, *L'Italia nell'Europa danubiana*, op. cit., p. 77.

51. See R. Lemkin, *Axis Rule in Occupied Europe* (Washington, Carnegie, 1944), pp. 99–106, 267–282. The book also gives useful information on Italian policy in its other annexed and occupied areas, as does F.P. Verna, *Yugoslavia under Italian Rule 1941–43. Civil and Military Aspects of the Italian Occupation* (unpublished Ph.D. thesis, Santa Barbara, California, 1985), particularly chapters 5, 7 and 8.

See also E.A. Radice, 'The Development of Industry', in M.C.Kaser and E.A. Radice (eds), *The Economic History of Eastern Europe 1919–1975*, Vol. 2 *Interwar Policy, the War and Reconstruction* (Oxford, Clarendon, 1986), pp. 446–47.

52. For the experience of Italian occupation of Yugoslavia, see Sala article given in note 50; T. Sala 'Fascismo e Balcani. L'occupazione della Yugoslavia', in Cherubini et al. (eds) *Storia della società italiana*, Vol. 22, op. cit., pp. 436–47; T. Sala, '1939–43. Yugoslavia "neutrale", Yugoslavia occupata', *Italia Contemporanea*, Vol. 32, (1980); T. Sala, 'Guerriglia e controguerriglia in Yugoslavia nella propaganda per le truppe occupanti italiane (1941–43), *Movimento di Liberazione in Italia*, Vol. 24 (1972); J. Vujosevic, 'L'occupation italienne', *Revue d'Histoire de la Deuxième Guerre Mondiale*, Vol. 22 (1972).

53. See Deakin, *The Brutal Friendship*, op. cit., p. 99, pp. 183–84, 189–90, 194–204; the exchange of letters between Hitler and Mussolini, February-May 1943, in V. Zincone (ed.), *Hitler and Mussolini. Lettere e documenti* (Milan, Rizzoli, 1946), pp. 128–59.

54. Clodius' reports of 17 and 20 June 1941, in *DGFP*, series D, Vol. 12, documents no. 641 and 652.

55. See Collotti, 'la politica', op. cit., p. 60; Lemkin, *Axis Rule*, op. cit., p. 185; entries for 6, 8, 10 October 1942, in G. Ciano, *Diario, 1939–1943* (Milan, Rizzoli, 1946), pp. 653–55.

56. See L. Poliakov and J. Sabille, *Jews under the Italian Occupation* (Paris, 1955); M. Michaelis, *Mussolini and the Jews. German-Italian Relations and the Jewish Question in Italy, 1922–1945* (Oxford, Clarendon, 1978), chapter 9; G. Bastianini, *Uomini. Cose. Fatti. Memorie di un ambasciatore* (Milan, Vitigliano, 1959), pp. 54–55, pp. 86–88, p. 152, p. 259, p. 277.

57. See, for example, the document, 'La penetrazione economica tedesca in Croazia in un rapporto della Legazione di Zagabria', July 1942, in Collotti and Sala, *Le potenze dell'Asse*, op. cit., pp. 177–80.

58. See Collotti, 'Il ruolo della Bulgaria', op. cit., pp. 86–90.

59. U. von Hassell, 'L'Europa sudorientale. Osservazioni per la composizione degli interessi economici tedeschi e italiani', January 1941, in Collotti and Sala, *Le potenze dell'Asse*, op. cit., p. 119.

60. See the document, 'Gli interessi dell'Italia nelle zone minerarie jugoslave in un rapporto dell'AMMI', April 1941, in Collotti and Sala *Le potenze dell' Asse*, op. cit., pp. 169–72.

61. See D. Alfieri, *Dictators Face to Face* (London, Elek, 1954), p. 157; F. Anfuso *Roma. Berlino. Salò (1936–1945)* (Milan, Garzanti, 1950), chapter 8.

62. 'Coscienza Europea', *Critica Fascista*, 15 September 1941, in *Critica Fascista 1923–43*, op. cit., Vol. 3, pp. 1431–32.

63. See Bastianini, *Uomini*, op. cit., pp. 84–85; Deakin, *The Brutal Friendship*, op. cit., p. 199.

64. Quoted in Collotti, 'La politica dell'Italia', op. cit., p. 63.

65. See Bastianini, *Uomini*, op. cit., pp. 90–91, p. 95, pp. 113–14, pp. 322–25; R. Bova Scoppa, *Colloqui con due dittatori* (Rome, Ruffolo, 2nd ed., 1949), particularly chapters 3, 7–12; Anfuso *Roma*, op. cit., chapter 9; L. Simoni, *Berlin. Ambassade d'Italie 1939–1943* (Paris, Laffont, 1947), pp. 397–404;

Deakin, *The Brutal Friendship*, op. cit., 137–42, pp. 244–70, pp. 303–15; Collotti, 'l'alleanza italo-tedesca', op. cit., pp. 500–08.
66. See Alfieri, *Dictators*, p. op. cit., 246.

4 The anti-Bolshevik Crusade and Europe

M.L. Smith

In June 1941, as her armies struck out across the eastern frontier of the *Reich* in a 'pre-emptive' attack on the Soviet Union, Nazi Germany declared to the world as a whole that she was leading a European crusade against Bolshevism. With a deliberate, if eclectic historicism, Nazi propaganda suggested that the Panzer brigades speeding across the Russian steppe were the Teutonic knights of the twentieth century; their mission the defence of western and European civilisation against the barbarians from the East. Communiqués, speeches and newspaper articles throughout Nazi-occupied Europe called for volunteers to enlist as foot-soldiers in this fifth crusade. Germany, so it was claimed, was directing a 'vast operation of European policing' to which all the constituent nations of Europe should contribute. Indeed, before the campaign was a month old, German troops were reported as about to be joined in their work by armies composed of men from every corner of the Continent. The years from 1917 and, in particular, the previous 2 years of European history in which Germany had begun the defence of the west had been only a prelude to the final settling of accounts with the enemy of decency, culture, civilisation, religion and peace.[1]

The practical outcome of this appeal to mount a crusade is not easy to judge. From Nazi-occupied western Europe between the Autumn of 1941 and early 1944 it is estimated that about 50,000 men volunteered for, or were cajoled into, active service in specially created Danish, Dutch, Flemish, French, Nordic and Walloon formations in German uniform on the eastern front. The impact of their presence must, therefore, be judged to have been insignificant; the very fact of their participation a stance so exceptional as to be easily ignored after the war.[2] Against this verdict, however, it must be acknowledged that, as the war progressed, the Wehrmacht did fight increasingly alongside those 'legions' for which German propaganda had called. A Spanish Legion, 200,000 Italians and a greater number of Hungarian and

46

Rumanian troops entered the eastern war as allies of Germany—their participation a tribute to Nazi diplomatic effort and coercive power. They, together with Baltic and Ukrainian forces and even a Russian army led by the former Red Army General Vlasov, provided increasingly international and, it must be admitted, increasingly necessary support for German arms in the last 2 years of the war.[3]

There is, then, a case to be made that from 1942 to 1944 the war in the East already possessed the dimensions of a systemic conflict that in part foreshadowed the fundamental divisions of the post-war world. For a very great, perhaps unprecedented, number of Europeans the notion of the supreme danger represented by Bolshevism and the necessity of eradicating it by force was given an everyday, pervasive, reality. By means of an incessant propaganda, the harsh conditions of life under occupation and the forced economic contribution that the Nazis imposed on their conquered and satellite territories, were justified in terms of the aid they brought to the campaign against Bolshevism. More, the very definition of what would make a healthy Continent was put forward as lying not simply in Europe's capacity to bring about the defeat of the Soviet Union (a defeat, of course, that became ever more remote after the battle of Stalingrad) but in its ability, in so doing, to challenge communism as a cohesive and compelling ideology. In this way, as the present essay will try to show, anti-Bolshevism was presented as the fundamental point of European unity; the depth of commitment to its cause as synonymous with the identity and the future existence of Europe.

Hostility to Marxism and, especially, to its contemporary appropriation to the interests of the Soviet Union pervaded pre-war European politics; and it will be suggested below that this history played a central role during the war in providing the Nazis with a certain broad base of intellectual support for their vision of Europe. Nonetheless, it is important to recognise that the acts that led to the outbreak of the Second World War and to its eventual and primary impetus (in German eyes) against the Soviet Union were in some sense the result of the particular functional link that existed between Nazism and anti-Bolshevism. Firstly, it is not difficult to see its functionality to the Nazi drive to achieve state power in Germany. The rhetoric of virulent and sustained attacks on communism as an ideology as well as on the German Communist Party as a Soviet surrogate, together with the Nazi claim to be able to supersede a politics based on class conflict, drew to them the elements of political and social support that proved crucial to their success in 1933. Anti-Bolshevism in this wide sense provided a rallying point for those groups, disparate in origin but united in their fear of national disorder and personal decline into poverty and proletarianisation, which formed such an essential component of the Nazi vote. The second element of functionality attached to arguments concerning Germany's international position. The

Nazis' geopolitical perspective that emphasised the adjustment of boundaries in the east drew to their support many in nationalist and conservative circles who were resentful, humiliated and unreconciled to the settlement after the First World War and to what they regarded as its deliberate exclusion of Germany from the centre of European politics. To them, the Nazi emphasis on restoring Germany's position and vital influence in eastern and central Europe was made credible in large part by virtue of its attack on the League of Nations which was portrayed as the oppressive vehicle for French malice. But equally attractive was the Nazi vision that portrayed the Soviet Union as the real beneficiary of Versailles inasmuch as the Treaty had provided the opportunity for Soviet expansionism. The overthrow of Versailles, therefore, would represent not only the freeing of Germany from its shackles but was the essential condition to halt the achievement of Soviet hegemony in eastern Europe which was every bit as destructive of the German future as the terms imposed in 1919.

Anti-Bolshevism, whether in the form of a counter to the ideological claims of Marxism or in the service of justifying the revision of the Treaty of Versailles played a vital role, therefore, in creating a climate of political and social opinion favourable to the rise to power of the Nazis and in the direction that the use of that power was to take. But in accepting that this was the case it is important not to underplay the broader ideological dimension that anti-Bolshevism possessed for the Nazis. The very success of the anti-Soviet rhetoric employed by them in arousing an aggressive and revanchist nationalism has made it tempting to see Hitler's strategies toward the east as following in large measure a line of continuity with historic and traditional German goals. In this analysis the Nazis believed simply that they had learned from the mistakes of the Second *Reich* to the extent that they could create the conditions for a decisive *Drang nach Osten*.[4]

There were, of course, elements of congruity and continuity of geopolitical assessment between the two *Reichs*, but these ought not to be allowed to obscure the distinct ideological thrust of the Nazis' strategy toward the Soviet Union. Hitler accepted, just as Bethmann-Hollweg had done earlier, that the vital achievement of economic autarky supposed that Germany had to dominate east and central Europe—had, therefore, to enter into the Russian sphere of influence. But Hitler held, first, that German (and consequently, Nazi) interests could not be satisfied except by the physical destruction of the Soviet Union, together with the elimination elsewhere in Europe of the ideology which it had used since 1917 to sustain itself in being. Second, and most distinctively, for Hitler the war in the east when it came was to be far more than the means to acquire *Lebensraum*—a space for colonisation and food supply. The battle with the Soviet Union and with Bolshevism would provide the testing, the *raison d'être*, of National Socialism itself. In Hitler's world picture not only did the survival of Nazism depend on the absolute defeat of Bolshevism by means of the annihilation of its centre in the Soviet Union, but even more, the Nazi regime itself derived its legitimacy from how well it could prepare German (and ultimately European) society for that struggle. In short, at the heart of Nazism lay a teleology and it is this that most distinguished Hitler from his German 'statesman' predecessors. It was this that shaped his policy and allowed that flexibility and ruthlessness in international affairs that so disconcerted his opponents. So too, this teleology provided the drive by which the Nazi state organised itself both politically and economically so that it would be capable of waging—and winning—the war that was always in view, first in the west, because of the refusal of Britain to be separated from her alliance with France and then, on the basis of the victories of May and June 1940, with the real enemy in the east.

If, for the Nazi leadership, their system would justify its creation by how far National Socialism could be seen in practice to supersede communism, the means to realise this imperative were not straightforward. Ultimately, arms and large-scale rearmament were necessary as the basic instrument to back any scheme to make a New European Order. Only if she were able to produce arms in quantity and within a reorganised and controlled economy would Germany be able to reshape the political contours of Europe with any confidence of success.[5] Thus, Nazi society had as far as possible to be made to attain a level of preparedness sufficient, first, to drive a fatal rift in the potential coalition of powers which her aggressive intentions might bring into being and, second, to fight the decisive war against the Soviet Union. However, the conditions of Nazi state power that put war, and particularly a conflict in the east, to the top of the agenda were not propitious to carrying through such preparations. For the Nazis may be said, *a priori*, to have come to power in a divided society; divisions which both the ideological character-istics and the operational structure of the regime served to perpetuate rather than heal. Once in power, therefore, the Nazis faced a circular dilemma. Their ideologically driven desire to promote rapid rearmament, if it were pursued with the vigour that they believed to be required, would damage their ability to create those other necessary conditions of social well-being and political stability on which to sustain the proper preparation for war. Moreover, those conditions—full employment, extended welfare and cultural provisions and the replacement of the 'sterile' politics of class conflict by the class and national harmony expressed in the concept of *Volksgemein-schaft*—were themselves at the very heart of any claim that the Nazis could make to be able to forge a new social construct that was superior to the Socialism practised in the Soviet Union striven for in the West and upon which the demand that the German population accept the burden of war was premised.

Yet if Nazism faced a dilemma about means and ends, Hitler's brinksmanship in the 3 years that followed the reoccupation of the Rhineland did nothing to resolve it. On the contrary the increased threat of war that his policies evoked made the domestic consensus that would enable Germany to realise her expansionist plans both more urgent and less plausible. And it was here that the device of anti-Bolshevism entered a second phase of its role in supporting Nazi claims—at one and the same time defining clearly the enemy against which all the resources of the nation were to be mobilised and providing the justification for the methods of the régime and the imposed structures of Nazi society.

Two indications of the form in which this anti-Bolshevik rhetoric was displayed can be given.[6] First, there was a somewhat crude denunciatory device by which life in the Soviet Union was portrayed as the antithesis of that in the new Germany. The ethos of the Five Year Plans with their forced movement of populations, the destruction of the village roots of Russia and the example of coerced, dehumanised, Stakhanovite labour norms were all brought forward regularly to serve as indicators of the systemic defects of communism in the land where it had been given full rein. This form of propaganda was not, as the scale of the Stalinist terror in the late 1930s leaked out, without plausibility or, therefore, a receptive audience. In any case it sought in a simple, but effective, manner to legitimise the transformational dynamic of the Nazi 'revolution' that had brought about economic recovery without recourse to Soviet methods. Second, and more extensive in focus, the link was made between disorder—initially in the Weimar Republic and then in the democracies as a whole—and the presence of powerful and ambitious Communist parties. These, it was suggested, were part of an international coalition that sought to strangle Germany and reduce her once more to dependent poverty. As evidence the experience of the popular fronts in France and Spain provided a powerful demonology. At the heart of this picture was the argument that employment, prosperity and peace were interlinked and depended on maintaining the new Nazi order with its pride in the nation. The gains made since 1933 were threatened both from within and without. Internally, there existed an enemy in the form of the remnants of Marxist Socialists—an enemy whose tenacity and support from outside provided the justification for the Nazi apparatus of preventative control. Externally, since it was Moscow and its allies which financed and manipulated these forces of disorder, the German state had no choice but to prepare to defend itself if necessary by war. By so doing it was also defending jobs, the newly achieved quality of life and, in the end, long-term peace.

Such perspectives were the constantly repeated bases of the theme of anti-Bolshevism between 1936 and 1939 when the drive to rearm was at its height. It may be objected that such propaganda was, in terms of its likely success, a

crude instrument in that it presented a deeply unconvincing picture of
Weimar and the democracies as well as of the current international situation.
Yet the two trump cards of the Nazi regime were that domestically it had
solved (or could lay claim to have done so) the problem of unemployment
and that, internationally, it had broken Weimar's humiliating economic
subservience to the revengeful victors of 1918. It did not necessarily matter
that the jobs ensured by the rearmament and public works programmes
scarcely compensated for the accompanying loss of union and political
rights—rights which, in any case, had been severely eroded in the years
immediately before the Nazis took power. Anti-Bolshevism was intended to
play on the insecurity engendered by a fear of returning to the conditions of
the past. In other words it did not in itself create consensus, nor was it
intended to do so. Rather, as the shape of the police and terror state emerged
more openly, anti-Bolshevism acted first to provide an explanation of the new
shape of society to those who wished to hear and second as the means of
providing a rationale that would make the price of full employment acceptable
to those who were its beneficiaries.

The real danger to the fulfilment of the expansionist programme of the
regime lay, in fact, elsewhere than in the sceptical response to its economic
and social claims. The propaganda emphasis on the distinctive and positive
achievements of Nazism by comparison with the chaos in those countries that
were still suffering from the effects of the Depression was not the same as
preparing the population to fight a real war. Anti-Bolshevism was a useful
tool to help ease the way to a widespread acceptance of the first stages of
repression and rearmament. It was less apt as the basis of a case for the
rightness of fighting a war that, given Nazi goals, would have to be on a
Europe-wide scale. Massive rearmament meant depressing the real living
standards of a large section of the population and, most problematically, of
the industrial working class. If the cost of the preparation and pursuit of
Germany's international revisionism was to be an unavoidable squeeze on the
value of wages and long-term provision of services, then it is not clear that the
Nazis were politically ever in a position before the war to be confident that
this would be paid. Anti-Bolshevism was functionally useful as the support
for an integrative strategy because it focussed attention on the positive
elements of the régime and helped to justify what would otherwise be taken
as negative characteristics, but it was quite another matter to emphasise the
power and danger of world communism to such an extent that only mass
sacrifice and hardship, as the prelude to an inevitable war, would give
Germany the chance to survive at all.

This problem, which threatened to counteract the integrative utility of
anti-Bolshevism, was partially solved by recourse to the strategy of *Blitzkrieg*
—the aim of fighting only that type of campaign which involved a limited

mobilisation of resources and the minimum possible reallocation of public priorities. It was hoped by these means to achieve the goal of expansion without the disutility of a high level of social and political unrest. How conscious or coherent the strategy of *Blitzkrieg* in fact was, has been much disputed.[7] Nonetheless, it may be argued that it became actual as a consequence of the Nazi-Soviet Pact (itself a strategically apt decision to avoid a two-front war in 1939) as a result of which the limited and successive lightening campaigns against Poland, Norway, the Low Countries and France were successfully concluded. *Blitzkrieg* as it was practised was the form in which the Nazis accepted that the German population remained opposed to—and could not easily and in time be made to welcome—the costs of an expansionist war. More specifically it sought to avoid the consequences of the failure of the working class to be integrated in the nation. As such, *Blitzkrieg* and the device of anti-Bolshevism were complementary. The former was necessary to avoid exposing and putting to the test the true disunity of Nazi Germany; in itself it reflected the failure of the Nazi system actually to address the conditions of social change as it claimed to have done. The latter, while it too had its roots in a failure, was directed toward different ends. Rather than providing the means to help disguise the real purposes of Nazi policy toward Europe the utility of anti-Bolshevism lay, as has been suggested above, in creating compliance with Nazi hegemony over German society by making recognisable the disintegrative dangers of political and ideological disunity.

Such complementarity continued, however paradoxically, in the period after the signing of the Nazi-Soviet Pact, an event which otherwise might appear to have weakened the credibility of any assertion that the Soviet Union was the major threat to European peace. Moreover, the subsequent campaigns in the west that the Pact made possible tended, by the very fact of their successful outcome, to undermine the case for a further and fundamental struggle against the new ally. Further, the superiority that the Wehrmacht demonstrated in its easy victories over the democracies (it must be remembered that Britain was not expected by many observers in 1940 to be capable of continuing the fight after the fall of France) helped to validate the claims the Nazis made about their system. Above all the victories seemed to prove the vulnerability of those countries which, in Nazi propaganda, had been dependent on Soviet promises before 1939 and whose own evident inability to act as cohesive nations had been fatally weakened by the domestic effect of communist infiltration. This moral, which was not unacceptable within a *Reich* whose population was relieved by the short duration of a war whose outbreak had been so long feared, was one that could also be shared in the defeated countries. Many, particularly from the pacifist Left, were prepared to agree that it was the Soviet Union who, by her aggressive posture in Europe, had provoked—or, more subtly, not worked to prevent—the war, only to abandon its partners at the crucial moment when its bluff was called.[8]

The Nazi-Soviet Pact, therefore, had surprisingly little effect on the presentation of the theme of anti-Bolshevism during the year after its signature. The Nazis continued to point to the ever-present danger from the inherent bellicosity of the Soviet Union. To this they now added a warning as to its unreliability as a partner. This emphasis on the betrayal of the Western powers by the Soviet Union was a useful and effective arm of a foreign policy that sought to create uncertainty among the countries of central Europe. It is less clear that it had any effect in preparing the population of the *Reich* to accept and celebrate the idea of renewed war.

How far the Nazis were from convincing their own population of the real need to embark on a final conflict in the east is evidenced by the nature of the outbreak of the war with the Soviet Union when it came. It was *Blitzkrieg* written geographically large; a war that it was hoped would be waged as the previous campaigns had been with the least amount of radical change to German society. For the Nazi régime, the crossing of the Soviet border by German troops was the inevitable but risky step necessary to achieve the New European Order. For its subjects the conflict was given the stamp more of routine than of Armageddon. As one Nazi propagandist wrote in the summer of 1941, in a statement that clearly sought to normalise what was actually happening and to contain its significance: 'Germany has rid the European Continent of war.'[9] Thus, the first months of the campaign, crowned as they were with extraordinary and apparently effortless success, saw anti-Bolshevism used as little more than a celebratory commentary on the inevitable victory to come. Here Nazi propaganda was somewhat a victim of its own previous duplicity. The evidence that the war was almost a parade march east (it was easy to believe that the troops might be home for Christmas) did not, naturally, lend itself well to a parallel picture of the enemy as supremely powerful and well-prepared, nor to a convincing argument about the scale of the threat to international peace posed by the Kremlin. In a sense the very momentum of the army provided its own justification for the decision of the leadership both to prepare for and then to prosecute the war. So, while dutiful analyses of the build-up of Soviet forces on Germany's borders since 1939 in breach of the Nazi-Soviet Pact were to be found—the Baltic States, Bessarabia and Eastern Poland had all, it was claimed, been mobilised as launching pads for an attack on the *Reich*—the real thrust of such articles was generally dismissive. The language in which the enemy was described was increasingly racial and pornographic. The Soviets were savage, animalistic, degenerate, their racial type at once the cause of their aggression and of their inability to organise their own defence properly. In the face of the almost disappointing ease with which the campaign was being pursued, propagandists temporarily turned away from their previous delineation of the threat of Bolshevism and concentrated instead on describing it as a force alien to European values. This change of emphasis to evoke a spiritual distinction between the two opposing forces gave rise to extraordinarily graphic fantasies in which the public was encouraged to see the German soldier as the modern *chevalier*. Through the summer and autumn of 1941 the Nazis and their imitators in occupied western Europe vied with each other to define this distinction; often, as in this flight of invention from the pen of the Frenchman Jean Castellano, with prurient falsity:

> The Bolshevik soldier, even if it is true that he fights with an implacable tenacity, does so without that quality of heroism that gives to war its grandeur. There is an enormous difference, a true abyss, between the European and the Russian soldier. In the case of the European soldier there is, at the moment of death, a human consciousness, a memory, a divine light in his eye and in his heart a sentiment that makes his death holy. The Russian soldier dies like a beast and, dead, no longer resembles a man. I have never yet seen . . . a dead Russian with a serene countenance.[10]

Such pictures, purporting to come from the front, encouraged the idea that there was a fundamental human difference between the representatives of the two sides and thereby eased fears that the war would either be long or end in disaster. Above all, the success of the first months allowed anti-Bolshevism to be used to serve an undisguised and grandly confident ideological perspective. Bolshevism was dismissed as no longer relevant to the reordering of the Continent; together with their co-conspirators the Jews, Bolsheviks were now to be considered as beyond the pale of European civilisation.

The campaign was, however, neither a parade nor the lightening war to which the German public had been accustomed and on which the régime had, hitherto, gambled. As *Blitzkrieg* failed so German society became vulnerable to the divisive effects of Nazi war aims that the strategy had sought to avoid: first, to the effects of mass conscription for the east and the rise in the number of casualties at the front; second, to the inevitable decline in living standards the longer the war continued and the greater its material demands. Each of these consequences, in its way directed popular aspirations towards peace and helped to expose the illusory social and political consensus of before the war. It was imperative, therefore, when victory in the east did not come, that the régime redefine an integrative focus; and it was unsurprising in view of the widespread fear about the final result of the war against the Soviet Union, that this should have taken the form of a renewed and recharged anti-Bolshevism. Once again attention was directed to the negative effects of communism on German and European political life—a theme which had been largely in abeyance during 1941. The consequence of failure in the present war was indirectly posed by concentrating on the legacy of Germany's defeat in the First World War. Once more, propaganda described the mass unemployment and divisive social conflict that had characterised the 'communist' inspired Weimar governments which had reduced Germany to a condition of internal and international proletarianisation. The treatment was a familiar one. But new life was provided for what were otherwise conventional Nazi themes by a changed context. Germany was in a real war that by now was impossible to picture as anything but unprecedented in its dangers. At first the emphasis was on raising fears of another Versailles. As the war progressed this emphasis changed to describing the consequences of the physical invasion of the *Reich* by the Red Army whose soldiers, as we have seen, were already fixed in the public mind as the successors to the Tartar horde. In the war of attrition that developed on the eastern front and which voraciously consumed men and materiel, anti-Bolshevism began to derive a unifying strength from its increasing closeness to a credible reality. Above all, after the débâcle of Stalingrad in January/February 1943, the possibility of defeat — or, at least of perpetual war — meant that anti-Bolshevism narrowed its focus and, in so doing, at last provided some real linkage between regime and population in forging a national defensive unity of purpose.

The focus of anti-Bolshevism in the *Reich* had shifted by 1943, then, from being the indirect means of preparing the conditions favourable to the Nazis' war aims, to being the channel through which to marshal a common patriotism. At the very time when the usefulness of anti-Bolshevism to bolster the Nazi claim that it was able to build a superior social concept was least plausible, if not actually disfunctional, it was enabled to take on new life, justifying the régime as the only agent able to create the forces necessary to defeat the external danger. It should not be forgotten that the one serious attempt, in 1944, to overthrow Hitler and seek a compromise peace was largely inspired by the fear not only of the horrific consequences of a Russian occupation of the *Reich* but as much by the belief that, unless the western Allies themselves took on the role of a shield against the Bolsheviks, the country would be consumed as much culturally as physically.

It may be that the direction of anti-Bolshevik propaganda after Stalingrad conforms to a more general pattern of response to be found within all societies under threat of invasion. Certainly, the portrayal of Bolshevism sought to confirm fears that had been built up over a considerable period. But the shift of focus, even if it did find a more ready audience willing to accept the terms in which a new sense of national integrity was projected, still operated within the necessary condition of Nazi hegemony over German and European society. The failure of *Blitzkrieg* may be said, with some irony, to have created the possibility for the Nazis to express, and tap into, that national unity whose existence they had doubted and for whose absence the strategy had been intended to compensate. But equally, that unity itself depended on disunity and exploitation: within the *Reich* self-evidently so; outside its borders too, insofar as Germany's ability to survive the assault from the Red Army depended on the successful exploitation of resources on a Europe-wide scale. Their exploitation required first, Nazi continental hegemony and, second, the very domination by force which the population of the *Reich* was being urged to oppose in the shape of the spectre of Communist occupation. The conditions in which the unifying force of patriotism could and did operate in Nazi Germany were, therefore, founded on its necessary absence elsewhere. It was to maintain this contradiction that anti-Bolshevism in the form of the European anti-Bolshevik crusade, was designed to play a central part.

To understand the function of anti-Bolshevism in helping the suppression of western Europe by. the Nazis, some explanation is needed of the relationship between Germany and the occupied territories before the war against the Soviet Union. The conquests of 1939 and 1940 had allowed the Nazis to open up the economies of developed Europe to their use. In so doing they partially freed themselves from the constraint on their field of action that had been imposed by their need to maintain some measure of domestic acquiescence, particularly from the working-class in the *Reich*. The economies of the occupied territories were, then, in varying degrees and forms subject to immediate plunder.[11] It was they, especially in the west of Europe, which provided the consumer goods (as well as a healthy surplus on the real costs of occupation) which were essential to the design of *Blitzkrieg*. In addition they helped free the resources that enabled the Nazis to build for their campaign in the east which, precisely because it was conceived and presented in terms of a short war, demanded in its preparation a far greater commitment to production and mobilisation than could be expected of the German population. It was the success of *Blitzkrieg* which had put at the disposal of the regime those means necessary for the final assault on Bolshevism. It equally permitted the Nazis to continue to disguise the true scale of the war that they planned, a scale whose extent may be judged by the fact that even with the extensive looting of western Europe it was still necessary in late 1940 to push through the deeply unpopular measure of freezing wages and increasing prices within the *Reich*.[12]

German independence on the European economies was both well established and built into her *modus operandi* before the attack on the Soviet Union. The failure of *Blitzkrieg* in 1942 did not, therefore, create a relation so much as make its smooth operation more urgent. If the change to all-out war found German society in many respects unprepared and the regime prey to the possibility of openly expressed discontent at home, this served to make the contribution of the occupied territories more vital than ever. Régime and population in the *Reich* were, by the logic of the circumstances of Nazi rule over Europe, increasingly bound together in a complicity to exploit resources elsewhere that would provide a cushion against the true material costs of the war and further, as the war began to go wrong, ensure the basis of national security itself.

The outlines of this complicity were in fact well developed before Stalingrad. It was within the period from the end of 1941 until early 1943 that western Europe, hitherto the object of a somewhat uncoordinated if generally effective plunder, took on a more integrated importance to the *Reich's* war effort. In March 1942 Fritz Sauckel was appointed as *Reich* General Plenipotentiary for Labour with the specific brief of recruiting mass drafts of manpower from the occupied areas—in particular from countries such as France which had remained relatively untapped in this respect—for work in the *Reich*. One month earlier Albert Speer had been named as Minister for Armaments charged with rationalising production, especially the under-utilised high technology resources of western European industry. Contracts for war work, the retooling of factories, the return, in countries such as Belgium and the Netherlands to high levels of employment in the engineering and electrical sectors and the increased draining off of surplus labour from the dole queues into largely menial jobs in the *Reich*, all interacted with each other and intensified during this period.[13] The war became for the Nazis an explicitly European conflict, fought not only by a growing European army but, as importantly, by European workers and productive capacity.

To sustain this level of exploitation the Nazis combined coercion and terror with a policy of encouraging collaboration at the political and administrative level. Just as the creation of jobs and the prospect of social peace in Germany after 1933 had helped to implant the regime there, so similar factors played a powerful role in the occupied West, shattered and defenceless after the thoroughness of the defeat. The social and political desirability of a quick return to full employment did not have to be argued by the occupier alone. Even less was this so in countries like the Netherlands in which a high rate of unemployment had persisted right up to May 1940. In the second half of 1940 and throughout 1941, hopelessly trapped officials—one thinks here of the Secretaries-General in Belgium and the Netherlands, or of the civil servants of the Inspectorate of Finances in France—put their expertise and authority more or less willingly behind the urgent task of restoring economic life. It was not a very great step to move from this to accepting an ever greater volume of German orders (including those that asked for the production of components directly useful in armament manufacture) and penetration in business activity. This cooperation at the economic level often started with a certain degree of good-will. In practice it was sustained against the developing reluctance of officials to consent to too close a collaboration with the German war effort, by the coercive presence of the Nazis' collaborationist allies. Small, often miniscule, National Socialist movements and ideologically imitative groups were freely used in the first year of the occupation to stifle complaints about the extent of economic exploitation by the simple threat that the Germans might allow them to exercise power themselves.

In fact the Nazis kept these clients tantalisingly impotent, relying on the contempt in which men like Mussert or Quisling were held by their countrymen to provide a sufficient incentive for collaborators to stay loyal. As we now know, the Nazis themselves shared this contempt. They were concerned, too, that to grant real authority to such groups risked ruining the cooperation that had already been achieved. Yet, as the resources and skills of developed Europe were more and more needed to replace those swallowed by the conflict in the east and, additionally, as the strain on social relations in the *Reich* caused by this haemorrhage, as well as by the effects of the Allied bombing, began to tell, so the Nazis could not afford to alienate their obvious allies. It was essential that they widen the basis of cooperation by providing as broad a spectrum as possible of their collaborators with a role and a future within their own societies. It was to this end that anti-Bolshevism and the anti-Bolshevik crusade proved its utility in yielding a key sustaining myth to link the Nazis with their partners. For that part of the spectrum in which indigenous National Socialists were to be found, the crusade provided the Nazis with an instrument by which they could test the loyalty and commitment of their most ardent foreign supporters. Participation in this area of the German war effort became the most public sign, from France to Scandinavia, of collaboration with, in the sense of subservience to, the Nazi cause. More cynically, the crusade served as a most useful means of removing figures who were too charismatic or independently-minded to be entirely subordinate. Doriot, the leading personality of the French collaboration and Degrelle in Belgium were prominent examples of collaborators who were encouraged by the Germans in their desire to fight on the eastern front, from which their hosts hoped that they would heroically fail to return. For these people the crusade against the home of world communism expressed the main shared point of reference between themselves and the Nazis and completed the history of a drift to Fascism that had often started in Spain and the battle against the Popular Front.

But for another and more loosely defined group who were also willing to cooperate with the Nazi New Order and who did not think of themselves as Fascists, the appeal of anti-Bolshevism was more subtle. In their own estimation they were realists to the extent that they believed, albeit reluctantly and with no pleasure, in the medium-term dominance of Germany in Europe. They reacted to the fact of occupation as having some positive, if initially unlooked for, features. Chief among these was the temporary absence of conventional politics, which they saw as providing the chance to make some of those changes in their societies that had been blocked before the war. Already profoundly anti-communist, both by inclination and political history, they had in the last years of the 1930s been increasingly forced to take up a string of negative positions, among which anti-Fascism, anti-parliamentarianism and anti-capitalism tended to be the most common elements. Curiously, what the anti-Bolshevik crusade, as now proposed by the Germans, offered was the opportunity to turn these negative and oppositional formulae in a constructive direction, in two ways. First, there was a sense of the possibility of picking up once more some of that momentum lost since 1940, inasmuch as, a year after defeat, the benefits of the new Europe had transparently failed to materialise. On the contrary, the worsening of material life and the increased demands of the occupying power effectively prevented the realisation of even the first steps toward forging a new society. The outbreak of war against the Soviet Union, insofar as its vigorous prosecution would bring the chance of permanent peace to Europe would, equally, at last allow economic and social reconstruction to start. More, the destruction of Bolshevism even appeared to offer the chance eventually to end Nazi rule. Victory, by creating general conditions propitious to the development of the Continent as a whole would ultimately diminish the ability of Nazism to continue to act as the hegemonic force over Europe.

Second, and following from the above logic, the focus of anti-Bolshevism itself permitted the shape of European reconstruction to be defined. Many within the broad ranks of what may be termed the Collaboration regarded the Soviet system as imperialist in a territorial as much as an ideological sense. For them, the defeat of Germany at its hands would open the way for the Bolshevisation of the Continent. Moreover, it would halt that process of change whose prospects were encouraged by a Nazi victory, and which they believed would be neither capitalist nor Marxist in orientation. Thus, however unattractive Fascism (and especially its Nazi variant) was, Germany represented, even in her current political form, the sole committed rampart against Communist expansion. Further, and crucially to the argument, she alone incarnated the possibility (perverted as this was at present under the Nazi regime) of achieving a new kind of Socialism. Those who before the war had been attracted by the various strands of revisionism centred round Hendrik de Man or, in France, *néo-socialisme*, together with others who, whether from the starting point of syndicalism or a renewed Catholic social policy, had looked to define a different social construct, were increasingly convinced that it was Germany, through her containment of Bolshevism which held the key to the partial realisation of their ideas.[14] The crusade, therefore, was both necessary for self protection and bound to a specifically Nazi impetus. As one subsequently collaborationist Socialist in France,

L. Zoretti, had put it at the very start of the war: 'It is no use beating Hitler if the Nazi regime disappears too. Any regime seems to us preferable to the revolutionary Stalinist regime.'[15] For such analysts, anti-Bolshevism provided the bedrock of a belief that they and National Socialism were, in this one respect, pushing toward the same ends. More, that in the pursuit of the destruction of Bolshevism lay the only guarantee of a European context in which social justice could flourish.

It was in exploiting this sense of a mutuality of interests that the anti-Bolshevik crusade had its greatest utility to the Nazis, serving a central role in sustaining their concept of Europe. It was argued that within the *Reich* anti-Bolshevism had progressed through two distinct stages in each of which it helped in a different way to avoid the disintegrative consequences of the Nazi revolution. Now, in the occupied territories anti-Bolshevism took on another role: that of undermining national unity and the sense of nation. This is most obviously seen in the reporting of the crusade as a military event in the occupied countries. The reiterated laudatory references to those nationals who were prepared to fight in a foreign uniform—and, what is more, that of the occupier—were intended to be divisive, for the volunteers bore constant witness to the thoroughness of the defeat of their own lands. More important, presented in this manner, the crusade promoted what might be termed a transposed patriotism according to which the betrayal of the national interest was suggested as being its most profound defence. In other words, anti-Bolshevism, as it was directed at the general population of each occupied country, helped to confuse and diminish the potential power of the very idea of patriotism; as directed at the allies of, and collaborators with, the Nazis, by acting as a substitute for the integration which they had failed to make in their own societies it tied their future ever more tightly to German success.

Of equal utility was the way in which the anti-Bolshevik crusade tried to subsume national interests in a specious new European identity. 'Bolshevism', as Seyss-Inquart defined it in a speech given in Amsterdam (but which could have been delivered at the time in any of the occupied western European cities) was the 'mortal enemy of European culture and decency'. The support of the German campaign in Russia was, he claimed, the first condition for the freedom of Europe and only thereafter, and as a consequence, also for the freedom of the individual nations of which it was historically composed.[16] At one level this idea extended the *Volksgemeinschaft* into the totality of a New European Order. Bolshevism, whether as a political expression confined temporarily to Russia or as an ideology with world pretensions was not, and could never be, part of the larger European community except in a wholly negative sense, but at another level it was the sequence Europe-to-nation that was central to the intended message. What Bolshevism threatened to destroy, it was argued, was not simply the individual nation but the means for the

Continent to survive as a creative cultural whole. It followed that the counter to Bolshevism must also be mounted on a Europe-wide scale since nations acting individually were incapable of effective action. A representative example of this line can be found in the widely read mass circulation periodical, *Signal* in early 1942, which put the case transparently:

> . . . Bolshevism will remain a latent danger to Europe so long as what is left of the Soviet armies has not been annihilated. It is not, then, a question of asking ourselves if we will have a German Europe or a Europe which, under the direction of Germany, will safeguard her essential values and her sacred traditions and lead her peoples to a better future. In reality the soldiers of the Reich are not just defending the cause of their own homeland so much as protecting every European nation worthy of that name.[17]

The message was plain: the crusade had relocated patriotism and displaced it from the level of nation to that of Europe and only Germany could provide the necessary leadership. She alone was willing to take on the burden of the fight against Bolshevism, and that in itself justified her European hegemony. Furthermore, that willingness itself reflected the transformation that the Nazis had made in their own country. For the ability of Germany to wage a war of such magnitude was due, first, to the Nazis' revival of the link between nation and people which had made her capable of acting on a perception of the real danger of Bolshevism and second to the fact that the link had in turn created the social and political revolution (of which the *Führerprinzip* was the guiding expression) that provided the will to translate ideas into practice. It was this particular strength of her own national identity above that of others that gave Nazi Germany the right to direct the European war effort. Of course, it also meant that in this respect German national interests transcended those of other countries. Indeed, it might be said that until Bolshevism was defeated and the conditions for the resurgence of separate European identities had been achieved, Germany alone could properly be called a nation. For the occupied countries, a national future depended on how prepared they were to work for the European unity of which the crusade was expression, first test and admission charge.

Such 'logic' was functional to the Nazis in many respects. Naturally, it helped to subvert and keep in check the idea of national revival in the occupied territories. Nations in the European conflict were insignificant and vulnerable entities. This was a proposition that was well attuned to the psychology of defeat. So too, it expressed in a veiled manner the truth that the partners in this unity of Europe would never be equal. Each had its own contribution to make, but only Nazi Germany could determine the form that this was to take. Most of all, the focus of the anti-Bolshevik crusade allowed the Nazi occupiers to create among their clients a climate ruled by a sense of powerlessness and detachment from previous loyalties. In the end they were left with a clear picture. If they witheld co-operation or if the crusade was unsuccessful the consequences would be even worse than the present reality. It was not so much that Europe, including its western part, would be overrun by a brutal Red Army (though this theme did become prominent in the last months of the occupation), as that the Germans would reassert the primacy of their own national interests and leave the occupied territories to the consequences of civil war and to the absolute abandonment of all those hopes for social transformation for which the defeat of communism was the precondition.

Collaborators, active anti-communists and people who wished fundament-ally to change the shape of their own societies even under the conditions of occupation were a small and, as the war progressed, declining minority. Although the anti-Bolshevik crusade was directed in part to retain their cooperation, this could never be its only purpose. Just as its themes were developed over time to accommodate changing realities so also it seems to have been intended to reach many audiences. It was natural that sympathisers in occupied Europe should have been central to its utility, because of their potential to undermine resistance in their own countries, but a broader audience was no less important and no less essential to the Nazis' purpose. For the population at large in occupied western Europe, the crusade served precisely to demonstrate that the European partnership which it embodied was nothing other than an enforced one. So far from seeking to disguise the nature of the new Europe that the war would bring about, the crusade was presented in such a way as to make plain the inequality and exploitative nature of the proposed relationship between Germany and her conquered territories. Themes reiterated almost to the point of incantation, such as the mass migration of workers in the service of European production, the grandeur of the gigantic construction schemes of the Europe-wide *Organisation Todt*, or the articles describing (often with patronising folkloric detail of quaint dress and customs) the foreign legionaries of the armed crusade itself, all were emphasised as being a part of the recognition by subject peoples that Germany was the brain and the spiritual centre of a European renaissance.

Such references were not intended to make subtle points. On the contrary, if the gap between what was portrayed and what people were experiencing as true seems bold in its cynicism, that also was part of the purpose. The greater the disparity, the less those living in occupied societies had a choice but to read a message that their future lay in the Nazi scheme of things. Further, the more Nazi propaganda painted the reality of life under Bolshevism, the more it became clear that what it was in fact describing was the actuality of its own 'Socialist' *Paz Germanica*. The two not only merged with each other but their signs were reversed. Thus, Bolshevism was said to suppress and pervert society, destroying difference and individuality. Its victory, therefore, would end the pluralism that underpinned European civilisation, a pluralism guaranteed only by the Nazi vision in which 'no-one believes in restraining diversity and nuanced abundance to make of Europe an arid empire of brute force and standardised life'.[18] This kind of rhetoric poured from the Nazi press in occupied Europe. The point could not easily be missed. The 'Bolshevism' that menaced Europe became increasingly a synonym, or a transparent code, for the predatory face of Nazism.

For the population within the *Reich* similar presentations were used to the different end of reinforcing and justifying the German domination of Europe. Whereas Bolshevism had a monolithic aim, the anti-Bolshevik crusade which opposed it did so precisely by harnessing and expressing the pluralism of the Continent. It was the crusade that provided the channel for the separate streams of the European tradition to converge in purposeful activity and in so doing made them stronger. Anti-Bolshevism, then, was the motor force of European unity and it was Germany which had called it into action. It was this that justified her physical and cultural hegemony and conferred on her an overwhelming moral right (as well as duty to the German nation itself) to make the demands that she did of other European countries. As Goebbels expressed it in a widely disseminated speech in February 1943 after the defeat at Stalingrad, if the German people had put their blood at the disposal of the war it was only right that the rest of Europe should put its work at their disposal.[19] The anti-Bolshevik crusade gave those countries which were less far-sighted and less resolute than Germany, the opportunity to redeem the sacrifice that she was making on behalf of Europeans and in order to bring them to true unity.

The argument outlined in this essay has tried to illustrate the process by which Nazism sought to appropriate European society and an idea of Europe to its own values. To the last, anti-Bolshevism was the form in which the Nazi state attempted to harness the destructive forces which its own ideological imperative had called into play. Those forces, by the logic of their origin, could not be confined within the boundaries of Germany. In this respect, if for no other reason, anti-Bolshevism is of interest in the way that it played a many-sided role on a continental level as a secondary repressive device helping to keep subservient the societies which Germany had overrun.[20] The unity that Nazi Germany offered to Europe through the medium of her anti-Bolshevik crusade was as illusory as were her hopes of final victory in the war. This does not necessarily make the means by which the illusion was sustained either uninteresting or inappropriate to view from a broader perspective than that of a mere series of propaganda tricks. The context in which enslaved peoples were asked to accept the idea of European unity was a corrupt one; and the path by which it was to be realised was spurious inasmuch as it was premised on Nazi hegemony, but neither the theme of the extent of Europe, nor its definition around the central point that the achievement of unity required a conclusive outcome to the battle between all-embracing ideologies, were trivial. With the defeat of Nazism those themes continued to resonate. The divided shape of the post-war world testified as much to the depth of the disunity from which the European conflict had sprung as to the difficulty of resolving it in a peaceful manner.

Notes

1. P. Mernet and Y.M. Danan, 'Les thèmes de propagande après le 22 juin 1941', *Revue d'Histoire de la Deuxième Guerre Mondiale*, No. 66 (1966), pp. 48–53.
2. See J. Forster, '"Croisade de l'Europe contre le bolchevisme": la participation d'unités de volontaires européens a l'opération "Barberousse" en 1941', *Revue d'Histoire de la Deuxième Guerre Mondiale*, No. 118 (1980), pp. 1–26.
3. For the Russian anti-Bolshevik forces: C. Andreyev, *Vlasov and the Russian Liberation Movement: Soviet reality and emigré theories* (Cambridge, CUP, 1987). Other useful studies and memoir accounts: W. Dannau (ed.), *Ainsi parla Léon Degrelle*, Vol. VIII: *Flamands et wallons au front de l'est* (Strombeek-Bever, Byblos, 1974); J. Vincx, *Vlaanderen in Uniform 1940–1945* (Antwerpen, Etnika, 1981–82); S. van der Zee, *Voor Führer, volk en vaderland sneuvelde . . . de SS in Nederland, Nederland in de SS* (Den Haag, Kruseman, 1975); O.A. Davey, 'The origins of the Légion des Volontaires Français contre le Bolchevisme', *Journal of Contemporary History*, Vol. 6 (1971), pp. 29–45.
4. A.J.P. Taylor, *The origins of the Second World War* (Harmondsworth, Penguin, 1964); K.H. Jarausch, 'From Second to Third Reich: the Problem of Continuity in German Foreign Policy', *Central European History*, Vol. 12 No. 1 (1979), pp. 68–82.
5. The precise relationship between German domestic production, the achievement of a European New Order and the outbreak of the Second World War has been one of the more bitterly contested topics in the historiography of Nazism. The reading, to which this present study is indebted, is extensive. A helpful recent summary of the debate may be found in :'Germany, "Domestic Crisis" and War in 1939', *Past and Present*, No. 122 (1989), pp. 200–40. See also I. Kershaw, *The Nazi Dictatorship: problems and perspectives of interpretation* (2nd ed., London, Arnold, 1989).
6. For a survey and discussion of Nazi propaganda themes and techniques: D. Welch (ed.), *Nazi Propaganda: the power and the limitations* (London, Croom Helm, 1983). Goebbels' direction of the propaganda machine is chronicled in E.K. Bramsted, *Goebbels and National Socialist Propaganda 1925–1945* (London, Cresset Press, 1965). A case study of Nazi propaganda aims and of popular resistance to them is in I. Kershaw, *Popular opinion and political dissent in the Third Reich: Bavaria 1933–1945* (Oxford, Clarendon Press, 1983). A useful summary of the Nazi control of the press throughout occupied Europe can be

found in O. Hale, *The Captive Press in the Third Reich* (Princeton, Princeton University Press, 1964).

7. See especially: A.S. Milward, *The German Economy at War* (London, Athlone Press, 1965); R.J. Overy, 'Hitler's War and the German Economy: a reinterpretation', *Economic History Review*, Vol. xxxv (1982), pp. 272–91; R.J. Overy, 'Mobilization for Total War in Germany 1939–1941', *English Historical Review*, Vol. ciii (1988), pp. 612–39.

8. For example the French trade unionist, pacifist and later Minister in the Vichy government, René Belin, who argued in October 1939: '. . . in respect of Machiavellianism, deceit, amorality, duplicity and imperialism, Stalin is leagues ahead of Hitler', cited in M. Sadoun, *Les socialistes sous l'occupation; résistance et collaboration* (Paris, Fondation Nationale des Sciences Politiques, 1982), p. 24.

9. *Signal*, No. 15 (Aug. 1941).

10. *L'Emancipation Nationale*, 9 August 1941.

11. See A.S. Milward, *The New Order and the French Economy* (Oxford, Clarendon Press, 1970); J.R. Gillingham, *Belgian Business in the Nazi New Order* (Ghent, Jan Dhondt Foundation, 1977); G. Hirschfeld, *Freundherrschaft und Kollaboration: die Niederlande unter deutscher Besatzung 1940–45* (Stuttgart, Deutsche Verlags-Anstalt, 1984).

12. S. Salter, 'Structures of Consensus and Coercion: Workers' morale and the maintenance of work discipline, 1939–1945', in D. Welch (ed.), *Nazi Propaganda*, op. cit., pp. 88–116.

13. For Speer and Sauckel's policies in relation to the Western European economies: A.S. Milward, *The New Order and the French Economy*, op. cit., Ch. VI; P.F. Klemm, *German Economic Policies in Belgium from 1940 to 1944* (Ann Arbor, University Microfilms, 1978); G. Hirschfeld, *Freundherrschaft und Kollaboration*, op. cit., pp. 117–54; P.W. Becker, *The Basis of the German War Economy under Albert Speer, 1942–44* (Stanford, Stanford University Press, 1971); E.L. Homze, *Foreign Labor in Nazi Germany* (Princeton, Princeton University Press, 1967), esp. Chs. V–VII.

14. For a wider discussion of this point see M.L. Smith, 'Ideas for a New Régime in the Netherlands after the Defeat of 1940', in M.J. Wintle and P. Vincent (eds.), *Modern Dutch Studies, Essays in Honour of Peter King* (London, Athlone Press, 1988), pp. 175–85.

15. *Redressement*, 1 November 1939.

16. A. Seyss-Inquart, *Vier Jahre in den Niederlanden. Gesammelte reden* (Amsterdam, Volk und Reich Verlag, 1944), pp. 67–79.

17. *Signal (Edition en langue française)*, No. 1 (1942), pp. 4–5.

18. *Signal (Edition en langue française)*, No. 6 (1943), p. 38.

19. In E.K. Bramsted, *Goebbels*, op. cit., pp. 264–68.

20. See, too, the statement by D. Welch in the introduction to his study of the effectiveness of Nazi propaganda: 'Historians of widely different political persuasions and approaches have testified to the crucial rôle it played in mobilising support for the Nazis', D. Welch, *Nazi Propaganda*, op. cit., p. 1.

5 Anti-Americanism in National Socialist propaganda during the Second World War

Peter M.R. Stirk

Europe has been urged to unite in the face of the American and Russian colossi since the early nineteenth century. The challenge which these powers posed to Europe was a complicated one. Sheer geographic extent and, increasingly, population were two of the simpler aspects of the supposed threat. Cultural characteristics, economic power and imperial ambitions completed and complicated the picture. During the twentieth century the challenge grew. From the war against Spain in 1898 onwards the United States emerged as an international power and her intervention in the First World War confirmed that status. Intervention and its consequences also helped to distill the political and ideological challenge which the United States presented. Despite the vagaries and compromises of the post-war settlement, Wilsonian diplomacy gave the United States a distinct profile, which survived the deceptive return to isolation. The growth of mass entertainment in the inter-war period added a potent cultural dimension to the political profile. Similarly, developments in the Soviet Union clarified the threat from that quarter. The victory of Bolshevism and the formation of the Comintern gave concrete shape to that spectre which Marx had said would haunt Europe. Communism and world revolution were, thereby, overlaid onto the older images of Slavic culture and Russian great power ambitions.

Both of the emerging superpowers could, then, be understood in terms of their respective ideologies, cultures, economies and political forms. Images of the United States, however, exhibited more ambiguity and flexibility than those of the Soviet Union. This difference has less to do with the inherent nature of the two states than with the nature of European politics because attitudes towards the United States and Americanism have never served to define political cleavages in Europe in the way that attitudes towards the Soviet Union and Bolshevism have.[1] There have never been 'Americanist' parties, nor even capitalist parties, as there have been communist parties in

Europe. This point is quite simple and sounds banal, which it is, but its consequences are not. It has been possible to try to exclude, or simply ignore, the United States whereas, after 1917, it was not possible to ignore the Soviet Union, especially during the years of Comintern hegemony over the European communist parties. The link between the Soviet state and the European communist parties and ideology has always been exaggerated by their opponents, but this is no objection. Communism was first of all a European ideology. It had existed and been feared prior to the existence of the Soviet Union. Attitudes to the Soviet state were taken as a reflection of political conviction in the domestic arena, even if efforts were then made to discredit advocates of Socialism at home by imputing subservience to a foreign power. Oddly enough the isomorphism of state and ideology was greater in the case of the United States/Americanism than in the case of the Soviet Union/ communism. As the very name indicates Americanism incorporates the supposed ideas, culture, behaviour and so on of a particular country. Americanism without the United States is inconceivable. Communism without the Soviet Union had been a reality. The fact that Americanism was not institutionalised in the heart of Europe facilitated a more flexible, sometimes even fickle, rather than balanced approach to things American. The National Socialists were no exception here.

Any attempt to discern the National Socialists' image of the United States/ Americanism is inevitably complicated by their understanding of the nature and role of propaganda. They placed great emphasis upon propaganda in accounting for their domestic political success. Hitler's carefully staged speeches and rallies, his use of radio and the marathon aerial tours in which he harangued hundreds of thousands, as well as his own testimony, confirm this central role which propaganda played in the self-perception of the *Führer*. In international relations too there was a primacy of propaganda. Hitler followed large numbers of ex-generals and apologists for German defeat in the First World War in seeing the Allied victory as a product of superior propaganda which had sapped the will and moral fibre of the German nation.[2] His master of propaganda, Goebbels, shared this view. As he witnessed the Allied advance into the *Reich* in 1945 he explained the greater resistance offered on the Eastern front as a consequence of the focus of German propaganda: 'So far we have treated the Anglo-Americans far too leniently in our propaganda. . . . With our anti-Bolshevist atrocity campaign we succeeded in reconsolidating our front in the East.'[3] The National Socialist view of propaganda was also characterised by an intense cynism, most crudely expressed in Hitler's assertion that the bigger the lie the more chance of its wholehearted acceptance. Both characteristics, belief in the efficacy of propaganda and cynical manipulation, were for a long time accepted by commentators and still are by many. Recently doubt has been cast on the efficacy of National Socialist propaganda and a more differentiated assessment of its successes and failures has begun to emerge.[4] Despite the analogous revision of views about the coherence of National Socialist doctrines, embodied most starkly in Eberhard Jäckel's *Hitler's Weltanschauung*, National Socialist propaganda has continued to be viewed as little more than a tissue of lies.[5] There is of course a large element of truth in this assessment, but it is not the whole truth. In the first place, the National Socialist leadership, especially Hitler, exhibited a curious reluctance to give hostages to fortune by making promises which they had no intention of fulfilling. This reluctance was at its strongest in discussions over the propaganda policy for the occupied territories in the East, but it also plagued the whole approach to the New Order in Europe.[6] Second, even where the propagandists were free to exercise their cynicism, they were guided by what they thought would be effective and that in turn reflected their own convictions. Third, propaganda, precisely by virtue of its very distortions and caricatures, can expose real fears and deep-rooted prejudices. Fourth, in seeking to influence other people the propagandists were well aware that they had to appeal to existing convictions, including ones which were not necessarily specifically National Socialist which is not to say that these convictions were not also held by National Socialists. There is, moreover, at least a *prima facie* case that this facet of propaganda would be of more importance in propaganda designed for foreign consumption or directed towards the populations of the occupied territories.

One of the reasons for the supposition of the unmitigated cynicism, and hence duplicity, of National Socialist propaganda has been the vacuity of the vision of the New Order which was offered to the peoples of occupied Europe. This vacuity is hardly surprising for with the possible exception of a transnational Aryan élite or of a more broadly based German nation or Nordic people which would incorporate the populations of states beyond the boundaries of the existing *Reich*, the intent was to subordinate the other peoples of Europe to the needs and ambitions of the Germans. In the light of these problems there was, then, a tendency, itself justified by the principles of National Socialist propaganda, to focus on the image of Germany's, and Europe's, enemies. The *Feindbilder* became a substitute for any clarity about the New Order. One of these enemies was the United States. The image of the United States as an enemy was, it will be argued, complicated not only by the multiple facets of National Socialist propaganda but also by the more general considerations which induced a less consistent approach to the Americans by all Europeans—National Socialists included.

Whatever else Europeans thought about the United States in the aftermath of the First World War they were impressed by, and often fearful of, the economic strength of the emergent superpower. It was the land of mass production and consumption, of Taylor and Ford. It was also the land of the open frontier portrayed in American popular culture.[7] Hitler proved susceptible to the charms of both. Indeed he was so impressed that, in accordance with his racial theories, he decided that the United States was not the racial melting pot it claimed to be. Such power and success could arise only from the predominance of a self-contained Nordic element. The impact of the Depression induced a revision of his estimation, as it did that of large sections of the European population. The United States now became the land of unemployment and the Dust Bowl. The new image was summed up in Steinbeck's *Grapes of Wrath*, the film of which Hitler watched several times.[8] Political developments in the United States brought forth yet another image with the coming to power of Franklin D. Roosevelt.

Roosevelt and his New Deal met with considerable approval from the National Socialist press and leadership. From the outset he was presented as following the road carved out by Hitler and Mussolini. A eulogistic biography, published in 1934, described the New Deal as an 'authoritarian revolution' and a revolution 'from above'.[9] Roosevelt himself was presented as a man of the new age. His Industrial Recovery Act had broken with the old American tradition of non-intervention. Roosevelt's economic achievements were supplemented by the virtues of his political style. He was said to be an economic dictator who appealed directly to the American people, bypassing Congress. The analogy between the policies and style of the New Deal Administration and Fasicism were widely commented on even by opponents of National Socialism. As so often in the history of National Socialist images of the United States, Roosevelt's domestic critics provided ammunition for these judgements. At the forefront of such praise stood the *Völkischer Beobachter*. When other organs pointed to the limitations of the New Deal, the *Völkischer Beobachter* chose instead to give Roosevelt credit for what he had managed to achieve in such difficult circumstances.[10] Only when the President adopted a principled opposition to the totalitarian states in his Message to Congress on 3 January 1936 did this positive evaluation give way to a more critical tone. From then on the New Deal was increasingly judged to have been a failure. Roosevelt's antipathy to the 'totalitarians' wasdescribedasacynicalattempttodivertattentionfromhisdomesticdifficulties.[11]

As Europe moved closer to war the points of tension and disagreement with the United States grew. The *Kristallnacht* induced widespread revulsion in the United States and in January 1939 Goebbels was still complaining, in an article entitled 'Was will eigentlich Amerika?', that 'Since the 10 November 1938 this agitation has increased immeasurably. American public opinion, especially so far as it is influenced by Jews, has applied itself to a completely intolerable intervention in our domestic German affairs'.[12] The general tenor of the article was that the predominately Jewish controlled press was the source of American criticism of Germany though he did not hesitate to describe the United States as a land of lynch justice, scandals and unemployment, whose culture, such as it was, was totally derived from Europe. All of these themes would become part of the repertoire of National Socialist anti-Americanism. However, at least up until the outbreak of war between the two countries there was strong pressure to mitigate criticism of the United States and Roosevelt and to play down evident points of conflict. Alongside the straightforward desire to delay a conflict which was becoming increasingly inevitable ran more complicated machinations. Thus, in July 1940 Goebbels ordered that America be treated as a negligible quantity, lest more interested commentary might include 'unconsidered remarks' which would provide ammunition for American Jews. Ever concerned about the efficacy of German propaganda, Goebbels had earlier, in September 1939, instructed that excessive enthusiasm for the isolationists in the United States should be avoided because he anticipated that they would lose the argument and feared that their failure could be seen as a German failure.[13]

With the outbreak of war, many of the previous restraints were cast aside and the full panoply of prejudice and caricature could be deployed. The themes were well enough prepared for the response to be immediate, though on 16 December 1941 Goebbels was inclined to keep some of his powder dry, since German hostility towards the United States was strong enough anyway.[14] Though much of the literature on National Socialist propaganda has concentrated, naturally enough, upon Goebbels and the *Reichsministerium für Volksaufklärung und Propaganda* the propaganda apparatus was as subject to the vagaries of polyarchy as other aspects of the Third *Reich*. The position was, as usual, particularly confused in the occupied countries.[15] Amongst those jostling for power and influence were the representatives of Max Amman, *Reichsleiter für die Presse*. Amman's able *Stabsleiter*, Rolf Rienhardt, built up a substantial press empire throughout occupied Europe. At its peak the *Europa Verlag*, which served as a holding company for these publications, distributed over a million copies on a daily basis. These papers are a rich, and relatively unexplored source of National Socialist propaganda. They are also a little unusual in that they generally enjoyed a greater degree of autonomy than was customary. In part at least this was due to the influence of Rienhardt, one of those well-educated and ambitious young National Socialists who proved such an irritation to their coarser overlords. These papers are of particular interest, for by virtue of their location they were bound to be concerned with the construction of the New Order and hence with the *Feindbilder* which bolstered, and served as a substitute for, it. The extent of their influence is difficult to gauge. They probably suffered from the general disrepute which afflicted National Socialist propaganda, especially as the war turned against the Axis. Amongst some sections of the population they were undoubtedly dismissed as mouthpieces of an occupying power—which they were. Yet they were also highly regarded by allied intelligence officers as a source of National Socialist views and it is mainly in this respect that they are considered here. The two things cannot of course be rigidly separated. As instruments of propaganda they were intended to influence people and it is important to consider exactly who they were intended to influence. For example, the paper which will be most frequently mentioned below, the *Brüsseler Zeitung*, naturally had a substantial German readership, since the occupation authorities undertook to purchase and distribute a substantial part of the daily issue. It also retained subscribers amongst the German army and occupation authorities when they were transferred to other areas.[16] It is also worth mentioning that the *Brüsseler Zeitung* was published in an area which was intended in the long run to be part of the Greater German *Reich*, and hence was writing for people of supposed Germanic stock even where it reached beyond the ranks of the occupying authorities.

The initial response of the *Brüsseler Zeitung* to the war between Germany and the United States was relatively restrained compared with some other sections of the National Socialist propaganda apparatus. Other organs took up the themes of Goebbels' article in the *Völkischer Beobachter* with vigour. The United States was presented as the land of decadent *Amerikanismus*. Typical of this approach was an article of 16 January 1942 in the *Völkischer Beobachter* by Richard Sallet. Rhetorically entitled 'Amerikanischer Jahrhundert?', the article depicted a land of persistent unemployment in which farmers, who were the backbone of the nation in National Socialist dogma, were the true 'stepchildren'; the education system was in such disarray that the US army had to reject 92,000 potential recruits within two months on the grounds of illiteracy. It was a land in which Jewish influence was rife, the cultural tone was set by parvenus, the *Readers Digest* and Hollywood. The prevalence of sexually transmitted disease, divorce and atheism completed the picture.[17] The theme of Jewish influence was carried to an extreme in articles like the one entitled '*Die Bedeutung Amerikas für das Judentum der Welt*'.[18] According to this Jews were involved in the very discovery of America and had gradually and increasingly grown in influence and number throughout the history of the United States. Scarcely any other group appeared in the article, save as a transient foil for the onward march of Jewry. Although anti-semitism and notions of cultural decadence are to be found in the initial response of the *Brüsseler Zeitung* they are more notable by their relative absence. This left room for other themes, themes which help to grasp the nature of the challenge which those not committed to the prophecies of the theorists of racial conflict saw in the United States. They were also themes which were deeply rooted in European society in the inter-war period.

The major threat posed by the United States lay in its economic strength as, in the language of Allied propaganda, the arsenal of democracy. The nature of this threat was quite complex as Dr Hunke, *Präsident der Werberates der Deutschen Wirtschaft*, recognised. According to the report in the *Brüsseler Zeitung* of 17 October 1943, he had warned that: 'The greatest danger for us is that we allow ourselves to be morally impressed by the possibilities of the enemy's war potential.' This 'suggestive nimbus' of the United States, as he called it, had to be thoroughly destroyed whereas the reality of American economic power could be countered through corresponding production.[19] Indeed, from the outset persistent efforts were made in the *Brüsseler Zeitung* to undermine this image of strength. The weakness of the economic giant was discerned in a shortage of raw materials. The United States was said to be short of bauxite (16 January 1942), scrap iron (14 February 1942) and rubber (6 March 1942)—amongst other things. Later on, labour was added to the list and even gained predominance over the shortage of raw materials, but the simple line of deficient supplies of materials was repeated in various guises throughout. Another prominent strategy was to focus on the financing of the war, which the United States was said to be managing only at the expense of massive and crippling budgetary deficits (20 February 1942). Again the theme was endlessly reaffirmed. There was an explicit comparison here with National Socialist Germany and the New Order. Whereas the United States, despite the vastness of its territories, was dependent upon 'external' and inadequate sources of raw materials, Europe was self-sufficient. And whereas the United States, despite its immense hoard of gold, was near financial collapse the New Order, liberated from the chains of gold, was financially sound.

For the most part, however, simple imperialism sufficed as a theme. It could be used both to confirm the weakness of Great Britain and to point to conflicts between the Allies. This was indeed the predominant response of the *Brüsseler Zeitung* to the entry of the United States into the war. Headlines like 'Diverging Strategies' (7 January 1942), 'USA will take over English bases permanently' (3 February 1942) and 'Roosevelt remains the victor over London' (5 February 1942) proliferated. In this period the articles contained the reassurance that the United States was more interested in the Pacific than Europe, but even so, American superiority over Britain was so heavily emphasised that it almost belied the other theme of its economic weakness. The motive for this inconsistency is not difficult to discern. The image being conveyed was of an Anglo-Saxon bloc against which Europe must unite, under German leadership.[20] On 8 February 1942, the *Brüsseler Zeitung's* editor, Heinrich Tötter saw the arrival of American troops in Iceland as a sign of a forthcoming Atlantic federation in which small states would lose their independence. The German New Order would, he claimed, not only exclude this alien power bloc from Europe but would permit each state within the New Order to act in the light of its own interests. Quisling's Norway served as an example of this autonomy!

The supposed threat of American imperialism grew in importance as the war progressed. The underlying basis was discerned in, amongst other works, *Dollar Imperialismus*, the title of a book by Peter Aldag published in 1942. Aldag sought to discredit American imperialism, implicitly leaving open the possibility of justifying other forms of imperialism, by claiming that it was unnecessary. This thinly populated land, this *Raum ohne Volk*, with all its wealth was not driven by any domestic pressure to expand. In a typical National Socialist ploy he derived from this lack of internal pressure the notion that American imperialism was unlimited. Whereas the expansion of peoples out of *völkisch* necessity had natural limits, imperialism driven by the greed of capitalist plutocrats had no such limit.[21] The same idea is evident in the *Brüsseler Zeitung*, in articles like 'Even against England unrestrained' (20 August 1943). By 1943 the simple assertion by Sumner Welles of the need to take account of national interest was taken as sufficient evidence in itself of rabid imperialism. Dollar imperialism was discerned in particular in Latin America, which figured prominently in Aldag's book. Another paper of the Amman empire, the *Pariser Zeitung*, presented the nefarious activities of the United Fruit Company in an article entitled 'In the tentacles of the banana trust' (1 April 1943), but financial power was seen as the main weapon of American imperialism in Latin America. While simple greed often provided sufficient motive in the eyes of National Socialist propaganda slightly more sophisticated motivations could be dredged up from the debates of the inter-war period. Thus, American imperialism was motivated, it was claimed, by the need to find markets for its surplus production, without which the United States would be stricken by renewed depression and unemployment. When dealing with its impact upon the European powers other factors came into play. England was frequently warned that the United States was seeking to establish a stranglehold on merchant shipping in the postwar world, as, for instance, in the *Brüsseler Zeitung's* article, 'USA displaces English shipping' (24 August 1943). American imperial ambitions were closely related to the perceived shortages of raw materials and production difficulties, so that, according to the *Pariser Zeitung*, Wall Street's five points included the creation of monopolies in oil and rubber, and a dominant position in civil aviation and shipping (6 January 1944). As with so much of National Socialist anti-American propaganda there was an implicit, and sometimes explicit, comparison with the New Order in Europe. Thus in the French language section of the *Pariser Zeitung*, 'Les limites du grand espace américain' (18 February 1944) claimed that the pan-American economic region was unviable since the surplus production of the member countries was too similar. This is a most interesting assertion, for it unintentionally reveals the assumption that the economic unity of regions rested upon the exchange between exporters of finished goods and exporters of raw materials and foods. Whether French businessmen perceived their fate as the former or the latter is a moot point. In any event it is illustrative of how National Socialist conviction manifested itself in National Socialist propaganda.[22]

The unrestrained character of American imperialism had other resonances, rooted in the way National Socialist doctrine borrowed from what it saw as American ideology and sought to turn this against the United States. Nowhere was this more prominent than in the use of the Monroe doctrine. The latter, suitably adjusted, formed the basis of Carl Schmitt's *Völkerrecht-liche Grossraumordnung*, which was first published in 1939 and went into several editions.[23] The rhetoric of the Monroe doctrine was taken up by Hitler in an interview with an American journalist in 1940, in which he declared 'America for the Americans, Europe for the Europeans. This underlying mutual Monroe doctrine . . ., were it observed by both sides, would not only secure a lasting peace between the new and the old world, but could also supply the most ideal basis for the peace of the entire world . . .'[24] It was especially appropriate while the National Socialists were trying to delay the entry of the United States into the war, but it persisted throughout, especially in the slogan of 'Europe for the Europeans'. The United States by exceeding its allotted region, as the National Socialists understood it, could be held guilty for violating its own principles.

That it did so was thought to be indicative of Roosevelt's irrational hatred of Germany and the imperfections and vices of his Administration. Roosevelt the war-monger was a prominent theme. It was Roosevelt who had dragged the unwilling American people into war against Germany and Europe. The contrast between anti-Bolshevik propaganda and anti-American propaganda is quite marked here. A distinction was drawn between the leadership of the United States and its people in a way which was not done in the case of the Soviet Union and the Soviet people. There were, to be sure, more ambiguities in the presentation of the occupied East than is often recognised, but not of the consistency and extent of the former. A typical article from the *Brüsseler Zeitung* in 1942 reported the views of a Wallonian Lieutenant under the title, 'The reality of Bolshevism'. According to this Lieutenant, Bolshevik 'materialist unculture' is directed wholly towards the annihilation of 'western culture'. Soviet soldiers are motivated by 'blind and stubborn fanaticism' which is as levelling and impersonal as the 'stupefied indifference of the civilians'. By comparison the American people were the victims of Roosevelt and his advisors. The miners' leader, John Lewis, was portrayed as a genuine leader, unlike Roosevelt, of the interests of US workers and, of course, as pro-isolationist. The coal miners' strikes of 1943 provided endless ammunition.[25] The distinction between an inimical leadership and the people could be difficult to maintain, especially when the American public declined to play the role allotted to it by National Socialist propaganda. In January 1943, one of several reports on the United States' White book on foreign policy expressed surprise at the lack of criticism which accompanied this publication. According to the *Brüsseler Zeitung* the text exposed great imcompetence on the part of the United States' government and should have called forth torrents of denunciation from its citizens. That it did not, was explained away by reference to the unspecified deficiencies of the 'typical American mentality.'[26]

The threat posed by the image of American economic power was countered, then, both by attempts to deny the reality of economic strength and by attempts to discredit it by associating it with imperialist ambition. Another major threat was more difficult to counter. The United States had long been seen by Europeans not only as a land of immense resources and wealth but as the New World, free from the wars, class distinctions and poverty of the old Europe. The power of this image is evident in its attraction for dissident Italian Fascists.[27] It was this potent image which Giselher Wirsing set out to destroy in his *Der masslose Kontinent* which was first completed at the end of 1941 and subsequently went through several editions.[28] By comparison with much of the National Socialist output, Wirsing's work was unusually substantial and sophisticated, even if it did not shrink from the full range of crude caricature and anti-semitism. Wirsing accepted that the United States had been the land of youth and opportunity which had spawned the American 'myth'. He took up the idea of the frontier, as expounded by F.J. Turner, as the key to this myth. He even admitted that after the disappearance of the frontier at the end of the nineteenth century the reality of opportunity, and even more so the myth of opportunity, persisted. Indeed, he pointed out that the emergence of gigantic trusts, which greatly restricted the economic opportunities of the lower strata, paradoxically confirmed the myth, for were these economic empires not the creations of self-made men? But the tide had turned. A new upper strata was emerging in the United States in which wealth and position were inherited, not earned. Moreover, this new strata had succumbed to the influence of the most reprobate representative of the old order, England, as American heiresses were married to the English aristocracy.[29] At the same time as this social and cultural transformation was taking place, the United States, from 1911 onwards, began imposing restrictions upon immigration. Wirsing took this as evidence that the United States now feared the formation of a new proletariat for whom the possibility of success was no longer open. He added that although Theodore Roosevelt had defended the American myth against the emergent trusts the battle was really lost. Subsequent Presidents put forth only a sham opposition to the new economic reality.

At this point Wirsing changed his point of attack. He had established, to his satisfaction, that the United States was in much the same position economically as contemporaneous European states. He then set out to claim that the title of youth and of the new world had passed back to Europe. The American myth had become an obstacle to progress, for the future pointed now to an interventionist state and a planned economy. The myth merely sufficed to endow the New Deal with an aura of revolution while it actually impeded the adoption of more radical measures. The New Deal was in fact dissipated amidst the conflict between the advocates of state planning—primarily Jewish—and the leaders of the trusts who resented any restriction upon their financial power. Once again the failure of the New Deal, compounded by rising Jewish and English influence, pushed President Roosevelt towards diversionary foreign adventures and war against Germany. Wirsing too felt obliged to find the Achilles' heel in the United States' economy. He discerned it not in the shortage of raw materials or even the vicissitudes of capitalist finance, but rather in the persistence of the conflict of forces which had undermined the New Deal. This left open the possibility, he admitted, that a unified leadership supported by a genuine mass movement could rectify the problem, but of that, he reassured his readers, there was no prospect. By the same token, German economic superiority lay in its political system and ideology. For Germany did possess the requisite leadership, mass movement and planning.

The New Deal, which had met with such a favourable reception at the beginning, continued to play a major role in National Socialist propaganda. Its failure was consistently cited in both the *Brüsseler Zeitung* and the *Pariser Zeitung* as one of the reasons for Roosevelt's warmongering. As National Socialist propaganda became increasingly concerned with Allied postwar planning in 1943, the failure of the New Deal took on a broader significance. As an obsolete and liberal economic order, sustained only by the conditions of war, the United States, were it victorious, would bring Europe only the unemployment and financial subservience which had characterised inter-war Europe. Despite the crash of 1929 and the ensuing withdrawal of American financial support to Europe, the idea that the United States, and it alone, could engineer European economic recovery remained strong. One inter-war advocate of European unity, Francis Delaisi, justified his support for the New Order and his selection of the United States as a symbol of the old, liberal system on the following grounds:

> firstly because the economic crisis which threatened to tear apart our whole social structure started there, furthermore, because the momentary power and quite recent wealth of the United States continues to influence a part of European opinion, which sees the enormous gold reserves of the American banks as the basis

for a reconstruction of the world economy. These Europeans have completely forgotten that the USA has already tried to meet this task after the First World War in 1921–1929.[30]

Yet the changes in the economy of the United States associated with the New Deal occasionally resurfaced, especially in the *Brüsseler Zeitung* and similarities between the New Order in Europe and developments in the United States were explained in much the same way as they had been earlier, although naturally a different emphasis was placed on them. Whereas earlier the similarities were regarded as a welcome imitation of National Socialist policies, now they were taken as evidence that the intellectually impoverished Americans had no ideas of their own, or merely promised what the New Order was already achieving.[31] The latter emphasis is evident in the response to Roosevelt's message to Congress at the beginning of 1942. The *Brüsseler Zeitung* proudly proclaimed that 'What he says of the struggle of the USA for tolerance, honour, freedom and belief, are programmatic points for which Germany and its allies are fighting against the Bolsheviks in the name of European culture.' Even more striking are the comments on the US war economy which appeared in 1943. In response to an article by Harry Hopkins which called for more radical measures for the mobilisation of labour, the *Brüsseler Zeitung* printed the rhetorical subheading 'Written by Dr Goebells?' (7 February 1943). Two days later an article covering Donald Nelson's pronouncements upon the same theme was more explicit: 'Even in the field of labour mobilisation the United States sees itself forced, as a consequence of the lack of any ideas of their own, to take over the measures of the authoritatian states.'[32] The idea that the United States had, after all, broken with the old liberal economic order was sufficiently widespread for it too to be used as a tool with which to discredit Allied postwar planning. Thus Friedrich Lenz argued in *Die Krisis des Kapitalismus in den Vereinigten Staaten* that, willingly or not the United States had been compelled to adopt many 'European' practices in the wake of the depression.[33] The free market had been abandoned in the land of its greatest advocates. A return to it was unlikely for social as well as economic reasons. Even Roosevelt had accepted the slogan of a 'right to work' and a return to the free market could only be achieved at the cost of 'social reaction and "plutocratic" class domination'.[34] From this position the Allied alternative to the controlled economy of the New Order appeared as hypocrisy; which was itself a favourite theme.[35]

These divergent interpretations can be accounted for in various ways. Propagandist opportunism is one evident option. So too is the simple fact that there was no single National Socialist image of America. Different ideologues had different views. Nor should it be forgotten that the United States did present ambiguities, which the more sophisticated National Socialists like

Wirsing and Lenz sought to take account of in their own way. Equally important is the fact that images of the United States, though often crude, were very potent and, as the National Socialist ideologues had frequent occasion to complain, difficult to remove even when contradictory images appeared. This supposition finds some corroboration from none other than Hitler himself. Despite his predominant contempt for the land of racial miscegenation, and unemployment in the wake of the Depression, he could occasionally give vent to earlier prejudices. Thus on the eve of war with the United States he commented that the American work ethic was closer to Germany's than the more modest desires and ambitions which he ascribed to the Spanish. In September 1941 and again in February 1942 he recalled the old idea that the development of engineering skills in America had been brought about by men of German stock. In April 1942 his admiration for the motorised society resurfaced. Germany he said had much to learn from American mass production which reduced the cost of vehicles to the point where every working man could afford to own and run one.[36] This did not prevent him from viewing America as a land of the greatest cultural depravity which could not produce a soldiery with the stomach to fight.

Such rabid anti-Americanism, interlarded as it usually was with anti-semitism, was initially relatively absent from the *Brüsseler Zeitung*. Although anti-semitic themes often appeared in such articles, as when the extension of US diplomatic activity in the British Empire was equated with the spread of Jewish influence, the predominant emphasis was on America's egoistic lust for power and wealth, the underlying weakness of the arsenal of democracy and so on. However, 1943 saw the emergence of a new line.[37] Here we find the archetypal anti-Americanism. It appeared most pointedly in the form of cartoons on the front page. One, entitled 'If the USA dominates Europe', showed a black American, significantly dressed in the uniform of a policeman, exhibiting the remnants of the European race, clothed in rags and living amidst ruins, to a group of American tourists (13 April 1943). Another, entitled 'The bearers of culture . . .', showed two American airmen, again black, with the legend, 'Their cathedrals? Only old piles of stone, without cinemas, bars or barbers' shops' (10 July 1943). The way for such crude caricatures had been prepared by extensive reportage of Allied bombing. Damage to cathedrals and churches, both in Germany and Italy, figured prominently. The *Brüsseler Zeitung* reported the bombing of Rome under the headline, 'The fight for Rome. Culture or dollars, cathedrals or skyscrapers?' (25 July 1943). The connection between this specifically anti-American, or anti-Anglo-Saxon, propaganda and the assertion that the United States and Great Britain would sacrifice Europe to the Bolsheviks was never far away. According to an article in the *Deutsche Allgemeine Zeitung* (4 July 1944) by Willy Beer, with their terror-bombing, '. . . the British and Americans are driving us step by step to outward proletarianism and wish to force us to the Bolshevist conceptions of existence'. Another variation on this theme was the claim that there was in some sense a fundamental similarity between American culture and Bolshevism. This appeared in an article entitled 'Homunculus? On the future shape of man' (11 August 1943). According to that article men had been reduced to automatons in both cultures. In the Soviet Union this parlous condition had arisen out of deliberate Bolshevik policy. In the United States it had been inevitable from the outset, for American culture had been based on a 'primitive colonialism'. This sort of attack followed on from the well-established theme of communist influence within the United States, but the idea that the two cultures were basically the same was relatively new.

The youth of Europe was seen as particularly susceptible to the siren call of *Amerikanismus*, as indeed it was, not least within the *Reich* itself. Efforts were made to counter this influence by portraying the true picture of youth within the United States. According to the title of one article, youth was the victim of the plutocratic economic system (22 October 1943). High rates of child mortality, the employment of child labour, parents who left children outside the factory gate were all invoked as a prelude to elaboration on the malign moral consequences of this economic exploitation. The respective conditions of youth had a double significance for it also formed part of the wider struggle for the title of the New, and youthful, world which was so important to National Socialism. For the National Socialist movement understood itself as a party of youth in a literal sense as well as a metaphorical one.[38]

Gangsterism figured prominently in many articles, though, perversely, one described the American fascination with the underworld as conclusive evidence of cultural depravity. Supposed connections between Roosevelt and gangsters were assiduously followed. Reports of American bombing raids included references to 'young Al Capones' and 'flying gangsters' who had no respect for culture, tradition or the lives of innocent civilians. The land of the gangster, as portrayed by the American film industry and disseminated throughout Europe before the war, was easily pressed into service. There was more reticence about the land of Ford and Taylor, which was hardly surprising since this would inevitably invoke images of economic strength. Even so some comment was made and reveals a consistent theme. Henry Kaiser, shipping magnate and folk hero in the United States, drew attention in the *Brüsseler Zeitung* (1 July 1943).[39] His success with the application of techniques of pre-fabrication and mass production was disparaged by reference to the personal rewards he received. More importantly, doubt was cast on the quality of the product. The *Pariser Zeitung* offered a different perspective on the theme of quality versus quantity in an article on 'Leistungskonkurrenz' (21 January 1944). Here the 'guided economy' of the

New Order was said to promote competition in terms of quality against a background of stable prices, whereas the alternative evident in the Anglo-Saxon world induced a violent competition to reduce prices at the expense of quality. The same theme was carried over into the military field when the *Brüsseler Zeitung* argued that in an age of mechanised warfare, qualities of heart and spirit became decisive (9 July 1943).[40]

The supposed moral superiority of the New World and American idealism were presented through the prism of arrogance. Attempts were made to reach the roots of this aspect of the American myth. The *Pariser Zeitung* saw the individualism of the pioneer era of American history as the source of its self-perception as the chosen people (10 March 1944). The opportunity to link this with the notion of Jewish influence was not missed. The main weapon against the moral standing of the United States remained, however, the persistent references to self-interest and greed which was made in practically every comment upon inter-Allied negotiations. As the cultural battle escalated so too did the deployment of anti-semitism, though it is worth noting that the *Brüsseler Zeitung* always lagged behind its sister paper, the *Pariser Zeitung* in this respect. There is indeed even a slight difference between the German language and French language sections of the latter. The coverage in French often outstripped the German in its anti-semitism. Indicative of this is the edition of 8 April 1943. Both sections included an article accusing Roosevelt of planning to hand over Europe to the Soviet Union. The respective titles were, in German, 'Roosevelt: Europa Stalins Einflussphäre' and in French, 'Roosevelt rumine des plans de bolchevisation de l'Europe'. The French language article alone was accompanied by a small piece on the American-Soviet Friendship Society, entitled, 'Aux USA les plus grands amis des soviets sont . . . des juifs naturellement'. These nuances, indicative as they are of a diffuse difference of emphasis, may well reflect the different climate of occupation and intended readership of the two papers in Brussels and Paris as well as the interest, in France, of appealing to the lowest and only common denominator of the collaborationist movements, namely anti-semitism. They also raise the question, alluded to above, of who were the intended readers of propaganda and the possibility that Axis propaganda may be a not insignificant register of conditions in occupied Europe.[41]

The slogan that the Americans intended to sacrifice Europe had been decreed by Goebbels at the beginning of 1943 to counter the belief that the British and Americans would save Europe from the Bolsheviks, a belief which he thought was particularly prevalent amongst intellectuals.[42] It formed part of what became a largely defensive propaganda strategy focussing on the fate of Europe in the event of an Allied victory.[43] The occupation of Sicily, which began in the summer of 1943, was used to warn Europeans that the Americans were incapable of governing Europe, lacking, as they did, the requisite experience. Alongside the idea that the parvenu could not match the skills of the European colonial tradition, and implicit criticism of his presumption in thinking he could, ran the notion that Sicily revealed the intent of the Americans to create a bridgehead in Europe for 'capitalist imperialism'. Such was the judgement of the *Pariser Zeitung* on 9 March 1944. More prominent, prior to allied invasions, were affirmations of the cynical intent of the United States to purchase Stalin's continued support, with Europe as the payment. In the *Brüsseler Zeitung*' headlines like 'Delivery of Europe to Bolshevism doesn't worry America' (28 March 1943) and 'Roosevelt's World Order: Sacrifice of Europe to the Soviets confirmed' (21 April 1943) set the tone. From then on every opportunity was taken to push home the message. Much was made of speculation in the Allied press about the shape of post-war Europe, each report serving to expose some further detail of the Allied treachery. Symbolic of this tactic was the headline, 'Betrayal of Europe takes shape: Benes will legalise Stalin's intentions' (25 November 1943). The cynicism of the Americans was emphasised in a report on the recent Teheran conference in the *Pariser Zeitung* (9 January 1944). According to this Roosevelt had sold Europe to Stalin in return for a 10,000 million dollar trade deal. In another follow-up the Americans were said to have realised only belatedly the full consequences of their duplicity. In ceding Europe to Stalin's sphere of influence they had expected to be able to export their goods to post-war Europe, but Nelson at least had begun to realise that the sordid deal was not good business. The Soviet Union would use its massive slave labour to exclude American goods and dominate Europe economically (24 January 1944). In the image presented by these organs, the Americans' cynicism was matched by their stupidity and servility in the face of Stalin. Cartoons presented the western Allies in general as puppets of the Bolshevik despot. The United States was said to have no independent policy in Europe, merely waiting upon the dictates of the Soviet Union.

Any attempt to gauge the efficacy of National Socialist anti-American propaganda is bound to be dubious in the light of the complexity of the phenomena involved. By its own exaggerated standards it should have been able to induce a Europe-wide resistance against the alien superpower and culture, yet Goebbels was dissatisfied even with the response of Germans to the 'invaders'. That, of course, says at least as much about his misjudgement of the potentials of propaganda as it does about anything else. The specific themes of its anti-American propaganda are however of importance in that they reveal something of the National Socialist perception of the American challenge. Sheer economic power, the charms of the New World and the anti-Bolshevik saviour were the main ones. The first was most difficult of all to dislodge. In the Netherlands, for example, the representative of the Foreign Ministry, had complained in January 1942 that the impression of Japanese successes was belittled by reference to the military potential of the United States. With apparent irritation he added that Roosevelt's claims about the latter were, of course, believed.[44] That the United States is an economic giant has been the common denominator of European perceptions in this century, regardless of whether the giant has been loved or hated, admired or despised.

There was however a grain of truth in Goebbels' comments. For all the venom poured out against *Amerikanismus*, the National Socialist attitude to the East and to Bolshevism had been harsher and more consistent than its attitude to the United States. This was, in part, a consequence of the victory of Hitler's dreams of a racially based German empire in the East over those who, for ideological or pragmatic reasons, looked for an alliance with the Soviet Union.[45] It also reflected the wider ambiguities of Europeans towards the United States. With the exception of the strength of the anti-semitism of much, but not all, of the propaganda apparatus there was little that was specifically National Socialist in the image of American virtues and vices. The National Socialists could, and did, seek to undermine and discredit the appeal of the United States, largely by mobilising other images of America which were just as deeply rooted and European as the ones they feared. Dollar imperialism, the arrogance of the American sense of mission, the threat to European colonial possessions, cultural shallowness, and mass unemployment were all part of Europe's view of the United States. It is this fact, rather than any supposed efficacy of National Socialist propaganda, which explains the persistence of these images beyond the end of the war.

Reflection upon National Socialist images of America during the war, of which the above is a pilot study, potentially tell us a great deal. It confirms the view that the content of its propaganda is an important source for understanding the perceptual world of National Socialism. It points to the difficulty National Socialists had in saying anything more positive about their New Order. It indicates the European dimension of part at least of National Socialist doctrine. The very vagaries of its propaganda cast doubt upon the cultural divide which the National Socialists sought to draw down the Atlantic, or sometimes across the Channel. Finally, it has the potential to serve as a useful tool for understanding the varied conditions of occupation in Europe.

Notes

1. Ernst Fraenkel, *Amerika im Spiegel des deutschen Politischen Denkens* (Cologne, Westdeutscher Verlag, 1959), p. 44.
2. See Jutta Sywottek, *Mobilmachung für den totalen Krieg* (Opladen, Westdeutscher Verlag, 1976).

3. Hugh Trevor Roper, *The Goebbels Diaries* (London, Secker and Warburg, 1978), p. 241.

4. See especially Ian Kershaw, 'How Effective Was Nazi Propaganda', in David Welch (ed.), *Nazi Propaganda* (London, Croom Helm, 1983), pp. 180–205.

5. Eberhard Jäckel, *Hitler's Weltanschauung* (Middletown, Connecticut, Weslyan University Press, 1972). For an assessment of the historiography of National Socialist propaganda see David Welch, 'Introduction' to Welch (ed.), *Nazi Propaganda* op. cit., p. 2. A strong form of the assumptions criticised by Welch is to be found in Robert Edwin Herzstein, *The War That Hitler Won* (London, Abacus, 1980), especially pp. 57 and 85.

6. See Alexander Dallin, *German Rule in Russia 1941–1945* (London, Macmillan, 1957) for the eastern front. The difficulty of dealing with the New Order in general is discussed in Peter Longerich, *Propagandisten im Krieg* (Munich, Oldenbourg, 1987), pp. 69–108. An illuminating example of the problem is the response of Rudolf Rahn, deputy Leader of the Information department in the German Foreign Office, to resistance to making tactical promises: 'Since when have we been so fearful and modest?' Quoted in Ludolf Herbst, *Der Totale Krieg und die Ordnung der Wirtschaft* (Stuttgart, D.V.A., 1982), p. 247.

7. For European attitudes in the inter-war period see Peter Berg, *Deutschland und Amerika 1918–1929* (Lubeck, Mattheisen, 1963); David Strauss, *Menace in the West* (Westport, Greenwood, 1978); Paul Cagnon, 'French Views of the Second American Revolution', *French Historical Studies* Vol. 2 (1962), pp. 430–449; Robert Boyce, *British Capitalism at the Crossroads, 1919–1932* (Cambridge, Cambridge University Press, 1987). Germany was often thought to be the most Americanised of European countries. See, for example, the aside by Ludwell Denny, *America Conquers Britain* (London, Knopf, 1930), p. 407.

8. Gerhard L. Weinberg, 'Hitler's Image of the United States', *American Historical Review*, Vol. 69 (1964), pp. 1006–10.

9. Helmut Magers, *Roosevelt Ein Revolutionär aus Common Sense* (Leipzig, Kittler, 1934), as described by John A. Garraty, *The Great Depression* (New York, Anchor, 1987), pp. 205–6.

10. Hans-Jürgen Schröder, *Deutschland und die Vereinigten Staaten 1933–1939* (Wiesbaden, Steiner, 1970), p. 104.

11. Ibid., pp. 109–10.

12. *Völkischer Beobachter*, 21 January 1939.

13. Willi A. Boelcke (ed.), *The Secret Conferences of Dr Goebbels* (London, Weidenfeld, 1967), p. 64; Michael Balfour, *Propaganda in War 1939–1945* (London, Routledge, 1979), p. 165.

14. Boelcke (ed.), *Secret Conferences of Dr Goebbels*, op. cit., pp. 194–5.

15. On polyarchy in the propaganda apparatus see Longerich, *Propagandisten im Krieg*, op. cit., pp. 14–21. On the *Europa Verlag* see O.J. Hale, *The Captive Press in the Third Reich* (Princeton, Princeton University Press, 1964), pp. 279–83.

16. On the *Brüsseler Zeitung* see R. Falter, 'Le *Brüsseler Zeitung* (1940–1944)', *Cahiers d'Histoire de la Seconde Guerre Mondiale*, Vol. 7 (1982), pp. 39–81. Falter says distribution peaked at 245,000 and refers to a distribution of 20–25,000

amongst German and non-German civilians. On other publications in occupied Belgium see Els de Bens, 'La presse du temps de l'occupation de la Belgique (1940–1944)', *Revue d'histoire de la deuxième guerre mondiale*, Vol. 20 (1976), pp. 1–29, which says only one French language and two Flemish language papers exceeded a distribution of 100,000. For a dismissive estimation of the influence of another paper in the Amman empire, *Die deutsche Zeitung in den Niederlanden*, see G. Hoffman, *NS-Propaganda in den Niederlanden* (Berlin, Verlag Dokumentation, 1972), pp. 89–91.

17. Hitler declared that this was the best article on America that he had read. *Akten der Deutschen Aussenpolitik 1918–1945* (Göttingen, Vandenhoeck and Ruprecht, 1969), Series E, Vol. 1, Doc. 129.

18. Peter Aldag, 'Die Bedeutung der Entdeckung Amerika für den Judentum der Welt', *Nationalsozialistische Monatshefte*, Vol. 13 (1942), pp. 684–93.

19. Heinrich Hunke sought to coordinate economic propaganda to counter the allied, and especially American, challenge in this field. See Herbst, *Der Totale Krieg*, op. cit., pp. 248–51.

20. Much of anti-American propaganda was simultaneously anti-British. The existence of an Anglo-Saxon bloc had been a prominent theme of American studies in Germany prior to the war. See the 1937 directive to Universities which prescribed that 'attention must be paid to the extension of English Civilisation to North America . . . the candidate must have a clear idea of the Anglo-Saxon world as a cultural and political *Gesamterscheinung*', quoted in S. Skard, *American Studies in Europe* (Philadelphia, Philadelphia University Press, 1958), Vol. 1, p. 283. There were also differences, not least because of the National Socialist desire to point to inter-Allied conflict.

21. Peter Aldag, *Dollar Imperialismus* (Berlin, Eher, 1942), p. 8. See also Curt Wunderlich, *USA Dollarimperialismus und Wallstreetterror* (Berlin, Staneck, 1943). The distinction between limited *völkisch* expansion and other forms had been drawn earlier by Rosenberg and the *Tatkreis*. See Peter M.R. Stirk, 'Authoritarian and National Socialist Conceptions of Nation, State and Europe', in Peter M.R. Stirk (ed.), *European Unity in Context: The Interwar Period* (London, Pinter, 1989), pp. 125–148.

22. On National Socialist conceptions of the *Grossraumwirtschaft*, see Eckart Teichert, *Autarkie und Grossraumwirtschaft in Deutschland 1930–1939* (Munich, Steiner, 1984).

23. Carl Schmitt, *Völkerrechtliche Grossraumordnung* (Berlin, Deutscher Rechtsverlag, 1941). See also Ulrich Scheuner, 'Die Machtstellung der Vereinigten Staaten in Zentralamerika', *Zeitschrift der Akademie für Deutsches Recht*, Vol. 7 (1940), pp. 309–11. The National Socialist appropriation of the Monroe doctrine is criticised in Lothar Gruchmann, *Nationalsozialistische Grossraumordnung* (Stuttgart, D.V.A., 1962). Schmitt did not lack critics at the time from the ranks of National Socialism, for example, Reinhard Höhn, 'Grossraumordnung und völkisches Rechtsdenken', *Reich, Volksordnung, Lebensraum*, Vol. 1 (1940), pp. 256–88.

24. Quoted by Gruchmann, *Nationalsozialistische Grossraumordnung*, op. cit., p. 12.

25. On the reality of the coal miners' strikes see Richard Polenberg, *War and Society*.

The United States 1941–1945 (Philadelphia, Lippincott, 1972), pp. 161–170.

26. For the wider response to the White Book see *Review of the Foreign Press* (Munich, Kraus Reprint, 1980), Series A, Vol. 8, no. 171 (18 January 1943).

27. J.D. Wilkinson, *The Intellectual Resistance in Europe* (Cambridge, Mass., Harvard University Press, 1981).

28. Giselher Wirsing, *Der masslose Kontinent. Roosevelts Kampf um die Weltherrschaft* (Jena, Diederichs, 1943). The *Nationalsozialistische Monatshefte* called it the best book available on the topic (Vol. 13, 1942, p. 724). It was enthusiastically reviewed in the *Brüsseler Zeitung,* 12 March 1942), and attracted attention in occupied Europe. See *Review of the Foreign Press*, op. cit., Series A, Vol 7, pp. 621 and 696. Wirsing had been a prominent member of the *Tatkreis*, served in the SS and became chief editor of *Christ und Welt* after the war.

29. This theme appears in 'Yankees and Lords', *Pariser Zeitung*, 16 May 1943.

30. Francis Delaisi, *Die Revolution der europäischen Wirtschaft* (Stuttgart, D.V.A., 1943). Delaisi had been a prominent advocate of European unity in the interwar period. See Carl Pegg, *Evolution of the European Idea* (Chapel Hill, University of North Carolina Press, 1983), pp. 71 and 136.

31. See also Hitler's rejoinder to Allied propaganda on 30 September 1942: '. . . they suddenly discovered our party programme after protracted effort, and we see with astonishment that they promise the world approximately the same for the future as we have already given our German people.' Max Domarus (ed.), *Hitler, Reden und Proklamationen* (Munich, Süddeutscher Verlag, 1965), Vol. 2, p. 1913. See also the earlier comments of 30 January 1942 (ibid., p. 1827).

32. Donald Nelson was head of the War Production Board until August 1944. He fell from that office as a result of what was seen as his premature commitment to the reconversion to a civilian economy. Polenberg, *War and Society*, op. cit., pp. 161–70.

33. Friedrich Lenz. *Die Krisis des Kapitalismus in den Vereinigten Staaten* (Stuttgart, Kohlhammer, 1943), p. 57. There are echoes of this disagreement over the extent to which the United States abandoned the free market and its ideology in the current discussion of the Marshall Plan.

34. For a different interpretation of this issue see 'USA Arbeitsgesetz nur bluff', *Pariser Zeitung*, 18 February 1944.

35. A similar ambiguity was recorded by *Review of the Foreign Press*, Series A, Vol. 7, Supplement no. 146: 'What matters most is that German readers should be given enough material to allay their doubts and fears about the United States as an enemy power. Consistency of presentation has sometimes to be sacrificed. . . . They are assured that the United States is a relatively young nation (*Berliner Börsen Zeitung*, 25 June), and three days later Megerle in the same paper assures them that the old-fashioned 'people of yesterday' caused the war in a desperate effort to force on the world the outworn ideals of liberal capitalism.' The *Review* thought that subsequent articles tended to confirm the latter option. Karl Megerle was Ribbentrop's *Beauftragte für Propaganda*. See Longerich, *Propagandisten im Krieg*, op. cit., pp. 67–8, 79–80, 87–9 and 94.

36. Trevor Roper, *Hitler's Table Talk 1941–1944* (London, Weidenfeld and Nicolson, 1973), pp. 43, 46, 279, 416.

37. The *Brüsseler Zeitung's* relative restraint was not typical. See the weary comment of the *Review of the Foreign Press*, Vol 7, no. 160 (26 October 1942), on the response to the 450th anniversary of the discovery of America: 'As usual a comparison between Germany's culture and American lack of it—"Coca-cola and chewing gum can have no effect on Europe's culture"—was the main burden of the articles . . .'

38. On National Socialist concern about the attractions of *Amerikanismus* for French youth see 'Frankreich spricht nach USA', *Brüsseler Zeitung*, 26 January 1943. The paper could not resist blaming this on the decadence of the French and the notion that they had no ideas of their own with which to counteract the American challenge.

39. Henry Kaiser reduced the production time for shipping prodigously and enjoyed wide popular renown. See Richard R. Lingeman, *Dont't You Know There's a War on? The American Home Front, 1941–1945* (New York, Putnam, 1970), pp. 130–31.

40. This idea had been· popularised by, amongst others, Ernst Jünger in the aftermath of the First World War.

41. The fact that the SS acquired substantial influence in Paris from April 1942 onwards, with the appointment of Karl Albrecht Oberg as *Höhere SS und Polizei Führer*, but did not acquire comparable influence in Brussels until July 1944, may well be an important aspect of differences in the prevailing climate. For details of the appointments see Norman Rich, *Hitler's War Aims* (London, Deutsch, 1974), Vol. 2, pp. 177–81 and 208–10. I am grateful to M.L. Smith, who has generously given me the benefit of his extensive knowledge of conditions in occupied western Europe, for this point.

42. Boelcke (ed.), *Secret conferences of Dr Goebbels*, op. cit., p. 333. The idea that the United States would be the arbiter of Europe's fate was widespread. For some French views see Robert O. Paxton, *Parades and Politics at Vichy* (Princeton, Princeton University Press, 1966), pp. 99–101, 214–15, 246. Salazar thought that the United States would save Europe from the Bolsheviks. See *Akten der Deutschen Aussenpolitik*, op. cit., Series E, Vol. 1, Doc. 256. He evidently continued such speculations. There is a fascinating attempt to exploit them without giving too much away in 'Um Englands Nachfolgeschaft', *Brüsseler Zeitung*, 5 December 1943.

43. Longerich, *Propagandisten im Krieg*, op. cit., pp. 101–2.

44. *Akten der Deutschen Aussenpolitik*, op. cit., Series E, Vol. 1, Doc. 138. See also the judgement of Herbst, *Totale Krieg*, p. 243.

45. Goebbels had sympathised with the pro-Eastern elements of the NSDAP and there may be elements of genuine regret in the lament for his supposed leniency in anti-American propaganda.

6 The integration of Czechoslovakia in the economic system of Nazi Germany

V. Průcha

The rise of the modern state of the Czechs and the Slovaks in 1918 was part of a process which started with the disintegration of the Austro-Hungarian Empire after the latter's defeat in the First World War. Political disintegration was accompanied by economic disintegration, as the market of the old monarchy was divided into the markets of the newly established succession states by the new custom-barriers. The period between the two World Wars was not favourable to integration in central and south-east Europe. Territorial disputes between the individual countries, frictions between nationalities, fears of German hegemony and of the resurrection of the Habsburg monarchy, as well as the different levels of economic development, standards of living, social policies, political structures and systems of government, made integration impossible. In the early 1920s the opportunity to reduce trade barriers between the successor states was missed. The military and the political alliance of Czechoslovakia, Yugoslavia, Romania, (the Little Entente) was rather unstable and the attempt to strengthen cooperation between these three countries by establishing the so-called Economic Little Entente failed completely in the early 1930s. The bonds between these countries were growing weaker.

These already considerable problems were compounded as Europe became part of the various spheres of interest of the world powers. The victory of the National Socialist Party in Germany in 1933 meant the start of a purposeful *Drang nach Osten*. Aiming to gain control of the countries of central and south-east Europe, the Nazis made use of various methods: capital infiltration, expansion of trade (particularly in the form of large purchases of agricultural products and raw materials), political pressure, activation of the German minorities, offers of alliances, military threats and, later on, direct aggression. Czechoslovakia bordering on Germany and possessing a relatively advanced economic potential, was the most exposed to pressure, threats and attempts to destabilise the country.

German economic expansion was based upon the theory of *Grossraumwirt-schaft*. In spite of the fact that this theory, in its Nazi variant, crystallised into an integral form as late as the beginning of the Second World War, it was deeply rooted in the past.[1] According to Nazi plans, Germany was to have become the core of an extensive economic whole comprising the greater part of Europe from Gibraltar and Scandinavia to the Urals and Cyprus. The supporters of *Grossraumwirtschaft* believed that the industrially, technologically and organisationally advanced German nation was destined to construct and control the European economic region beyond German borders. Under the hegemony of the Third *Reich* a strange type of economic integration was to be forced on the other European nations, not as Germany's partners but as objects of exploitation.

In the autumn of 1939, when the German economic sphere already fully covered the territories of Austria, Czechoslovakia and Poland, an institution was founded in Berlin by one of the Nationalsozialistische Deutsche Arbeiter Partei (NSDAP) ideologists, Werner Daitz, under the name of the *Gesellschaft für Europäische Wirtschaftsplanung und Grossraumwirtschaft*, in order to resolve the problems associated with the creation of a European *Grossraumwirtschaft*. A complex draft for a further advance in that direction was put forward by the German Minister of National Economy, Walter Funk, immediately after the fall of France. In August 1940 this draft was approved by Hermann Göring and, in February 1941 another research institute was founded in Dresden under the name of *Zentralforschungsinstitut für Nationale Wirtschaftsordnung und Grossraumwirtschaft*. When, towards the end of the war, the German economic empire was breaking up under the pressure of the Allied armies, Nazi propaganda changed its tone to emphasise the necessity of creating a European economic community on the basis of mutual cooperation between the European countries.[2]

The German *Grossraumwirtschaft* was to have been completed in full after the assumed victory of the Fascist powers, but its profile and the final aim was clear enough during the Second World War. Not only theoretically, but also from the point of view of practical experience, the economics of *Grossraumwirtschaft* can be viewed as a tool of German economic aggression and as a means for the systematic exploitation of the subjugated European nations. This economic policy also posed a serious threat to the allies of the Third *Reich* and to the uncommitted countries. The Fascist regime in Italy, for instance, considered the territory round the Mediterranean to be its economic sphere of interest and it rightly feared that this sphere might not be able to compete either with the German *Grossraumwirtschaft* or with its Japanese counterpart in the Far East. As early as 1939, the Slovak government tried to slow down the rate of German exploitation of the country by reducing exports to Germany to the level of imports, the government of Finland openly voiced its fears that the economic alliance with Germany might result in a decline of Finnish manufacturing industry and Sweden saw in German economic policy a menace to its sovereignty.[3]

Austria and Czechoslovakia had been the first to be subjected to German rule and the Nazi regime had longer to implement its economic plans in these countries rather than elsewhere. The process of incorporating Czechoslovakia into the economic system of the Third *Reich* and the role of the Czechoslovak economy in the *Grossraumwirtschaft* exhibits four main characteristics.

First, in contrast to Austria and some of the countries of south-east Europe, Czechoslovakia was initially able successfully to resist the attempts to tie it economically to Germany. The position of German capital remained relatively weak in Czechoslovakia and the German share in Czechoslovak foreign trade turnover in the years 1929 to 1937 fell from 30 to 16 per cent.[4] Second, the agreement concluded in Munich in September 1938 involved, among other things, approval by the governments of the United Kingdom, France and Italy to Czechoslovakia's incorporation into the economic sphere of Nazi Germany. In view of the preceding state of affairs the transfer involved a rapid re-orientation of the external economic relations, which was completed within barely a year, although certain differences persisted between the Czech frontier regions, the Czech central regions and Slovakia. This re-orientation inflicted upon the country did not take any account of the needs of Czechoslovakia and was dictated by exclusively German interests, but for the mauled Czechoslovakia there was no other alternative in the period between the Munich agreement and March 1939. Economic ties with the annexed frontier regions could not be broken off immediately. Moreover, Germany was in an advantageous position, for it had a number of very effective means of applying pressure. It could, for instance, discontinue the supply of coal and electricity from the annexed regions to the rest of the country. It could disrupt transport across these regions, making it difficult for the hundreds of thousands of Czechs moving inland from the region ceded to Germany. Autumn 1938 also brought significant changes in the ownership of capital in four directions: an influx of German capital, the ousting of Czechoslovak capital from the frontier regions, the ebb of west European capital, and the transfer of Jewish property to the west.

Third, the economic policy implemented by Nazi Germany in the different parts of Czechoslovakia was quite different. In Slovakia it resembled German economic policy in the Balkans or in Hungary. Slovakia was to become a supplier of raw materials, food and unskilled manpower, a buyer of the products of German manufacturing industry and a sphere for the profitable investment of German capital. However, the Czech lands were looked upon as an integral part of the Third *Reich* and therefore as part of the industrial core of the European *Grossraumwirtschaft*. For this reason no dismantling of industrial potential was foreseen after the expected victory of the German armies, as it was in the case of Poland or France. Nor was any substantial restructuring of industry in favour of the raw materials' sectors planned.

Fourth, the incorporation of the Czech lands into the German *Grossraumwirtschaft* was to be started with the restriction of Czech influence in the economy, and completed with the full Germanisation of the region and the population. The racially acceptable Czechs were to be Germanised, part of the population expatriated and the others physically liquidated.[5] These plans would have been fatal for the Czech nation, not only in the event of a German victory but also in the event of a military stalemate, for even in this latter case the Czech lands would most probably have remained part of Germany. In spite of the fact that Germanisation of the Czech economy had made great progress during the war, 'the decision concerning the final solution of the Czech problem' was put off until after the war for fear that the undue haste might adversely affect the smooth running of the armaments industry. Restraint was also induced by the simple fact that Germany was rather short of people who could be entrusted with colonising Czech territory.

The occupation of the Czech lands in 1938–39 and the conversion of Slovakia into a vassal state were of immense political, military and strategic importance to Nazi Germany and had a far-reaching economic effect. At that time, Czechoslovakia was the most industrially advanced country in the region to the east and south-east of Germany and Czech industry was considered to be one of the main suppliers of German industrial goods and armaments during the war.

Although Czechoslovakia was in no way rich in raw materials, its contribution to the German effort to achieve self-sufficiency in raw materials should not be overlooked in view of the strained balance of raw materials in Germany immediately before the war started. In Slovakia, Nazi economic policy was aimed particularly at the exploitation of the raw material base of the country, whereas in the Czech lands the occupier's main interest focussed on manufacturing industry. From the point of view of military preparations for the war, Czech heavy industry was of particular importance—viz. armaments factories, metallurgical and chemical works, mines and a number of large engineering enterprises which were readily capable of being converted to military production. In no other occupied country, with the exception of France and perhaps also Belgium, did Germany gain such a substantial military potential as in Czechoslovakia, where, moreover, manufacturing industry suffered little war damage. It is also worth recalling that, in 1939, Germany took possession of the modern armaments of the Czechoslovak army without having to take any military action.

The occupation of the Czech lands also improved the economic standing of Hitler's Third *Reich* in agriculture. Drawing on the surplus produce that had been accumulated during the protracted agrarian crisis in Czechoslovakia in the 1930s and taking advantage of the high intensity of farming production in the central regions of Bohemia and Moravia, Germany hoped to be at least partially able to alleviate its food shortages, which had been exacerbated by the annexation of the less fertile areas of Austria and the Czech frontier regions.

The effort to make maximum use of the human and material resources of the economically advanced occupied country for their own purposes determined the tactics of the Nazis in the Protectorate of Bohemia and Moravia.[6] The methods of Nazi policy in the Protectorate differed in a number of ways from the methods applied in the other occupied countries. The economic measures imposed by the occupation authorities and the constraints placed upon the activities of the bourgeoisie may have been more severe than in the occupied countries of northern and western Europe, but, on the other hand, looting was less prominent and terrorisation of the population less drastic than in Poland, Yugoslavia or in the occupied territories of the Soviet Union. Fear that a temporary vacuum might arise in the Protectorate and impair the smooth running of the economy, caused the implementation of some of the Nazi projects to be postponed until after the end of the war, especially the complex project of Germanisation of the Czech economy and of the entire 'Czech region'.

The economic importance of the Czech lands during the war also shaped some of the social and political policies of the occupiers. Although they were increasingly resorting to terror in the Protectorate, the Nazis were trying to keep up the appearance of a 'normal life' and they even considered it dangerous to allow the living standard of the Czech population to decline too steeply, because the situation in the Protectorate would have become even more explosive. Economic stability was also strengthened by social demagogy aimed at the wavering and nationally and politically less mature strata of the Czech nation.

The position of Slovakia was considerably different from the position of the Czech lands particularly in the initial period of the occupation. Instead of annexing Slovakia openly, Nazi Germany formally declared it independent and sovereign, and military occupation of the territory did not take place until 1944. A totalitarian dictatorship of the clerical and Fascist type was established in Slovakia under German auspices by the Slovak representatives of the Catholic Slovak People's Party headed by J. Tiso.[7] Whereas in the Czech lands occupation generated unequivocal antagonism between the Czech population and the occupiers, in Slovakia the clerical and Fascist regime was at first able to rely on a relatively broad social basis, which only gradually dissipated.

A similar differentiated approach was also characteristic of German economic policy in the Czech lands and Slovakia. Their differing degrees of dependence on Germany followed not only from the political aims of the Nazis, who supported Slovak separation with the intention of breaking up the Czechoslovak state and fomenting discord between the Czech and the Slovak nations, but also from the rather different economic and social structures of the two countries. Bohemia and Moravia were highly developed industrial regions, whereas in Slovakia half of the population depended on agriculture for their living. Slovakia lagged behind the capitalist development of the Czech lands by several decades, its bourgeoisie was relatively weak, and the industrial proletariat less numerous and concentrated. One consequence of this difference was that the small-scale nature of production in the Slovak economy proved more difficult to control than economies with a high concentration of production and capital. Precisely for this reason the exploitation of Slovakia had to be effected to a large extent with the help of a Slovak administration.

Although the economic dependence of Slovakia upon Nazi Germany may not have manifested such an immediate and pervasive character as the dependence of the Czech lands, the 'sovereignty' of the Slovak economy should not be overestimated even in the period immediately following 14 March 1939 (date of the Second Partition). The methods that Nazi Germany invariably used for enforcing its hegemony were varied and refined. From the legal point of view these methods of enforcing supremacy were based upon the relevant paragraphs in the Protection of Slovakia Treaty concluded by the German and the Slovak Governments which, among other things, legalised military occupation of the westernmost part of the country, as well as supreme German control over the Slovak armed forces and Slovak foreign policy. The semi-colonial character of the position of Slovakia immediately after its separation from the Czech lands is most clearly documented by the provisions of the protocol concerning the 'economic and financial cooperation' between Germany and Slovakia, which virtually gave the Third *Reich* free access to the economic resources of Slovakia.

On the basis of the secret protocol which was signed immediately after the foundation of the Slovak state, Germany gained absolute control of Slovak agricultural production, forestry and timber production and mineral resources. Industrial production was to be expanded in harmony with German requirements and Germany was to cooperate in the development of the Slovak transport system and to take part, through advisers, in all the more important financial decisions. The Protection of Slovakia Treaty and its economic annexe legalised a situation whereby German experts not only suggested important measures but also enforced them directly.[8]

The two documents of March 1939, together with the development of the situation in the following years, show clearly that Slovakia was assigned the task of becoming a strategic base for the German invasion of eastern and south-east Europe during the Second World war and were a raw material and agrarian reservoir for Germany. The economic dependence upon Czech capital, typical of the inter-war period, was replaced by German supremacy and the hopes of the Slovak ruling circles of being masters in their own house quickly dwindled.

The incorporation of Slovakia into the Nazi *Grossraumwirtschaft* led to constant exploitation of Slovak resources by Germany. More than 150,000 Slovaks were assigned to work in Germany at different periods, tree felling and mineral mining were stepped up, a disadvantageous rate of exchange between the crown and the mark was imposed on Slovakia,[9] and German debts to Slovakia were frozen in blocked mark accounts. Payments for supplies and services to the German armed forces, payments for transport and transfers of the pay of Slovak workers in Germany swelled these blocked accounts.[10]

The incorporation of the Protectorate of Bohemia and Moravia into the Nazi *Grossraumwirtschaft* was closely linked with the processes of militarisation, Germanisation and exploitation. In order to accelerate these processes, the occupiers made use of the system of *gelenkte Wirtschaft* (controlled economy) imported from Germany and applied as early as 1939. In Slovakia this system was introduced a little later and was certainly less widespread. The principal characteristics of *gelenkte Wirtschaft* included: compulsory organisation of businessmen in the individual branches of the national economy; central management of production, distribution and capital goods; central distribution of fuels, raw materials and other products; obligatory deliveries of farming produce and prohibition of the free sale of agricultural products; strict control over foreign trade and international payments; state-controlled pricing, allocation of labour and control of wage levels; a system of rationing of consumer goods.

The so-called labour offices were the most fearsome institutions of the controlled economy because they were the main agencies for the system of forced labour. Conscription of labour for work in Germany applied to all young Czechs of certain ages—at first this applied only to men, but later on women born in 1924 were also conscripted for work in the German aircraft industry. Excluding the tens of thousands of prisoners and migrant labourers who commuted across the frontier every day to work in Germany, approximately half a million Czech nationals worked in Germany, few of them voluntarily. Of the total number of foreign labourers in Germany at the beginning of 1941 the Czechs and Slovaks made up approximately 13 per cent though in spring 1944 this share fell to 5–6 per cent.[11]

The controlled economy became an efficient tool for the militarisation of the Czech economy, which manifested itself in every aspect of life. The structure of industrial production underwent particularly radical changes.

The metal industry, including metallurgy, accounted for 54 per cent of all the workers in the industrial sector in March 1945. At the beginning of 1945 the aircraft industry alone had 141,000 workers in its 135 enterprises in the Czech lands, including the frontier regions, 25 times more than before the war. In comparison other industries demonstrated a marked decline of production, with the exception of wood-working and the optical industries. Farming and construction also declined and house building practically ceased.[12]

The link between the controlled economy and Germanisation was equally transparent. German nationals were invariably assigned to key posts in the newly established administration of the controlled economy and they, of course, systematically pushed through various measures designed to weaken the economic positions of Czechs. The measures taken by the occupiers soon resulted in the liquidation of a large number of Czech enterprises in the manufacturing industry, crafts, trade and banking. German enterprises, on the other hand, were strongly favoured. German influence in the economy was also strengthened by the confiscation of Czech and Jewish property, the penetration of German capital into Czech joint stock companies and the confiscation of land owned by Czech farmers and peasants.[13]

The incorporation of Czechoslovakia into the Nazi *Grossraumwirtschaft* was followed by the systematic exploitation of the country, inflicting considerable damage upon its economy. Amongst the most prominent and damaging measures were the undervaluation of the crown in its relation to the mark, the compulsory introduction of the mark into circulation beside the crown in the Protectorate of Bohemia and Moravia, and the abolition of the customs boundary between the Protectorate and Germany from October 1940. The Czech lands were dragged into financing the German war effort by being obliged to pay a regular 'protection' fee—in effect a tax imposed upon the Czech population—and Slovakia was forced to increase its military outlay.

The German occupation wrought havoc in all spheres of the economy. In addition to direct war damage and casualties there were increased health problems. Alongside the exploitation of labour outside Czechoslovak territory there was, in the Czech areas an added distortion of human resources as the replacement of the older generation of the intelligentsia was inhibited by closure of the universities and reductions in the intake of secondary, technical and grammar schools. The Germans froze immense Czechoslovak assets in Germany and furthermore, material goods were drained by a distorted exchange rate. The currency and state finances were disrupted, savings were devalued by inflation, exchange reserves and gold were stolen, forests were depleted by excessive felling and Czechoslovak rolling stock and vehicles were scattered all over Europe.

The record of German economic domination of Czechoslovakia in the war years is important not only because of the damage and misery which it inflicted but also because of its long-term consequences. The experience of occupation and the memory that this occupation was part of an enforced integration served to discredit the very idea of economic integration. The aversion to participation in any larger political and economic formation was also effectively fed by memories of the period preceding 1918, when the Czech nation, as part of the Austro-Hungarian Empire, had for centuries been faced with the prospect of Germanisation and the Slovak nation had been threatened with extinction by integration into Hungary.[14]

The consequences of the two world wars had both a disintegrating effect and an integrating effect on Czechoslovakia, in that they promoted the economic, political and cultural integration of the Czechs and Slovaks into a single sovereign state. Any plans for supranational formations drafted either during the inter-war period or after the Second World War met with extreme mistrust and were suspected of threatening hard-won national independence. In a small country located in the heart of Europe, in close proximity to Germany, at a point where the interests of the world powers clashed and, after 1945, the boundary between two worlds, that mistrust was fully understandable.

At present, political integration and the plans for supranational formations are far from being of topical interest to the Czechoslovak population, but there has recently been a marked trend towards a more positive attitude to economic integration. An ever growing part of the population realises that the efficiency of the national economy is at present dependent upon the level of integration achieved by the members of the Council for Mutual Economic Assistance (Comecon), and the old question of whether to integrate, has changed into the question of how to integrate. The initiative taken by the Czechoslovak government in this direction at the recent sessions of Comecon is thus in full conformity with public opinion in Czechoslovakia. The Czechoslovak public also supports economic cooperation with the non-socialist countries and the establishment of contacts between Comecon and the EEC.

Notes

1. J. Chodorowski, *Niemecka doktryna gospodarki wielkego obszaru 1800–1945*, (Wroclaw, Zaklad Narodowy im Osslińskick, 1972).
2. Cz Luczak, *Polityka ekonomiczna Trzeciej Rzeszy v latach drugej wojny światowej* (Poznan, Bykom, 1982), pp. 35–39.
3. Ibid., p. 41.
4. *Zahraniční obchod Republiky československe v roce 1937*, Vol. 2 (Prague, Statni Urad Statisticky, 1938), p. 35. In the same period the share of Austria in Czechoslovak foreign trade fell from 12 per cent to 6 per cent and the share of

Hungary from 6 per cent to 2 per cent. Amongst the Balkan countries Bulgaria and Yugoslavia are the best examples of the reorientation of foreign trade towards Germany. A. Teichova, *Kleinstaten im Spannungsfeld der Grossmachte* (Munich, Oldenbourg, 1988), p. 182.

5. The plan for Germanisation was the subject of a classified document by *Reichsprotektor* J. von Neurath and Secretary of State K.H. Frank. This document was approved by Hitler. *Reichsprotektor* R. Heydrich, in his speech to German officials in the Protectorate on 2nd October 1941, estimated that from the point of view of race, Germanisation could be applied to 40–60 per cent of the Czech population. He added that the attitude of each individual to Germany was also an important criterion. Heydrich claimed that in the Czech lands 'a Czech has in the end nothing to adduce to justify his presence there'. He recommended expatriating part of the Czech population and moving it to the Arctic Ocean. Anyone who resisted Germanisation was 'to be stood against the wall'. The documents have been published under the title *Chtěli nás vyhubit*, (Prague, Ministerstvo Informaci, 1961), pp. 62–75, 132, 152, 184. See also the publication *Československo a norimbersky proces* (Prague, Ministerstvo Zaranicnich Veci, 1946).

6. The Protectorate of Bohemia and Moravia was founded in the western part of the post-Munich Czechoslovakia. The principal items of Hitler's decree of 16 March 1939 concerning its establishment had been copied from the colonial treaty concluded between Tunisia and France in 1881. The highest representative of the occupying power was the *Reichsprotektor* and the autonomous Czech administration was represented by the President and the government of the Protectorate. The power of the autonomous Czech administration was however gradually curbed. Prime Minister A. Eliáš was sentenced to death in October 1941 and executed in June 1942. In the government, reorganised at the beginning of 1942, the greatest power was concentrated in the hands of W. Bertsch, a German entrusted with the management of the Ministry of National Economy. The other Czech ministers had German deputies, who actually managed the individual ministries.

7. The founder of the party was a Catholic priest, A. Hlinka, who opposed the policy of the two Czechoslovak presidents of the inter-war period, T.G. Masaryk and E. Beneš. After his death in 1938 the party was led by another Catholic priest, J. Tiso. When Slovakia was made 'independent' on 14 March 1939, Tiso became Prime Minister and from October 1939 until April 1945 he was President of Slovakia.

8. For the text of the two documents see *Československo a norimbersky proces*, op. cit., p. 342.

9. The rate of exchange of the mark to the crown was fixed at 1 to 8.33 in the Czech frontier regions, at 1 to 10 in the Protectorate and at 1 to 11.65 in Slovakia, but the real purchasing power of 1 mark in the period 1938–39 was approximately 6–7 Czechoslovak crowns. The adverse rate of exchange between the mark and the crown, 1 to 11.63, was maintained in spite of the fact that, e.g. in the years 1941–42 the purchasing power of one German mark was only 4 Slovak crowns.

10. L. Kováčik, *Slovensko v sieti nemeckého finančneho kapitálu* (Bratislava, Pravda,

1955), p. 86.
11. Calculated from the data quoted in J. Kuczynski, *Die Geschichte der Lage der Arbeiter in Deutschland von 1789 bis in die Gegenwart*, Vol. II/1 (Berlin, Tribüne, 1953), pp. 239 and 264.
12. *Statisticky zpravodaj* (Prague, Statni Urad Statisticky, 1945), p. 7; *Ustredni svaz cs. prumyslu v roce 1945* (Prague, 1946), p. 89.
13. *Státní hospodaření za války a po revoluci* (Prague, SNPL, 1946), p. 83; L. Chmela, *Hospodářská okupace Československa, její methody a důsledky* (Prague, Orbis, 1946), pp. 107–110.
14. The following works dealing with the economic problems of the Second World War may be of interest to the reader: R. Olsovsky et al., *Přehled hospodářského vývoje Československa v letech 1918–1945* (Prague, Statni naklad politike literatury, 1961); V. Průcha, *Základní rysy válečného řízeného hospodářství v českých zemích v letech nacistické okupace*, in *Historie a vojenstyi*, 3; J. Faltus and V. Průcha, *Prehl ád hospodářského vývoja na Slovensku v rokoch 1918–1945* (Bratislava, VPL, 1969); V. Průcha et al., *Hospodářské dějiny Československa v 19. a 20. století* (Bratislava, Pravda, 1974); V. Průcha et al., *Hospodářské dějiny evropských socialistických zemí* (Prague, SPN, 1977(; V. Průcha et al., *Historia gospodarcza Czechoslowacji XX wieku* (Warsaw, Panstowe Wydawnictwo Navkowe 1979); V. Průcha et al., *Rozwój gospodarczy europejskich krajów socjalistycznych* (Warsaw, Panstowe Wydawnictwo Ekonomicze, 1981); V. Průcha et al., *Nástin hospodářských dějin v období kapitalismu a socialismu* (Prague, Svoboda, 1982, 2nd amended edition, Prague, Svoboda, 1987); V. Průcha, *Landwirtschaft und Ernährung in der Tschechoslowakei während des Zweiten Weltkrieges*, in B. Martin, A.S. Milward (eds.), *Landwirtschaft und Versorgung im Zweiten Weltkrieg* (Scripta Mercaturae Verlag, Ostfildern BRD 1985), pp. 128–142.

7 Making the new Netherlands?: ideas about renewal in Dutch politics and society during the Second World War

J.C.H. Blom and W. ten Have

'The old world is dead. The future lies with those who can resolutely turn their back on it and face the new world with understanding, courage and imagination,' states the closing sentence of E.H. Carr's *Conditions of Peace* first published in 1942, a work that through the underground network of the Resistance became widely known in the occupied countries of Europe.[1] In many of these countries the experience of the Second World War produced both a surge of activity and a widely-felt need for reflection or taking stock. This can be seen, for instance, in a revival of an interest in religion, but most of all it took the form of an active consideration and discussion of the shape of the future. In the eyes of many people pre-war society with its many defects could not be allowed to return unchanged. After the war a better world and a better society were to be created. Thus, many people in the occupied countries shared Carr's opinion. Expectations for the future ran high with the tensions engendered by the war and occupation acting as a kind of pressure cooker of ideas.

It would be wrong to think that opinion was undivided as to the nature of the world that was to be reborn. In retrospect, the basis of agreement consisted of not much more than a common aversion to the pre-war situation and a shared state of mind after the defeat which was characterised by the need to do something positive. What this did mean was that, in spite of the many internal differences of opinion, the same catchwords reappeared. In the Netherlands these manifested themselves as the desire to create more unity in a country that was traditionally highly segmented and the determination to pursue active policies that would eliminate the evils associated predominantly with the effects of mass unemployment. The spirit of the time was encapsulated by the idea of renewal. Old ways must go: existing ways must be changed.

Before analysing further those concepts of renewal which prevailed during the occupation, it is important to review briefly the critical ideas that had surfaced during the previous decade. For discussion during the war years inevitably had its origins, in the Netherlands as elsewhere, in the unease that had already been generally expressed in the 1930s. It was in part the ideas put forward in these years that, through the force of war, helped lead to the concrete formulations of renewal in the post-war period.

What were the central issues that occupied the nation and provided the main lines of subsequent innovatory thinking? Four issues which were substantially interlinked may be said to have dominated all others:

1. The problem of government authority.
2. Questions surrounding the socio-economic basis of Dutch society.
3. National unity.
4. A discussion of what changes in mentality were required to break the rigidity of the political system.[2]

Let us look first at government authority. There was a widespread belief that the pre-war governments had failed to act with sufficient energy in both social and political matters. The existing political arrangements between parties were widely held to be the prime cause of this, but there was considerable diversity of opinion as to the remedy. Some thought that a policy that consciously strove for and was based upon an idea of national unity would bring about the desired improvements. Others, however, blamed the political system itself. Parliamentary democracy within a constitutional monarchy, it was argued, prevented both the prime minister and the cabinet from vigorously asserting government authority. The plethora of political parties was thought to contribute to this inaction insofar as they were suspected of letting their own interests prevail over the general, national, interest. There was also disagreement as to the areas in which government authority needed to be expressed more forcefully. Some critics focussed on law and order. They saw an absence of discipline in society and a lack of respect for authority, the existing order and government. They noted with distaste the low prestige of the armed forces in society. For others the problem lay more in the socio-economic sphere where they wished for a greater and more energetic government intervention.

This brings us to the second issue: the socio-economic order. The Netherlands' economic system was an extreme example of liberal, *laissez-faire*, *laissez-aller* capitalism. To an increasing number of people in the 1930s this was objectionable. They set against it, as an alternative, *ordening* (order) a word that came almost to typify the period. It could be a socialist order established by revolutionary or peaceful means. It could equally mean the cooperation of the various interests in society, either under government auspices or on a voluntary basis. Such ideas in turn led to proposals for the establishment of new bodies with statutory powers over economic life and social relations. In any case, it was increasingly felt that the free play of social forces and the unbridled pursuit of egotistical interests must be counterbalanced by a new public spirit.

With this we have come to the third issue of pre-war discussion: national unity. This has already been touched on in terms of the question of the lack of government authority. The multiplicity of political parties and the resulting fragmentation of Dutch political life tended to create a general dislike of politics and to encourage a preference for an entirely different system in which only the 'national interest' counted. (In 1933, 54 political parties contested the elections, of which 14 succeeded in entering a parliament in which there were only 100 seats.) More influential still were the moves to restrict the increase of new parties and, more especially, to end the peculiarly Dutch system of party formation known since the 1930s as *verzuiling* (literally pillarisation, or compartmentalisation). This term was used to describe the division of the Dutch population into a number of segments, each possessing its own common and distinct denominational and/or ideological base and each organising itself socially and politically within this boundary. To the critics of *verzuiling*, the system pushed the real problems and essential choices of the country as a whole into the background, simply by existing. First, it preserved artificial divisions and so hindered the process of national unity. Second, inasmuch as those pillars organised on a denominational basis held within themselves a number of divergent and even contradictory opinions, they tended to mask the difference between progressives and conservatives and thus prevented a political re-alignment on a national scale. As a result, both the political system and the machinery of government were regarded as inefficient and ineffective.

The fourth issue, which centred on the desire to break the rigidity of the system through a change of mentality, was closely bound up with one of the consequences of the segmentation of Dutch society. *Verzuiling*, it was felt, had caused a type of fossilisation of political life, which was perceptible in the way in which power was distributed. Because of the thoroughness of *verzuiling*, the number of seats held by the different parties in parliament remained roughly constant. In the 1930s the Catholic Party usually obtained about 30 seats, as did the Protestant parties within their pillar; the Social Democrats could expect a little over 20 seats and the Liberal parties between 10 and 15. This distribution was only occasionally disturbed by smaller parties who managed to gain an isolated seat or two. The result, according to the critics, was ossification, since politics became a business largely of negotiations about the formation of coalitions controlled entirely by the party élite. The prevailing mentality was, therefore, one in which discussion about principles and essential issues in society did not have a high priority. The party élite remained closed to ideas of renewal both in terms of its personal demeanour and in its inability to be receptive to new ideas. It was this rigidity that needed to be broken. A new élan, a new style and a new sense of involvement in the pressing social issues of the time had to be created. Only the reintroduction of a debate about principles would restore the dynamism missing in political life and make possible a start in solving the huge problems facing the nation.

The various ideas about renewal, then, were closely bound up with each other. For this reason it is possible to talk of a common tendency in the criticisms that were expressed against the existing order, but there was no question of there being one coherent and widely supported alternative. Much of the criticism was rooted in an undefined feeling of unease about the present to which very few people gave a more concrete expression. Even then it was apparent that there were great differences in both the analysis and the solutions proposed.

Nevertheless, three distinct centres may be discerned which provided the matrix around which debate was conducted during the occupation. First— though not most influentially—there were the groups with a right-wing authoritarian focus which, in the Netherlands as elsewhere in Europe, were conspicuous from the end of the First World War.[3] In the early days after the war these groups had been inspired by Mussolini and Fascism without knowing much about either. They were attracted by the impression of energy given by Fascism in its striving for national and social recovery and seduced, especially, by its stance of radical opposition to parliamentary democracy. For a long time the numerical importance of these movements was minimal. This changed when the *Nationaal Socialistische Beweging* (National Socialist Movement or NSB) was formed in 1931 around a programme largely copied from the German NSDAP. This movement succeeded where the others had failed. Solidly organised, it soon drew to itself a large following. In the elections of 1935 for the Provincial Estates it was, in Dutch terms, extra-ordinarily successful, polling almost 8 per cent of the votes. Although unable to sustain this level of support it remained a potential force right up to the invasion of 1940.

Second, there was a focus of anti-democratic and corporatist ideas among young predominantly Catholic intellectuals and artists who had turned away from the big Catholic Party, the *Rooms Katholieke Staats Partij*. Concerned at the inability of the official Catholic Party to tackle economic and social problems within the existing system, they argued for a rejuvenated, assertive Catholicism. Their determination to end the political squabbling brought them close to the authoritarian movements in this respect. In other respects the basis of their thinking was to counterpose the idea of a united nation against the 'pillarised' reality. Much of their effort was directed at an attempt to break the rigid denominational and ideological boundaries in Dutch society by promoting contact between sections of the population who were otherwise separate from each other.

Third, there was a movement from within the pillars themselves. Even though the pillars and their corresponding political parties formed the basis of the existing political system, it would be wrong to think that there was a complete lack of thought about change. During the 1930s in particular, a group within the large Protestant Party, the *Christelijk Historische Unie* (CHU) began to oppose *verzuiling* and to call into question the validity of the confessional basis of party formation. In the Social Democratic Party (SDAP) a growing reformist current offered a series of plans as an alternative to the unsuccessful conservative anti-crisis policy of the government coalition. The *Plan van de Arbeid* (Labour Plan), which was adopted in 1936 as official Party policy, contained a far-reaching and detailed set of prescriptions for socio-economic policy both in the short and the long term. It was this very subject of the socio-economic order which also exercised minds in several other established parties. The young especially and those outside the circle of the party élites explored the lines of a more actively interventionist government role in tackling the economic crisis. Naturally, differences between groups remained. The very choice of the words in which the criticisms were formulated expressed as much: some spoke of a corporatist order; others of functional decentralisation. Yet there was a sense of working in a similar frame in spite of the difficulty of crossing the traditional dividing lines between the pillars. 'From all sides there is a call for order' wrote a young Social-Democrat with innovatory ideas, M. van der Goes van Naters in 1935, citing the Labour Plan and the widely-discussed Papal Encyclical *Quadragesimo Anno* as examples from either end of the spectrum.[4] The desire for renewal was voiced increasingly frequently and often stridently, but as the war approached it is true to say that it had as yet touched only a minority. The 'traditionalists' remained on top. It took the shock of war and occupation to loosen the bonds of tradition.

The German invasion, the rapidity of the Dutch capitulation and the occupation caused an enormous shock in the Netherlands.[5] The first violently expressed emotions were followed by a return to everyday life as if in a trance. It was 'business as usual', or so it seemed. In public life in general and in political life in particular lethargy reigned. Parliament had been dissolved and, after the first indignant protests against the German invasion and the capitulation speech made by the Commander-in-Chief, little or nothing was heard from the government or politicians. The German military and the authorities who began to organise an occupation régime that might well prove to be a lengthy one, behaved in an exemplary manner. It was for this reason that the attention of the general public focussed largely on the

NSB. They were expected to show a new confidence, and this they did through their arrogant behaviour in the streets and the confident assertion in their press and public meetings that they would shortly help form a government.

In these circumstances, and with the traditional political parties seemingly moribund, a new political movement presented itself to the Dutch people in July 1940, the *Nederlandse Unie* (Netherlands Union). In its Manifesto the key words were unity and renewal. The first of these made the *Unie* a home for the many people who wished to remain Dutch and who, in the conditions of uncertainty as to the direction that the still novel occupation would take, looked upon the NSB as traitors who wanted to hand over the country to the German Nazis. The call for the unity of all those who had been divided before the war found receptive ears. Within just a few months the new movement had 8–900,000 members, more than all the pre-war political parties put together had ever had.[6]

In addition, the *Nederlandse Unie* argued in favour of renewal. It was the first organisation to come forward during the occupation with a new formulation of ideas about the shape of a future—independent— Netherlands. The rejection of the pre-war system was both implicitly and explicitly the point of their departure. The part of their programme that called for the maintenance of the national character was addressed specifically to the situation of the occupation, but it also had another, long-term, significance that referred to the necessity of tolerance and freedom of conscience. Thus the idea of unity was both a call for a united front against the NSB and a development of the pre-war opposition to the disunity of *verzuiling*. Slogans such as 'the unity of the nation', 'organic ordering' and 'stronger state power' also stood in a line of continuity with the neophilia of the pre-war. These aims of the *Unie*, which were close to much of the new thinking throughout Europe during the war did, it is true, show a certain affinity with the terminology of the National Socialist occupier. Nevertheless, and perhaps even partly because of this, the *Unie* became, until its dissolution by the Germans in December 1941, the point of assembly for those who wished to preserve a Dutch nation in the future, however uncertain that future was. Discussion of renewal contributed powerfully to this aim while, at the same time, the very weight of numbers gathered in the *Unie* made plain to the occupier the dangers in favouring the NSB.

Such adaptations to present circumstances were widely to be seen. Apart from a certain tendency to leave everything as it was for the time being and wait and see, a widespread urge toward unity was noticable in social life. In many areas, clubs and organisations that had been strictly 'pillarised' and divided on confessional lines before the war merged with each other. For the most part this was spontaneous, although later in the occupation it was often advanced by the Germans. One important consideration behind such mergers was always to keep the NSB hand 'off the tiller'.

In July 1940 a series of consultations took place between the leaders of the main political parties. There was no immediately obvious result, yet the meetings provided the sign of a new willingness to move towards closer cooperation. If the political parties themselves did not initiate a discussion about political and social renewal, individuals within them began increasingly to do so.

In this respect, the contacts first made in the early period of the occupation and developed subsequently in the camp at St Michielsgestel took on a great importance for a part of the political élite. This camp in the south of the Netherlands was the place in which a large group of those who were most prominent in public life were brought together as hostages by the occupier in 1942. In terms of religious and political affiliation the group was very heterogeneous. The many discussions at St Michielsgestel resulted in a formulation in terms of renewal and a plan for its realisation after the Liberation. It was agreed that *verzuiling*, with its system of political parties based on confessional principles, had to be broken through. A new 'party of the whole nation' should be formed based on the ideology of personalist socialism. Here the influence of the circle round the French periodical *Esprit* was obvious. Personalist socialism, as articulated by the *Esprit* group's founder, Emmanuel Mounier, was a social philosophy in which the spiritually and ethically inspired individual took responsibility for the achievement of a just society. The argument for its applicability to the process of renewal in a post-war Netherlands which was conducted at St Michielsgestel involved, not surprisingly, many of those who had played a prominent part in the *Nederlandse Unie*.[7]

If we leave aside the attitude of the Dutch National Socialists— unquestionably also centred on a form of renewal—the further development of innovatory concepts was to be found increasingly in the underground movements and the underground press. In the later stages of the war three main currents can be distinguished. First, there were those who argued for a more authoritarian system of government, often advocating a more significant role for the monarch. Second, sustained effort for renewal among Marxist and radical Socialist groups may be detected. The Communists in particular tried to reach out to a wider constituency than before through an appeal for greater openness. In spite of the sympathy for the Soviet Union as an ally, the attempt was mainly unsuccessful. Part of the reason lay in the fact that the Social Democrats were continuing what they had started before the war, moving toward cooperation with other established parties. In doing so they were drawing near to the third current of proposals about renewal: that advocating more solidarity and a greater spirit of community along the lines that had already been manifested in the *Nederlandse Unie* and at St Michielsgestel. All of these groups shared a strong desire for solidarity and cooperation and, normally, the belief in the necessary re-ordering of social and economic life.

Such matters were debated, often heatedly, in the underground press.[8] from the discussions in these papers it is clear that the aim of renewal was flatly rejected only in the orthodox Protestant circles around the Anti-Revolutionary Party (ARP). *Trouw*, the underground paper which best represented the voice of the ARP, dismissed the idea of a future that was based simply on opposition to the situation before May 1940. It criticised, too, the prevailing scepticism of parliamentary democracy as well as the call for a greater role for the government. Here the *Unie* came in for particularly harsh criticism. Towards the end of the war others joined *Trouw* in regarding the *Unie*'s original striving for renewal as having been conducted in too close a contact with the occupier. *Het Parool*, for instance, also turned against the *Unie* but accepted that its supporters had been disillusioned with the old political parties. It agreed that these were now finished for good because they had lost their authority. Should they return after the Liberation then so would the sterile political disputes: questions from before the war such as whether to play football on Sundays or the acceptability of cremation would resurface. With this in mind, *Het Parool* pleaded for a ban on new party formation for 6 months after the Liberation to allow a new, free, public opinion to develop. In its view, a new party based on progressive social and economic policies had every chance of success, including among Catholics. Such a party would define itself on a 'spiritually acceptable basis' and guarantee the rights of all groups within society. Personalist socialism, it was thought, offered a good starting point. With this *Het Parool* came strikingly close to the plans for breakthrough that had been formulated in St Michielsgestel and thus, close also to the position of the *Unie*. In their own various illegal newspapers former *Unie* members argued for the same type of renewal. *Christofoor*, a paper dominated by Catholics (and some Protestants) who wanted a new non-confessional party, stood up for the discredited *Unie* by pointing to the 'vote of confidence' that had been given to it by some hundreds of thousands of people. Nor was the focus on *ontzuiling* ('de-pillarisation') confined to these ex-*Unie* circles. *Vrij Nederland*, operating on the left wing of the Resistance, considered party formation based on religion to be the most important obstacle to the achievement of renewal.

Although even *Trouw* could not avoid some association with ideas of unity and renewal (it argued, for instance, in favour of the realignment of all 'positively Christian' Protestants in one political party) it provides an emphatic counter to the view cultivated by most of the underground press that during the occupation the renewers had a monopoly. Some people envisaged a new conservative grouping which would be an effective block against renewal ideas. At its core would be an alliance between liberal supporters of *laissez-faire* capitalism and opponents of 'de-pillarisation', such as were to be found in *Trouw*. Somewhat less prominent were those who preferred the existing order without substantive change. The employer D.U. Stikker, for example, who played a role in the Resistance was clearly opposed to policies of radical government interference in economic affairs. In trade union circles there was considerable hesitation about the search for unity. Many showed that they preferred to maintain the existing (or pre-war) structure and to concentrate on restoring their previous position. They had to compete, however, with renewers both within and outside their organisations. A very good indication of the place that the renewers held in the spectrum of illegal groups is provided by an example from late in the war. When, toward the end of the occupation, a coordinating committee of the unions was set up and, in order to achieve parity, allocations to left, right and centre had to be made, the renewers—even if they had their origins in the *Unie*—were placed firmly on the left.

There was one topic about which ideas of the future were developed during the occupation which was not linked with comparable ideas from before the war. This was the position of the Netherlands in Europe.

The illegal press took different views on the question. In the early part of the occupation the *Unie* had already argued that after the war, whatever its outcome, there would be a need for a thoroughgoing cooperation with other parts of Europe. The German invasion had made it clear that the Netherlands could no longer stand alone. Later in the war *De Ploeg* embroidered on this theme: from the time of the German attack the main issues had been cooperation and economic unity on a European scale; these would not disappear once the war was over. In its turn, *Het Parool* proposed a military alliance with France, Belgium and Britain as the basis for a post-war customs and currency union. *Vrij Nederland* dismissed German propaganda which suggested that the Third Reich was fighting for 'Europe'; but it conceded that this propaganda had had the effect of putting the 'task' of Europe for the Netherlands on the public agenda. On this question *Trouw* once more took a deviant line, finding the thought of European Union obnoxious inasmuch as it was reminiscent of that German imperialism from which the Continent was now suffering.

The declaration in favour of a European Federation, framed in Geneva in 1944 by representatives of the Resistance movements from a number of occupied countries, caused scarcely any reaction in the Dutch underground press.

Yet there was no doubt that the united front against the German oppressor had brought about a spirit of fraternity and solidarity between the occupied nations of Europe.[9] The Resistance in the Netherlands, however, showed itself too preoccupied with the concerns of everyday life and of the future of the country to dedicate itself to the working out of concrete plans for European cooperation after the war. It was less a lack of concern than a matter of priority.

Finally, brief mention must be made of the position of those Dutch people who had fled to England in 1940. Many of them were also renewers. Queen Wilhelmina in particular, unlike her Ministers, was a firm advocate of renewal. She had her own strong views—some of which she had expressed just before the war—about the fossilisation of public life and the gap between the élite and the mass. England provided her with a forum for renewal insofar as it gave her the opportunity to make contact with those she considered to be the real representatives of the future Netherlands, in particular young members of the Resistance movements. Her views found an echo in London and some found their way back to be widely circulated in the Dutch Resistance.

From the moment of the Liberation it was clear that the period immediately following would be crucially important for the successful realisation of plans for renewal.[10] In this respect it was of great significance that the Netherlands was liberated in two stages. The southern, predominantly Catholic, part of the country was liberated in the Autumn of 1944; the remaining part not until May 1945 at the very end of the war in Europe. In between lay the 'hunger winter' which affected the west of the country and, especially, the cities, resulting in terrible deprivations and a complete disorganisation of society. Most advocates of renewal in the liberated South decided to postpone the realisation of their plans until the whole country had been liberated. Renewal, they argued, must involve the whole country. The result of this delay was that other parties and organisations not committed to renewal were able to retake their positions without encountering competition and, in their turn, begin to organise a resistance against renewal. In retrospect it is also apparent that as material conditions worsened in the last winter of the war, so too did the prospects of political and spiritual renewal. Among other considerations, the job of reconstruction demanded too much of the country's energy.

After the final liberation of the whole of the country many of the personalist socialists and the anti-*verzuilers* created the renewal movement, in the shape of the *Nederlandse Volksbeweging* (Dutch People's Movement or NVB), that they had prepared for in the hostage camp at St Michielsgestel. For a short time it seemed as if it might sweep all before it. One of the Movement's leading figures, W. Schermerhorn, became Prime Minister almost entirely on the grounds that he was a renewer. During the period before the first post-war elections, the NVB received enormous and favourable publicity. In addition, it benefited from the distance between itself and the more authoritarian currents of renewal. These latter showed themselves in the end to be without widespread support in large measure because in the circumstances after the Liberation it was not easy to argue against parliamentary democracy. So too the NVB could be distinguished from renewal proposals associated with radical Socialists as well as the revived Communist Party and its newspaper *De Waarheid*. These groups scored some success in the field of trade union re-organisation, in particular with the creation of a new unified trade union council, the *Eenheid Vak Centrale* (EVC). However, their position was weakened to the extent that they took the blame for the manifestations of unrest that occurred after the war (notably the dock strike) and which were pictured as hindering the process of reconstruction. Moreover, the dominant role of the Communists in the EVC prevented a linkage at élite level, deterring above all the Social Democrats.

The ardent renewers of the NVB did succeed in inducing a few groups to merge into the intended 'new party for the whole nation', most notably the Social Democratic and the radical Liberal Parties. To their great disappointment, however, only a few isolated individuals joined from the Confessional Parties. The old Confessional Parties simply stayed in place, sometimes in a new shell, as was the case with the Catholics, who created a new *Katholieke Volkspartij* (KVP). The election result of May 1946 was clear-cut. In spite of all their propaganda in favour of renewal, the new *Partij van de Arbeid* (Labour Party or PvdA) barely polled the number of votes that the parties which it had absorbed had gained separately in the last pre-war elections. In these terms the radical socialist renewers had produced a greater electoral swing: the Communist Party in its new form won 10 per cent of the vote, compared to its 3 per cent before the war.

After the election, a governing coalition was formed between the PvdA and the KVP who, in their pre-war guises, had briefly worked together in the last coalition before the occupation. Regarding policy the renewers had to swallow many disappointments. Insofar as the problems of material reconstruction, the post-war purges and trials and the escalating Indonesian crisis left time to think about renewal, most of it failed. Aside from the political parties themselves, which presented a nearly unchanged spectrum, the best example of this failure is perhaps in the realm of broadcasting. Before the war broadcasting had been pre-eminently pillarised, being made up of separate Catholic, orthodox Protestant, Social Democratic and general (more or less Liberal) services. In spite of frenetic attempts to replace this by one national broadcasting system, here too *verzuiling* remained largely intact. The results were similar in other areas. The socio-economic field saw some change inasmuch as the role played by government was, for a time, much greater than it had been before the war. Moves were made to develop separate corporatist bodies with their own statutory powers, and yet the impetus for interference came more from the requirements of reconstruction than from any ideological conviction in renewal as such. What was proposed in legislative terms was only a pale reflection of what the renewers had wanted; what was carried into practice was a paler reflection still. Only in the field of foreign policy was there a distinct change of course with the abandonment of the pre-war policy of neutrality. This did fit with what many voices during the occupation had been saying, but the main reason for the shift lay in the fact of the world situation. The Netherlands had little alternative but to participate in the Atlantic and European Alliance.

Doorbraak (breakthrough) was the word used after the Liberation to express the idea of a new party system and a new direction for the Netherlands that would do away with the pillarised relations of the past. It has to be admitted that this utterly failed to happen; both the supporters and the opponents of *doorbraak* agreed on that. Just as had been the case before the war, the elections of 1946 put the desire for renewal in perspective and left its advocates without a chance of success. Does this mean, then, that they had been chasing shadows? Did the 'vision' of the occupation founder on the harsh post-war 'reality' as the author of a study published some 15 years after the Liberation suggested?[11] If we take a broad perspective the case is hard to dispute. It is clear that *verzuiling* was, if anything, strengthened in the coming years; liberal capitalism flourished rather than withered away in the post-war boom; the composition of the social and political élite and its ponderous style of governing scarcely differed from before the war.

There remains a question, however, as to whether this is the whole story about the renewal movement. Renewal as such may not have triumphed but it is possible to detect a number of shifts of emphasis in the social and political order. In the first place the movement against parliamentary democracy with its accompanying calls for a more authoritarian style of government disappeared completely—though this is a phenomenon that can be observed throughout western Europe. Second, in spite of the failure of breakthrough in a strict sense, its influence did penetrate the political establishment. The ideas of the renewers played a key role in the policy development of the PvdA and also, crucially, the KVP. In addition, the renewers' insistence on the practice of cooperation from which none of the major political groupings would be excluded was clearly confirmed. Third, after the end of the emergency situation of the immediate post-war period, the role of government was unmistakably greater than it had been even before the war when there had been unprecedented intervention brought about by the economic crisis of the 1930s. There was a clear general wish to continue and expand this role in the long term, which manifested itself in new legislation (albeit sometimes rather half-hearted) on socio-economic affairs.

On the other hand, the radical socialist movement, particularly the variant represented by the Communist Party, became weaker as time went on. Thus, it may be that innovatory thinking critical of strongly exclusive stances began to shift and create nuances in terms of *ontzuiling* in an otherwise strengthened pillarised order. It is possible that this paradox played a part in developments in the future, especially in the 1960s. 'If there was a decisive transformation in the contemporary history of the Netherlands this should be sought in the 1960s rather than in the Second World War', was how one of the present authors summed up the problem of continuity.[12] Did the innovatory lines developed during the occupation have to wait over a decade to be realised? At first sight, and from a narrow point of view, the answer would appear to be no. Not only was there no obvious line of continuity in terms of people or organisations but, most important, there is no clear affinity between the changes proposed in the 1960s and those advanced during the earlier period. Yet, looked at in a wider perspective, a line of continuity can be traced. It is indisputable that much of what happened in the 1960s was motivated above all by an urge toward *ontzuiling*, in part, perhaps, because the increased government role of the post-war had finally undermined the position of the pillars in the social and political order of the country.

Any conclusion, in the absence of wide research on the 1960s in the Netherlands, must be a tentative one. For this reason it is possible to offer only a suggestion as a final thought. It was during the 1960s that a keen interest in the 1930s, the occupation years and the immediate post-war period developed. Might it be that this interest played its own role in the processes of transformation? Topics such as that of authority, the nature and style of government and of social relations or of the place of religion and the churches in Dutch society, were at the centre of debate. It is not hard to perceive a line of influence, even if this was indirect, coming from the earlier period. Perhaps, finally, it is not completely by chance that the official exhibition commemorating the Liberation of 1945 held in the 1960s should have carried the title 'Wonderful Liberty?' with a question mark.

Notes

1. E.H. Carr, *Conditions of Peace* (London, Macmillan, 1942), p. 275.
2. This paper is largely based on the available literature on Dutch history for the period 1930–50. The main general surveys are *Algemene Geschiedenis der Nederlanden*, Vol. XIV and XV (Haarlem, Fibula-Van Dishoeck, 1979 and 1982); E.H. Kossman, *De Lage Landen 1780–1980* (Amsterdam, Elsevier, 1986)—an earlier version was published in English as *The Low Countries 1780–1940* (Oxford, Oxford University Press, 1978); H. Lademacher, *Geschichte der Niederlande. Politik—Verfassung—Wirtschaft* (Darmstadt, Wissenschaftliche

Buchgesellschaft, 1983); L. de Jong, *Het Koninkrijk der Nederlanden tijdens de Tweede Wereldoorlog*, Vol. I–XII ('s-Gravenhage, Staatsuitgeverij, 1968–88).
3. Much has been published about Dutch Fascism and National Socialism. The major surveys are A.A. de Jonge, *Crisis en critiek der democratie* (Assen, Van Gorcum, 1968); L.M.H. Joosten, *Katholieken en Fascisme in Nederland 1920– 1940* (Hilversum, Unieboek, 1964) and de Jong, *Het Koninkrijk*, op. cit.
4. M. van der Goes van Naters, *Ordening door nieuwe organen* (Amsterdam, Arbeiderspers, 1935), p. 5.
5. The main literature for this section is de Jong, *Het Koninkrijk*, op. cit.; J.C.H. Blom, 'Nederland onder Duitse bezetting 10 mei 1940—5 mei 1945', in *Algemene Geschiedenis der Nederlanden*, op. cit., Vol. 15, pp. 55–95; W. Warmbrunn, *The Dutch under German Occupation 1940–1945* (Stanford, Stanford University Press, 1963); G. Hirschfeld, *Freundherrschaft und Kollaboration. Die Niederlande unter deutsche Besatzung, 1940–1945* (Stuttgart, Deutsche Verlags-Anstalt, 1984).
6. On the history of the *Nederlandse Unie* see J.C.H. Blom, 'De Nederlandse Unie. Een bespreking', *Tijdschrift voor Geschiedenis*, Vol. 89 (1976), pp. 60–69; and, in English, G. Hirschfeld, 'Collaboration and Attentism in the Netherlands', *Journal of Contemporary History*, Vol. 16, pp. 467–486; M.L. Smith, 'Neither Resistance nor Collaboration. Historians and the Problem of the *Nederlandse Unie*', *History*, Vol. 72 (1987), pp. 251–278.
7. The discussions in St Michielsgestel are covered in M. de Keizer, *De gijzelaars van St Michielsgestel. Een éliteberaad in oorlogstijd* (Alphen aan den Rijn, Sijthoff, 1979).
8. The following analysis of the debate in the underground press is based on the documents in B. Bakker, D.H. Couvée and J. Kassies (eds.), *Visionen en werkelijkheid. De illegale pers over de toekomst der samenleving* (Den Haag, Daamen, 1963). Unfortunately, this book gives no precise references. It is not possible, therefore, to annotate the quotations from the illegal press which appear here.
9. W. Lipgens (ed.), *Europa-Föderationspläne der Widerstandsbewegungen 1940– 1945. Eine Dokumentation* (Munich, Oldenbourg, 1968), pp. 262–310.
10. For the post-war period see the literature cited in note 2 above; also P.W. Klein and G.N. van der Platt (eds.), *Herrijzend Nederland* (Den Haag, Nijhoff, 1981) and *Nederland na 1945* (Deventer, Van Loghum Slaterus, 1980); D Barnouw, M. de Keizer and G. van der Stroom (eds.), *Onverwerkt verleden?* (Utrecht, HES, 1985) and H.W. van der Dunk et al. (eds.), *Wederopbouw, welvaart en onrust* (Houten, De Haan, 1986). All these books are collections of articles.
11. J.C.H. Blom, 'The Second World War and Dutch Society: continuity and change', in A.C. Duke and C.A. Tamse (eds.), *Britain and the Netherlands. War and Society* (Den Haag, Nijhoff, 1977), p. 248.
12. ibid, p. 255.

8 Shaping a new Belgium: the CEPAG—the Belgian Commission for the Study of Post-war Problems, 1941–44 [1]

Brigitte Henau

This paper investigates the way in which the Belgian intelligentsia in exile during the Second World War envisioned the Belgium of the post-war world. In contrast to what had happened during the First World War, the last thing the exiled Belgians wanted after the war was a return to the 'pre-war world'. They were painfully aware that something had been amiss with the system as it had functioned during the inter-war period and meant to spend their time preparing for a better Belgium and a better world. Their views can be seen in the work of the Commission Belge pour l'Etude des Problèmes d'Après-guerre (CEPAG), which functioned as the think-tank of the Belgian government in exile in London from early 1941 until the Liberation of Belgium. CEPAG was set up to prepare ready-to-use plans for the government's return and suggestions for long term structural reforms.*

The CEPAG in theory and reality, 1941–44

The Commission pour l'Etude des Problèmes d'Après-guerre was based in London under the direct authority of Prime Minister Pierlot. It had a threefold task:

---

* This account of the CEPAG is almost exclusively based on archival sources, chiefly the personal papers of its President, Paul van Zeeland, and of its Secretary-General. These papers contain a full set of reports written by and for CEPAG members, the usual institutional records (minutes of meetings etc.) and correspondence in connection with CEPAG. Private papers of other CEPAG members and of other actors in the period were consulted.[2] After a brief discussion of how CEPAG was established and how it functioned, the bulk of the paper analyses the ideas for the structural reform of Belgian society and economy after the Second World War put forward by CEPAG members.

1. To study problems pertaining to the reforms to be implemented in the political, economic and social sphere.
2. To study and prepare (in cooperation with the Ministerial Departments concerned) the measures to be enforced at the moment of the Liberation to re-establish a normal life.
3. To maintain a liaison with its private or official counterparts in allied countries, so as to inform the government of general developments in planning for the post-war period.

CEPAG was headed by a Central Committee which coordinated and guided the work in progress, allotted the tasks, surveyed and coordinated the writing of the general reports to the government and met periodically with cabinet members. It was subdivided into seven 'sections' which were concerned respectively, with foreign policy, the reform of the State, education, economic policy, social problems, reconstruction and colonial problems. The option to create additional sections was left open. A New York branch was created to inform the government of developments in America, to secure the collaboration of the Belgians in exile on the other side of the Atlantic and to help maintain a Belgian presence there.

This was the formal and legal definition of CEPAG. Its real development was somewhat different: it started functioning in January 1941, but was not given legal status until June 1942.[3] As a thorough study of the CEPAG as an institution has already been made,[4] we can limit ourselves to a rough sketch of the way it worked.

The idea of creating a study group with the express purpose of preparing for the post-war period seems to have originated with the exiled Prime Minister Pierlot.[5] On 15 January 1941 Jef Rens (friend and Chief of Cabinet of former Prime Minister Spaak and second in command of the Belgian socialist trade union) was nominated 'counsellor of the Government', a title created especially for the occasion.[6] He was specifically entrusted with the mission of setting up a study group for the post-war period and was appointed its Secretary-General.

Both Rens and Foreign Minister Spaak favoured asking former Prime Minister Paul van Zeeland, then based in New York, to preside over CEPAG.[7] It was an elegant means of securing the collaboration of one of Belgium's leading men without having to include him in the government.[8] Moreover, van Zeeland, with his host of prominent British friends, would be very useful in remedying the lack of contacts between British Government circles and CEPAG.[9] At the official request of the government, van Zeeland set out for London, arriving on 27 June 1941.[10]

CEPAG mostly relied on its Central Committee (half a dozen members) and on a small but highly qualified full-time staff. Amongst the members of the central Committee who played a role in the discussions about social and economic problems was Paul van Zeeland, a Catholic economist and financier, who after a career at the National Bank of Belgium had headed a government (1935–37) which fought the Depression by restoring the profit margin for Belgian business via a devaluation of the franc. For years van Zeeland had felt the need for a better organised economy and, as Prime Minister, had launched a study group for possible reforms to obtain a more stable framework for the economy, industrial relations and relations between industry and government. Vice-President Louis de Brouckère was one of the first Belgian socialists ideologically opposed to reformist tendencies in his party. He had a long career behind him both on the national level and with the League of Nations, but still clung too much to his old principles really to fit in with the new ideas defended by the majority of CEPAG. Vice-President Raoul Richard was a businessman whose main job within CEPAG was to negotiate for the goods that Belgium would need after the Liberation. Julius Hoste was a Flemish Liberal with progressive views on society. In 1942 he joined the government as Under-Secretary of State for Education. Gustave Joassart was a captain of industry with a genuine concern for social problems who brought his great practical experience of industrial relations to CEPAG discussions. In 1942 he became Under-Secretary of State for Refugees, Work and Social Security. Secretary-General Jef Rens represented the trade union view. He also created a Belgian trade union in exile and was active in the International Labour Organisation. Because of van Zeeland's long absences from London, Rens organised the daily running of CEPAG, leaving the orientation of the work to the President.[11]

Most of the research work for CEPAG was done by over 100 volunteers, mainly highly qualified Belgians who donated their time to study one or another problem at CEPAG's request. CEPAG never met in plenary session, but worked through its different sections. These sections discussed and analysed various problems and reported their provisional conclusions to the Central Committee. The Central Committee used these reports to draw up its own reports to the Government which contained specific proposals for discussion and comment. But CEPAG could not go beyond researching and gathering information. To by-pass this problem, special application committees were created, in which CEPAG members went so far as to draft bills in close collaboration with the Ministries concerned.[12]

CEPAG observed a strict separation between measures for the immediate post-war period and proposals for long term structural reform. The former were worked out in detail, so as to have a complete set of legislative measures ready to put into place as soon as the country was liberated. For the long term, thorough discussions and a careful study of tendencies in allied countries were the basis for general reports that could be used by subsequent governments to initiate permanent reforms and could help the people in Belgium to make choices after the Liberation.[13]

The most striking feature of CEPAG was the flexibility it displayed: although some sections had a fairly steady existence, others would spring up or die away, dissolve into sub-groups and re-unite; application committees appeared and disappeared again, according to the work to be done, the people and information available. The system of relying mostly on volunteers meant that CEPAG could seek the advice of a whole range of experts. Drawbacks were that the work was very uneven and sometimes assignments from CEPAG got limited attention from people absorbed by other professional activities. Also the different sections, sub-sections and committees sometimes infringed on each other's terrain.

President van Zeeland's arrival marked the real start of the CEPAG's activities. Until then only a few sections had really set to work. Van Zeeland set out the lines along which CEPAG was to work. His aim was to obtain, as soon as possible, provisional studies concerning the outlook for the reconstruction of a new world after the war and Belgium's place therein. He advocated very pragmatic and realistic working methods, that could lead to immediate government action.[14] Van Zeeland emphasised the importance of giving priority to the study of social and economic aspects, even if it meant postponing the study of other aspects.[15] Without the provisional reports of the economic section, other sections could not get started.[16] Van Zeeland also stressed the importance of the United States in peace talks and the future world, and pleaded for a special division of CEPAG in New York.[17]

The CEPAG's vision of post-war Belgium

The international dimension

Considering the openness of Belgium's economy, it is not really surprising that the study of social and economic problems was seen in an international framework and that it was deemed 'impossible to leave the solution of the economic post-war problems to the arbitrary and unilateral disposal of individual nations'.[18] The time to build a new system had come: the war had wiped out positions that had been taken for granted, including international trading links. Since it was vital for Belgium to be integrated into a broader economic and political system that did not take national and regional interest to be incompatible, it was decided actively to promote the kind of international organisations that would bring it advantage.[19] Van Zeeland's basic idea was that problems should be handled by the lowest tier capable of doing so. The national state would form part of a federal regional group (copied from the

US federal system), consisting of a customs union, a common credit policy and a monetary unit managed collegially by the different central banks (similar to the United States Federal Reserve System). World-wide problems (such as colonialism and access to raw materials) were to be tackled on a world scale.[20] The view of the world as one economic unit and of the need for Belgium to be part of it was by no means new.[21]

Throughout its existence, the CEPAG devoted much time and effort to studying the evolution in the international policies of allied governments and study-groups and in defining Belgium's position towards them.[22] We will focus on their ideas about domestic economic and social problems, keeping in mind that the system devised was intended to fit into a larger framework.

An economy and society to serve the people

All CEPAG's thinking about structural reforms gravitated toward the concept 'human being'. Even though the different CEPAG members approached the concept from different philosophical and political backgrounds, their conclusions converged toward seeing the goal of man as developing his personality harmoniously, which could only be achieved in society.[23] Some added the religious dimension that humans must have the opportunity to lead their lives in a manner worthy of that of a child of God, which allowed for the full blossoming of the spiritual life.[24] All acknowledged the right for a person to live decently. As the vast majority of people could only do so by earning their living through their work it was logical to claim work as a right along the same lines as the right to live. Work was seen to be more than just a way of earning a living, it was both a service and a duty to society and a human need as the citizen derived much of his dignity from his utility to the community.[25] Work was thus considered to be all-important, and CEPAG proposed that the right to work be enshrined in the Constitution.[26]

Society and economy had to adapt to this vision of man. The ultimate goal to which the interests of labour and capital would be subordinate was now of a social kind, building a regime in which *all* enjoyed security and could satisfy their legitimate needs.[27] The future Belgian government would have to devise an economic policy that organised the economy sufficiently to meet the people's social wishes, but also allowed as much individual freedom as possible.[28]

Building a framework of security around the citizen

The principles underlying the social aspects of the work of the CEPAG were to speed up the evolution from social assistance via insurance towards social security, encompassing not only working, but also living conditions for all citizens.[29] Under social security CEPAG included the security of earning a living (at least an equitable minimum wage), respect for the human dignity of the worker, the reasonable assurance that an orderly and prolonged effort would better the living conditions of the worker's family, a preventive and curative medical service at everyone's disposal and the protection of workers, of the young and of the weak in general. Social insurance should thus cover all aspects of a person's life that escaped the individual's control, plus some additional benefits: unemployment, hygiene, sickness, accidents at work and industrial illnesses, burial costs, premature deaths, old age pensions, child benefits, maternal insurance, marriage and childbirth grants.[30]

CEPAG did not succeed in outlining a definite plan to implement the social security system. Its members could not agree on whether the existing private insurance institutions (mostly religiously and/or politically orientated) should be maintained, or whether one official and neutral institution should handle all matters and contacts with the public.[31] On the financial side, since the underlying principle was one of general solidarity, in the sense advocated by Lord Beveridge,[32] it was clear that tax revenue and not individual contributions should be the prime source of finance. Citizens would contribute according to their means and benefit according to their needs.[33] The reports to the Government suggested that the work-force, the employers and the State should each bear a part of the total costs of the scheme.[34] Overall it would make no difference to public finances, because the cost would be made up through rising economic prosperity and national income.[35] Some members thought it premature to make precise plans, considering the many unknown factors, and pleaded for a slow, progressive evolution.[36]

As a result of the major role ascribed to work in the life of the citizen, it is no wonder that CEPAG considered that endemic and widespread unemployment was intolerable. The constitutional right to work implied that the authorities would take measures to enable the citizens to exercise that right and to remedy the shortage of employment through economic policy.[37] Should people become redundant despite all efforts, then compulsory unemployment insurance would enable the unemployed to provide for themselves and their families. The members of CEPAG adopted the principle of collective responsibility for unemployment and thus the duty of collectively sharing the expense of supporting the unemployed. The schemes proposed by different members to implement this varied somewhat.[38]

This deep concern for the victims of unemployment did not blind CEPAG members to the dangers of abuse and all agreed on very stringent controls. It was imperative that unemployment should not be seen as a comfortable, secure state to live in at the expense of the community. Much emphasis was put on helping the unemployed to find a new job and on their being obliged to accept any work suiting their qualifications. Certain members toyed with the idea of a more flexible version of the system practised by some British trades, where employment was guaranteed on the condition that the workers accept any work that they were assigned in that trade. As a real remedy to the problem of the unemployed, CEPAG envisioned constant training and re-training to adapt the work-force to the demand for labour.[39]

The economic support for the social paradise

The consensus within (and also outside of) CEPAG was that the economy should be brought back to its real purpose: serving human needs.[40] As these needs were defined in terms of giving all members in society the chance of happiness and security, it was essential that the economy was able to provide the material means necessary for their realisation. This demanded the adaptation and development of production. Belgium had traditionally fed its large population by using it as relatively cheap labour to convert imported raw materials into semi-finished goods for export. In exile, CEPAG members had seen the fabulous technological progress made in some countries and realised that the 'new', unoccupied countries were well on the way to a technical level equal to that of Belgium's export industries. Therefore, they thought it imperative that Belgium move toward more advanced technologies, convert its industry to highly skilled production and build up a reputation for high quality goods.[41] They set up a technical bureau, consisting of a small number of engineers, to study technical progress in industry.[42] CEPAG's proposals to help Belgium move into high technology included the creation of a special commission responsible for promoting new techniques that would give Belgium patents with a high exporting value, and for documenting changes abroad, especially in the United States and Great Britain.[43] Pleas for generous funding of scientific research were a logical consequence. The profit of commercialising results obtained through community funding should go to the community.[44]

Besides 'innovation', 'expansion' became a key-word. Everything should be done to raise production and the amount of goods at the disposal of the people. While general overproduction was excluded because human needs were unlimited, it was recognised that defective organisation of the economy could lead to imbalances and overproduction in certain sectors, because potential consumers lacked the means to exchange something for the coveted goods, as the result of insufficient production in another sector.[45] From this standpoint, the obvious requirements were the coordination and organisation of production. The CEPAG looked for *une solution véritablement neuve*,[46] a middle road between extreme interventionism and liberalism (both of which had failed in fulfilling social needs), a delicate balance combining the maximum of individual freedom compatible with the progress of the community.[47]

CEPAG's President consistently referred to this solution as 'planning'. When tackled by other members who preferred the word *dirigisme* or who stressed that 'planning' by no means implied management of the economy by the state, but only advice and control,[48] van Zeeland emphasised that he wanted to promote the use of the word 'planning', in a more flexible sense than was usually the case.[49] A 'plan' meant no more than a general programme. Very strict limits were set on state intervention: it should remain in the 'policy' phase and certainly not come into the 'execution' phase, which remained the realm of traditional economic actors. It did not go beyond supervision, emphasising the avoidance of error, not the positive obligation for citizens to act. However, when it was really necessary to remedy the failing of the private economy, the State should do so (for example via a public works policy).[50] The President emphasised that private initiative and political freedom should be preserved. Belgium would have a regime of 'organised freedom'. CEPAG members were well aware that good results were being obtained within the constraints of the war economies, but felt that these constraints would not persist in a democratic regime, nor that they would be efficient.[51]

Adapting the structure of the state to its new duties

The existing state structure was far from being adequate to cope with the new public role.[52] A more stable executive branch of government was an absolute necessity, as was a thorough change in political habits, a return to real democracy, in order to give the country a sense of responsibility and the feeling that politics were being conducted seriously.[53]

To start with, the Ministries, in particular those of Economy and Finance, had to be reorganised.[54] If the public authorities were to have their say in running the economy, it was imperative that they should be well-equipped to do so correctly and efficiently. A reorganisation of the statistical services and the creation of an institute for the study of the trade cycle were foreseen, to provide the executive with reliable figures and tools for devising its policy. CEPAG members were impressed by the British way of government and retained some of its traits in their thinking. A restricted number of 'super-Ministers' would outline the general policy. Other, subsidiary Ministers would implement policies in specific areas. All Ministries having economic responsibilities would be coordinated by one 'senior Minister' for the economy, who would keep supreme executive powers, but be helped by the creation within the Ministry of a Central Office of Coordination.[55] That body would be composed of three sections: the first would coordinate the work of subsidiary offices, the second would study the overall trade cycle and the third would be an administrative board of appeal in economic matters. The Central Office of Coordination would only work through a number of bureaux whose task it was to prevent acts injurious to the economy. Of these bureaux, some would monitor credit movements (to stop over-investment) and the banks, others would control those prices that were not formed through competition (monopolies, subsidised industries), others would monitor imports and exports or tackle problems of social security. These bureaux would enjoy a certain autonomy, and be composed of civil servants, with the possibility for frequent collaboration with experts from outside the civil service.[56]

CEPAG wanted to integrate the permanent economic and social power groups in the political system and associate them with public action. Given they already had great influence on political life, they might as well openly contribute to the elaboration and execution of economic policy.[57] This would unmask the hidden influences in the economy and involve the public more closely in industrial activity. The whole point was to incorporate the existing power groups by creating a framework within which private initiative would be left free.[58] But however important the role of the economic and social actors, the ultimate decision was to remain with the legislative and the executive.[59]

CEPAG's emphasis on designing a system of industrial organisation was the logical continuation of a process that had started well before the war, but whose enactment had been interrupted.[60] In November 1938 a bill had been presented to Parliament for discussion but it had been put aside when more urgent international matters claimed attention.[61] Such an organisation fitted in with the general wish for a better regulated and more stable economy and of the collaboration between the economic actors advocated by the Catholic Church. The government wanted people with practical knowledge to collaborate in order to avoid the ghastly errors of the inter-war years. This drive grew stronger during the war, because if the Government wanted to abolish the compulsory and corporatist organisation that the Germans had built in Belgium, it had to have a replacement ready.[62] Moreover, close economic cooperation among the economic actors would help control the still mobilised economy in the immediate post-war phase. Cooperation was also necessary for Belgium to play its role in future international economic organisation.[63] All these reasons, but most of all the urge to implement the new industrial organisation immediately after liberation, account for the fact that by the end of 1943 CEPAG had ready bills that provided for industrial groupings, parity commissions and collective conventions, institutions that the government thought essential to replace the German structure.[64] The CEPAG proposals followed closely the bill presented to Parliament in November 1938 and which CEPAG had, at the request of the government, taken as the basis for its work.[65] Plans for other aspects of the reorganisation did not reach the form of actual bills: discussions within sub-sections were still in full swing in the summer of 1944. This reflected the state of affairs at that time.

CEPAG held the view that healthy industrial organisation (not resembling corporatism) relied in the first place on free collaboration under a higher body of all existing voluntary and private trade unions and industrial and inter-industrial groupings. These would remain private, but should be encouraged (but not compelled) to obtain legal status. However, those who did would enjoy certain privileges and be involved in the future organization of the economy, whereas it seems that the others ran a serious risk of being excluded.[66] This would of course jeopardise the latter's chances of fulfilling their task, namely defending the common interests of their members.[67]

Whereas the workers and employers were well organised, the self-employed were not. CEPAG pleaded for a strong organisation of the self-employed, preferably using the already numerous existing groups. Their role would be to express the demands of the people they represented and to provide them with technical and practical help.[68]

Beside the existing private groupings, the government would create official industrial councils (30 at the most) which would be the forum for workers and employers of the same industry to confer about all subjects falling outside the scope of the parity commissions.[69] CEPAG members wanted a guaranteed 50:50 representation of employers and workers and an absolute majority for decisions (the 1938 bill had left the former to the discretion of the Government and wanted a 75 per cent majority for the latter).[70]

This double structure would be crowned by a higher body. CEPAG's President had outlined a 'Higher Council for the National Economy' composed of 24 representatives of economic interest groups (industry, workers, banks, agriculture, consumers, etc., but mainly producers) and aided by a technical staff composed of six economists appointed for life. It could subdivide itself into different sections and possibly attract help from outsiders. It would advise the legislative and executive branches of government and be able to take initiatives in all economic matters. It would also study the trade cycle and advise the Ministry of Economic Affairs on the coordination of economic activity, and monitor the functioning and organis-ation of industrial groupings.[71]

The application committee on economic organisation deviated from the President's proposal in that it wanted industrial councils instead of interest groups represented on the Higher Council for the Economy. It also rejected the 1938 proposal to have representatives of both employers and workers for every industry and broadened the powers of the Council: the executive and legislative branches would have to consult it on all economic matters. In addition to its full right to take the initiative, the Council would even have the obligation to do so at the request of 75 per cent of its members, and its proposals would enjoy a speedier route through Parliament.[72]

On the social level, collective bargaining on an equal footing between employers and employees in a given industry would take place through the so-called parity commissions. Their task was to discuss general conditions of labour, to prevent or solve industrial disputes, to encourage cooperation between management and workers within enterprises, and to make suggestions about labour law.[73] The negotiations within the parity commissions between representatives of labour and management had led to collective agreements which, in the past, had been very effective in smoothing industrial relations. In practice most of the parties involved, including those who had not signed the agreements had observed them, but some had not. CEPAG was in favour of making those agreements binding on the whole of the industry concerned. From a legal-technical point of view this could be achieved in different ways. For CEPAG's Social Section it mattered only that the contents of the collective agreements would become real legal rules and that these rules would also bind minorities which had not actively participated in their elaboration. The application committee for industrial organisation was more careful and eliminated possibly confusing statements about the obligatory power of the agreements. It also insisted that the proposal allowing that collective agreements be made binding for a whole industry be put through Parliament separately, instead of being included in the general project for industrial organisation after Liberation.[74]

In order for the system of collective agreements to function properly it was necessary to have a parity commission in each industry. These would be crowned by a General Parity Commission (or Social Council) covering all industries, the social equivalent of the Higher Economic Council. It would give advice to the legislative and executive branches of government and have the right of legislative initiative. Supplementary bodies would be created to incorporate groups not represented within the main body. In principle the CEPAG accepted the addition of a council of sociologists.[75]

Even though an early, unpublished, CEPAG Report[76] claimed that industry should be based on collaboration between employers and workers, not only through the parity commissions, but also on the level of the individual enterprise, with real participation of the workers in its management, CEPAG's proposals were very timid and did not go beyond creating company delegations to enhance the spirit of collaboration between workers and management.[77]

These proposals on the organisation of the economy did not enjoy unreserved support from all the CEPAG's members. The most common fear was that it would lead straight to corporatism, which was loathed because it curtailed freedom and had been so brutally imposed by the Germans.[78] Some CEPAG members saw the representation of interests as an artificial creation, non-existent in reality: people could not be subdivided into categories and even less so could the wishes of the social groups be seen as a valid alternative for the sum of the wishes of their individual members. Setting up different group interests against each other would not yield a common interest.[79] If only groups were heard (for example, the trade unions as speaking for the workers), non-members would be excluded, which was anything but democratic. Thus some members proposed that individuals vote on major initiatives.[80] Some feared an outburst of bureaucracy, or that the designed framework would fail to grasp the complexity of the economy and paralyse it. They pointed out that other attempts at planning had failed in the past. Counter-proposals included the creation of public services, with equal influence from both producers and consumers, the public ownership of certain sectors (i.e., banks, insurance) and the establishment of direct links between the state and the people interested in a particular area, via the creation of a special bureau within the Ministry of the Economy staffed with specialists for each sector.[81] Van Zeeland did not deny the risk of bureaucracy in the plans, but his aim was to simplify what already existed in a scattered fashion. The crucial factor would be the spirit in which the new institutions were made to function.[82]

It is not easy to assess the influence of CEPAG. Even though we cannot say that it reformed Belgium, we need not go to the other extreme in viewing it simply as a way for the Government in exile to keep busybodies out of their way.[83] The truth seems to lie somewhere in between. Many people who collaborated within CEPAG were respected experts in their own fields, and sometimes the government had a lot of trouble coaxing them into helping CEPAG at the expense of their other activities, which suggests that it really did desire a study of post-war problems. This was done mostly along the lines of the ideas that had been put forward by pre-war projects to reform the economic structure of the state. To those were added some more 'daring' aspects, reflecting what the exiles had seen in the United States and Great Britain.

With hindsight, it seems that the Belgians in exile were not fully aware of the changes that had taken place in occupied Belgium. Several study groups, ranging from small extremist groups to serious bodies supported by the establishment, had been active in preparing their own visions of post-war Belgium. Employers and trade unionists had learned to work together[84] and, together with civil servants and politicians, they had secretly elaborated a

Social Pact under the occupation. Both industrialists and workers made some concessions, recognising one another as forces to be reckoned with.[85] This agreement, made when facing a common enemy (and probably also in the hope of getting better conditions than in peace-time), proved much more attractive than the elaborate structures developed by CEPAG in London.

Social security is the most obvious example of this: CEPAG's plans for a national system covering everyone and everything were supplanted by those of the Social Pact. This proposed a compulsory social security system for workers, covering old age and premature death, involuntary unemployment, child benefits and paid holidays, illness and disability. The first five would be run by official agencies, the last two by private insurance, as had been the case before the war. This system was carried through very quickly after the Liberation for most employees and workers.[86]

The new parity commissions drew heavily on the 1938 scheme.[87] The General Parity Commission was set up in December 1944 by employers and workers, according to the outline of the Social Pact. It soon changed its name to General Parity Council and in 1952 it became an official body, the National Labour council.[88]

One of the first major acts of the government after its return in September 1944 was to abolish the economic organisation put in place by the Germans, thus creating total chaos and losing precious time.[89] In November 1944 the government installed a provisional organisation, consisting of industrial boards representing all people active in a certain industry. Their role was to foster collaboration between the different enterprises and between the enterprises and the government. Inter-industry boards had the same task for several sectors.[90] Heavy opposition to this system arose because it was compulsory, because it had a monopoly of representation, and because of a number of arbitrary decisions. It was quickly abolished.[91]

The thorough 'organisation of the economy' was not enacted until 1948, and then only after long debates. A Central Council for the Economy was established with members representing producers and trade unions and half a dozen coopted specialists or technocrats. Its aim was to advise the executive and legislative powers about economic topics and voice opinions expressed within it.[92] For some industries professional councils would be created, their main task being to inform the government and the Central Council for the Economy of the different opinions and suggestions within their trade.[93] Within each enterprise with at least 50 workers,[94] a mixed council consisting of employers and workers was to be created, with the job of airing opinions on working conditions and the factors influencing the profitability of the enterprise, monitoring the correct application of legislation to protect workers and receiving regular information on the economic and financial situation of their enterprise.[95]

The organisation of the economy as enacted in 1948 did not go as far as CEPAG had proposed, nor was it in line with what would probably have come out of studies terminated by the Liberation. The few bodies that were organised in 1948, like the General Council for the Economy, did not live up to expectations. More often than not the Central Council was used by the government as a convenient way to gain time when faced by thorny problems, and its advice was often ignored. Only a few professional councils were created over the years and the achievements of the councils within enterprises varied greatly from case to case.[96]

On the technical side, progress was made after the war: research centres were created in 1947 for some sectors as well as a Centre for Economic Studies within the Ministry of the Economy,[97] but all of these had many precedents and it is very hard to discern the decisive influence in their formation

On the whole, many of CEPAG's wishes were not fulfilled: the right to work was never written into the Constitution, trade unions have always declined to accept juristic personality, the self-employed did not set up a coherent organisation, the system of social security did not apply to all citizens and unemployment was never banned.

Even though CEPAG did not propose any 'shocking' new ideas, it did tend to go further than the Belgians who had remained at home, if only because of the close contacts in countries with more developed systems of social security and economic planning. CEPAG's proposals failed to convince those Belgians who had lived in the country during occupation and were superseded by the pragmatic plans, worked out in Belgium itself, along more traditional lines. Van Zeeland's view that he would gain the public's full support for post-war structural reform proved over-optimistic. His 'comprehensive, clear and daring' programme, centred on economic recovery through the creation of wealth and the installation of social security, was not implemented.[98]

Notes

1. I am grateful to Dr Dirk Luten (Vrije Universiteit te Brussel) for her pertinent and much appreciated comments on the manuscript, to Dr Peter Solar (Katholieke Universiteit te Leuven) for his kind help in preparing the English version of this paper, to Viscount van Zeeland for the permission to consult the van Zeeland papers (see note 2); and to the Belgian National Fund for Scientific Research and the Vlaamse Leergangen te Leuven for their financial help.
2. The Archives Générales du Royaume, Brussels (henceforth AGR) hold the Paul van Zeeland papers (henceforth PvZ), and the 'CEPAG-file' collected by Jef Rens in his capacity as the CEPAG's Secretary-General. The Centre de Recherches et d'Etudes Historiques de la Seconde Guerre Mondiale, Brussels (henceforth

CREHSGM) holds other Rens papers (henceforth PR5) as well as a rich collection of papers of other actors in the Second World War, including the papers of de Gruben (PG6), Debeve (PD17) and De Vleeschauwer (PD40).

3. *Moniteur belge* (London), 30 June 1942, p. 268.
4. Diane de Bellefroid, *La Commission pour l'Etude des Problèmes d'Après-guerre (CEPAG (1941–1944)*, Louvain-la-Neuve, unpublished thesis for the degree of 'licencie', 1987.
5. Jef Rens in an interview with V. Deckers on 6 February 1983 (cited in Victor Deckers, *De plannen voor de na-oorlogse periode opgebouwd door de staten betrokken bij de oorlog in Europe (41–45)*. *Het geval Belgie*, Brussels, unpublished thesis for the degree of 'licencie' (Royal Military School, 1983), p. 12). The 'paternity' of CEPAG has been debated. A good survey is provided by de Bellefroid, *La Commission pour l'Etude*, op. cit., pp. 61–5, who adheres to the view that the initiative was taken by the government.
6. Deckers, *De plannen voor de na-oorlogse periode*, op. cit., p. 15.
7. Spaak to van Zeeland, 25 February 1941, AGR PvZ 532; Vanlagenhove to van Zeeland, 23 January 1941, AGR PvZ 585.
8. The relationship between the Belgian government in exile and some other prominent Belgians in unoccupied territories was, to say the least, rather strained. After the German invasion of Belgium on 10 May 1940, the Belgian Government provisionally settled in France and arrogated to itself full executive powers. On 18 June 1940 the government announced its intention to resign. Their plea to return to Belgium was rejected by the Germans. Health Minister Marcel-Henri Jaspar left France for London on 23 June and proclaimed his unconditional intention to continue the war at the side of Britain. His colleagues, left behind in France, disavowed him. Jaspar immediately started to rally other prominent Belgians in the free world. On 9 July the Minister of Colonies arrived in London and persuaded the British not to recognise Jaspar as Belgium's official representative, but to bring over the rest of the Cabinet instead. Minister of Finance Gutt arrived in August 1940, Prime Minister Pierlot and Foreign Minister Spaak in October 1940. Once settled in London, the four distributed all the portfolios amongst themselves, excluding Jaspar. Other Belgians in exile recognised the authority of the Pierlot government, but resented being left out completely. A move to include all former Ministers in exile in the cabinet was rejected. Personal dislikes and pettiness stood in the way of friendly collaboration. Minister of Finance Gutt seems to have borne a grudge towards van Zeeland, on a personal level in addition to a dispute over monetary policy (Gutt wanted to save the franc from inflation through a sharp reduction of money in circulation, whereas van Zeeland favoured devaluation). In August 1942 three more Ministers arrived in London, one of them was reintegrated into the cabinet in October 1942, the other two not until April 1943. Luc Schepens, *De Belgen in Groot-Brittanie, 1940–1944. Feiten en getuigenissen* (Nijmegen, Gottmer; Brugge, Orion, 1980), pp. 13–46; 'Renseignements de M. Gutt' (undated, handwritten by de Gruben), CREHSGM, PG6, 54.
9. 'Procès-verbal de séance du Comité Directeur de mercredi, 2 juillet 1941', p. 3, AGR PvZ 711.

10. Spaak to van Zeeland, 19 April 1944 and van Zeeland to Spaak, 24 April 1944, AGR PvZ 532; 'Rapport liminaire sur les travaux de la Commission Belge pour l'Etude des Problèmes d'Après-guerre' (July 1941), p. 24, AGR PvZ 712.
11. de Bellefroid, *La Commission pour l'Etude*, op. cit., pp. 115–33. For a full list of members and short biographical sketches see ibid., pp. 115 et seq.
12. Jef Rens, 'Belgium's Post-War Plans', in *Oxford Mail* 16 October 1943, CREHSGM PR5, 314; *Rapports de la Commission pour l'Etude des Problèmes d'Après-Guerre (CEPAG) (1941–1944)* s.1. [1944] (henceforth *Rapports . . .*), pp. 107–8; *P.V. CC/17 Procès-verbal de la séance du Comité Central du jeudi 25 [sic] février 1942*, p. 1, AGR PvZ 711.
13. 'Les Belges de Londres et la préparation de l'avenir', pp. 2–5, CREHSGM, PR5, 300.
14. 'Procès-verbal de séance du Comité Directeur de mercredi 2 juillet 1941', pp. 1–4, AGR PvZ 711.
15. P.V. CCent/2 'Procès-verbal de la 2eme séance du Comité Central tenu [sic] le 7 juillet 1941', pp. 2, 5, AGR PvZ 711.
16. P.V. S4/1 'Procès-verbal de la première réunion du mercredi 16 juillet 1941', p. 1, AGR PvZ 737.
17. van Zeeland was left at liberty to set up a New York division of CEPAG. To avoid dispersion of the effort, it was made clear that New York would act only in support of the London headquarters. The New York division received very scant financing, but performed well even so. 'Procès-verbal de séance du Comité Directeur de mercredi 2 juillet 1941', pp. 1, 3, AGR PvZ 711.
18. P.V. S4/2 'Procès-verbal de la 2eme séance tenue le mardi 22/7/1941', p. 1, AGR PvZ 737.
19. PV CCent/4 'Procès-verbal de la séance du Comité central du mercredi 30 juillet 1941', AGR PvZ 711.
20. P.V. CCent/3 'Procès-verbal de la 3e séance du Comité Central tenue le 9/7/41', p. 1, AGR PvZ 711.
21. That case had been argued frequently by Belgians, not in the least by the future CEPAG's President. see, for example Paul van Zeeland, *A View of Europe. 1932. An Interpretative Essay on Some Workings of Economic Nationalism* (Baltimore, Johns Hopkins University Press, 1933); and the *Report presented by Monsieur van Zeeland to the Governments of the United Kingdom and France on the possibility of obtaining a general reduction of the obstacles to international trade* (London, HMSO, 1938) (Cmd. 5648).
22. The importance given to the international framework is obvious within the economic section too: out of the first nine assignments given to its members, all but one were concerned with international problems: P.V. S4/3 'Procès-verbal de la 3eme réunion tenue le mardi 29 juillet 1941', AGR PvZ 737.
23. S5/38 Jean Leroy, 'Problèmes du Travail', pp. 2–5 (May 1944), AGR Rens-CEPAG, 11 (1).
24. This religious dimension does not appear in the printed version of the second report, however it does in the mimeograph version: 'Deuxième rapport de la commission belge pour l'étude des problèmes d'après-guerre. Avril 1942', part IV, section II, pp. 5''–6, AGR PvZ 714.

25. S5/38 Jean Leroy, 'Problèmes du Travail', pp. 2–5 (May 1944), AGR Rens-CEPAG 11 (1); 'Deuxième rapport de la commission belge pour l'étude des problèmes d'après-guerre. Avril 1942', part IV, section II, pp. 5''–6, AGR PvZ 714; Louis de Brouckère went as far as to see man as being essentially a Homo Faber rather than a Homo Sapiens (S5/1 Louis de Brouckère, 'Rapport provisoire sur le chômage et le placement' (July 1941), AGR Rens-CEPAG 11 (1).

26. S5/21 Roger Roch, 'Les assurances sociales', pp. 3–12 (January 1943), AGR Rens-CEPAG 11 (I).

27. S5/1 'Procès-verbal de la première réunion du lundi 7 avril 1941' [social problems section], pp. 1–3, AGR Rens-CEPAG 11 (1); Jef Rens, 'Belgium's Post-War Plans', CREHSGM PR5, 314; S5/3 A. Delierneux, 'Les associations profession-nelles et le réferendum (September 1941), AGR Rens-CEPAG 11 (1); *Rapports* . . ., pp. 107–8.

28. Jef Rens, 'Belgium's Post-War Plans', CREHSGM, PR5, 314.

29. S5/28 'Rapport final sur les travaux de la section sociale', p. 7 (Projet), AGR Rens-CEPAG 11 (1).

30. S5/21 Roger Roch, 'Les assurances sociales', pp. 3–12 (January 1943), AGR Rens-CEPAG 11 (1); *Rapports* . . ., pp. 52–4, 65–7, 100–1.

31. It was mostly the confessional side which pleaded to maintain private institutions. For instance, Prime Minister Pierlot was adamant that it was part of the citizen's freedom to be able to appeal to institutions of his own opinion or creed for matters relating to health care etc. [Hubert] Pierlot 'Note sur le rapport de la section sociale', 31 August 1943, pp. 7–8, 11, CREHSGM PD40, 287.

32. William Beveridge, *Social Insurance and Allied Services*, (London, HMSO, 1942).

33. S5/21 Roger Roch, 'Les assurances sociales', pp. 3–12 (January 1943), AGR Rens-CEPAG 11 (1); 'Cinquième rapport de la Commission belge pour l'étude des problèmes d'après-guerre. Août 1943', pp. 142–3, AGR PvZ 717.

34. The second report mentions it as all three parties paying equal parts in the insurance fees, the fourth report states that the bulk of the cost would be borne by the State, thus reinforcing the graduation of the tax system (*Rapports* . . ., pp. 52–4, 65–7, 100).

35. *Rapports* . . ., p. 103. This financial optimism was not at all shared by the government. 'Note sur le rapport de la section sociale (Commission des Problèmes d'Après-guerre)' (undated, originated with the Cabinet of the Minister of Colonies), CREHSGM, PD40, 284.

36. Note of Joassart to Wauters, 9 June 1943, annex to Document S5/28, CREHSGM, PD40, 284.

37. S5/21 Roger Roch, 'Les assurances sociales', pp. 3–12 (January 1943), AGR Rens-CEPAG 11 (1); S5/38 Jean Leroy, 'Problèmes du Travail', pp. 2–5 (May 1944), AGR Rens-CEPAG 11 (1).

38. One thought that the best system would be dual organisation: private bodies would provide the dole from members' dues, the government would double that amount. Once an unemployed had used up all his dues, government and employers would continue to support him (S5/1 Louis De Brouckère, 'Rapport provisoire sur le chômage et le placement' (June 1941), AGR Rens-CEPAG 11 (1). Another distinguished three phases: one phase in which the unemployed drew on what he

had previously paid as insurance fee, one phase in which the funds were provided by the employers and a phase in which the community paid (S5/8 Max Gottschalk, 'Le problème du chômage' (March 1942), AGR Rens-CEPAG 11 (1).

39. S5/1 Louis De Brouckère, 'Rapport provisoire sur le chômage et le placement' (July 1941), AGR Rens-CEPAG 11 (1); S5/8 Max Gottschalk, 'Le problème du chômage (March 1942), AGR Rens-CEPAG 11 (1); *Rapports* . . ., pp. 52–4, 65–7.

40. 'Deuxième rapport de la commission belge pour l'étude des problèmes d'après-guerre. Avril 1942', part IV, section II, pp. 5''–6, AGR PvZ 714.

41. Rens to del Marmol, 2 August 1943, pp. 4–8, CREHSGM PR5, 229; Rens to LFE Wouters, 29 October 1943, CREHSGM PD17, 10.

42. P.V. CC/36 'Réunion du Comité Central du 3 novembre 1942', AGR PvZ 711.

43. S4/72 Capt. Gevers, 'Projet de Commissions à créer', AGR PvZ 741.

44. P.V. S4/3 'Procès-verbal de la séance du mardi 4 avril 1944' (section économique), pp. 2, 4, AGR PvZ 737.

45. *Rapports* . . ., pp. 124–5.

46. Their italics. P.V. CC/18 'Procès-verbal de la séance du Comité Central du 4 mars 1942', p. 1–2, AGR PvZ 711.

47. *Rapports* . . ., p. 45; S5/38 Jean Leroy, 'Problèmes du travail', pp. 6–10 (May 1944), AGR Rens-CEPAG 11 (1).

48. P.V. CC/17 'Procès-verbal de la séance du Comité Central du jeudi 25 [sic] février 1942', p. 2, AGR PvZ 711.

49. Note from van Zeeland to de Brouckère, 8 August 1941, AGR PvZ 163.

50. *Rapports* . . ., pp. 45–6, 51–2, 126.

51. P.V. CC/18 'Procès-verbal de la séance du Comité Central du 4 mars 1942', p. 1–2, AGR PvZ 711; P.V. CC/23 'Procès-verbal de la séance du Comité Central du 7 avril 1942', AGR PvZ 711.

52. Jef Rens, 'Belgium's Post-War Plans', CREHSGM PR5, 314.

53. 'Note pour les membres du Comité Central. Observations relatives au second rapport du Président. IIeme partie I–A', 4.4.1942, AGR PvZ 715; *Rapports* . . ., p. 40. CEPAG also devoted quite some time to studying the means to achieve that political stability, like amending voting legislation, Parliamentary procedures etc.

54. Jef Rens, 'Belgium's Post-War Plans' in *Oxford Mail* 6 October 1943, CREHSGM PR5 314.

55. P.V. CC/23 'Procès-verbal de la séance du comité central du 7 avril 1942', AGR PvZ 711; Rens to del Marmol, 2 August 1943, pp. 4–8, CREHSGM PR5, 229; *Rapports* . . ., pp. 49–50.

56. *Rapports* . . ., pp. 51–2.

57. P.V. CCent/5 'Procès-verbal de la 5e séance du Comité Central du mercredi 6 août 1941', p. 5, AGR PvZ 711.

58. P.V. S4/3 'Procès-verbal de la séance du mardi 4 avril 1944' (section économique), p. 2, AGR PvZ 737.

59. *Rapports* . . ., p. 46.

60. Dirk Luyten, 'Wetgevende initiatieven m.b.t. Bedrijfs-organisatie in de jaren 30 in Belgie', *Belgisch Tijdschrift voor Nieuwste Geschiedenis*, 19 (1988).

61. 'Projet de loi sur l'organisation des professions et la reglementation économique', *Parliamentary Documents. Senate. Session 1938–1939* Nr. 7.
62. S5/15 'La question de l'organisation professionnelle en Belgique' (not signed), pp. 5–7 (October 1942), AGR Rens-CEPAG 11 (1); Joassart to Pierlot 24 June 1943, AGR Rens-CEPAG 1.
63. S2/89 'Organisation professionnelle. Rapport de la sous-commission contrôle de l'Etat', p. 3 (July 1944), AGR PvZ 741.
64. Jean Deguent, 'Note pour Monsieur Rens', 20 December 1943, AGR Rens-CEPAG 16; documents CAOP/8 to CAOP/21, AGR Rens-CEPAG 1.
65. Pierlot to Joassart, 21.6.1943; Joassart to Pierlot, 24.6.1943, AGR Rens-CEPAG 1. The 1938 bill had proposed the creation of 30 professional councils, a National Economic Council at the top and a Council for Economic Regulation, showing much analogy to the first CEPAG line of thinking.
66. *Rapports . . .*, p. 87–8; P.V. CC.23 'Procès-verbal de la séance du comité central du 7 avril 1942', AGR PvZ 711.
67. S5/16 'La question de l'organisation professionnelle en Belgique' (not signed), pp. 5–7 (October 1942), AGR Rens-CEPAG 11 (1); *Rapports . . .*, pp. 47–8; CAOP 12 'Projet d'arrête-loi sur l'organisation des professions, les conventions collectives et les commissions paritaires' (October 1943), AGR Rens-CEPAG 1.
68. *Rapports . . .*, pp. 48–9.
69. This includes everything except working conditions, preventing or solving disputes and making collective conventions.
70. S2/89 'Organisation professionnelle. Rapport de la sous-commission contrôle de l'Etat', pp. 5–7 (July 1944), AGR PvZ 741.
71. P.V. CC. 23 'Procès-verbal de la séance du Comité Central du 7 avril 1942', AGR PvZ 711; *Rapports . . .*, pp. 47–8.
72. S2/89 'Organisation professionnelle. Rapport de la sous-commission contrôle de l'Etat', pp. 5–8 (July 1944), AGR PvZ 741; S4/5, 'Compte-rendu de la séance du 12/5/44 à la CEPAG', pp. 1–2, AGR PvZ 737. The application committee's Council thus had 30 representatives (one from each professional council) plus 10 members nominated by the government (out of which four to represent liberal professions) ('sous section contrôle de l'Etat 21.4.1944', AGR Rens-CEPAG 10 (2)).
73. CAOP 12 'Projet d'arrête-loi sur l'organisation des professions, les conventions collectives et les commissions paritaires', pp. 9–12 (October 1943), AGR Rens-CEPAG 1.
74. CAOP 22 Roger Roch, 'Note relative 1) aux projets de rapport au conseil et arrête-loi sur l'organisation des professions, les conventions collectives et les commissions paritaires 2) au projet de loi sur l'extension à des tiers de conventions collectives et de leur force obligatoire', pp. 2–5 (November 1943), AGR Rens-CEPAG 1; CAOP 19 'Projet de loi relatif à l'extension à des tiers des conventions collectives et de leur force obligatoire', AGR Rens-CEPAG 1. *Rapports . . .*, pp. 88–91.
75. P.V. CC/26 'Procès-verbal de la séance du Comité Central du lundi 14 avril 1942', p. 1–2, AGR PvZ 711; *Rapports . . .*, pp. 52, 91.
76. 'Deuxième rapport de la commission belge pour l'étude des problèmes d'après-

guerre. Avril 1942', part IV, section II, pp. 5''–6, AGR PvZ 714.

77. CAOP 12 'Projet d'arrête-loi sur l'organisation des professions, les conventions collectives et les commissions paritaires' (October 1943), AGR Rens-CEPAG 1. Of course, we do not know what the proposals might have been in future discussions.

78. 'Sous section contrôle de l'Etat', 12.5.1944 and 22.5.1944, AGR Rens-CEPAG 10 (2).

79. S2/28 H. Speyer, 'Rapports entre les pouvoirs politiques et les organismes sociaux' (October 1941), AGR Rens-CEPAG 9.

80. S5/3 A Delierneux, 'Les associations professionnelles et le referendum' (September 1941), AGR Rens-CEPAG 11 (1); *Rapports* . . ., pp. 107–8.

81. Richard, Joassart and Hoste supported van Zeeland's views, de Brouckère and Rens were more sceptical (P.V. CC. 23 'Procès-verbal de la séance du Comité Central du 7 avril 1942', AGR PvZ 711). S2/89, S4/90 Robert Hirsch and Philippson, Organisation professionnelle. Rapport de la sous-commission contrôle de l'Etat. Rapport minoritaire' (August 1944), AGR PvZ 741; PV S4/10 'Rapport de la séance du 10 juillet 1944' [contrôle de l'Etat], AGR Rens-CEPAG 10 (2).

82. P.V. CC 23 'Procès-verbal de la séance du Comité Central du 7 avril 1942', AGR PvZ 711,

83. Marnix Gijsen, *De loopgraven van Fifth Avenue. De oorlogsjaren in New York*, (Amsterdam, Meulenhoff, 1980), p. 53; José Gotovitch, 'Views of Belgian Exiles on the Postwar Order in Europe' in Walter Lipgens (ed.), *Documents on the History of European Integration*, vol. 2 (Berlin, de Gruyter, 1986), p. 415.

84. Robert de Smet to van Zeeland, 10 October 1944, AGR PvZ 859.

85. B.S. Chlepner, *Cent ans d'histoire sociale en Belgique*, (Brussels, Institut de Sociologie Solvay, 1958), p. 243.

86. 'Projet d'accord de solidarité sociale', pp. 6–8, CREHSGM PD40 12; *Moniteur belge*, 30 December 1944 and 28 March 1945; Hans Slomp and Tjeu van Mierlo, *Arbeidsverhoudingen in Belgie* (Utrecht, Antwerpen, Het Spectrum, 1984), 2 vols., II, pp. 9–19; J. Engels, *De evolutie van de verplichte ziekte-en invaliditeits-verzekering*, monthly wages (8 per cent borne by the workers, 15.5 per cent by the employer; for employees: 8.25 per cent and 15.25 per cent). Not until the 1960s was the whole of the population allowed to join.

87. *Moniteur belge*, 5 July 1945, p. 4350; 'Social pact', p. 10; 1938, p. 46.

88. Wouter Dambre, *Geschiedenis van de ondernemingsrade in Belgie (1945–1967)*, Ghent, unpublished thesis for the degree of 'licentiaat', 1983, 2 vols., I, pp. 43–4; Slomp and van Mierlo, *Arbeidsverhoudingen* . . ., op. cit., I, p. 121.

89. Fernand Baudhuin, *Histoire économique de la Belgique 1945–1956* (Brussels, Emile Bruylant, 1958), p. 36.

90. *Moniteur belge*, 19 November 1944, pp. 1002–7.

91. Dambre, *Geschiedenis van de ondernemingsraden*, op. cit., I, p. 42.

92. *Moniteur belge*, 27–28 September 1948, pp. 7768–9.

93. *Moniteur belge*, 27–28 September 1948, p. 7768.

94. That was the legal disposition. In practice it started in enterprises with at least 500 workers, and gradually smaller enterprises were included.

95. *Moniteur belge*, 27–28 September 1948, pp. 7772–3.

96. Chlepner, *Cent ans d'histoire sociale*, op. cit., p. 402; Baudhuin, *Histoire économique de la Belgique*, op. cit., pp. 188–9.
97. Ibid., p. 179.
98. P.V. CCent/5 'Procès-verbal de la 5e séance du Comité Central du mercredi 6 août 1941', p. 5, AGR PvZ 711.

9 Reality not rhetoric: Belgian-Dutch diplomacy in wartime London, 1940–44

Pierre-Henri Laurent

Historians of the Second World War period whose interests are not military have only recently begun exploring European government activities in London. Many have been properly preoccupied by continental resistance and collaboration and few interested in the London locale for any reason other than military planning. In very recent years, students of post-war Europe and especially those interested in the emergence of the European unity or integration movement have found developments among the London governments-in-exile to be paramount in comprehending post-war Europe.

This paper will examine and analyse one bilateral relationship from 1940 to 1944 in which a major breakthrough was achieved not simply in terms of a Belgian-Dutch *rapprochement*, but in the construction of a basic model of economic integration. It will be argued that a relatively unique set of circumstances, highly dependent on time and place, strategic personages, a novel approach to treaty-making and, eventually, an extremely pragmatic economic diplomacy, forged the central process leading to Benelux. Whereas the vast majority of the London governments in exile discussed and debated post-war solutions at highly rhetorical levels and accomplished nothing concrete, the Belgians and Dutch found that they could address with realism their collective economic future with a new outlook and statecraft.

To comprehend Lowlander relations during the war necessitates a broad stroke background analysis of pre-1940 connections. Since the emergence of the Belgian state in 1830, Brussels and The Hague had laboured to address numerous residual issues of the 1839 Treaty of London with limited success. The inter-war years had resulted in few concrete ameliorations of the basic conflicts in their relations. There were still controversies about agrarian policy and deflation as a policy against economic hard times. In particular, many transport conflicts such as control over the Scheldt, river drainage, railroad and truck haulage questions remained points of extreme difference.

Many issues revolved around the basic low-tariff model of the Dutch and the much higher protective tariff concept and historical reality of the Belgians. And of course, the steady rise of the Flemish issue in Belgium, as that segment of the population moved further into socio-political visibility and participation, escalated in its importance in the relationship between neighbouring states.[1]

It is evident that in 1940 the two nations were not eager to leap into bed with each other, but sought means by which many of their differences, particularly the economic ones, might be overcome.[2] As Kossmann has noted in his study of the Low Countries, by the outbreak of the Second World War statesmen had still not managed to reach an agreement on those hard economic questions which had led to the painful economic crises of the 20's and 30's.[3] If the bitterness and accompanying stubbornness on both sides which dated from the nineteenth century was mostly gone, the basic nature of Dutch/Belgian ties was still strained and uneven in 1940. Therefore, it is fair to say that on the eve of the outbreak of war, the two states had been working to lay aside some of their differences and draw closer together but economic/commercial and linguistic/cultural divergences of paramount importance to both still remained unsettled. The state of affairs was now far from hostile but not close or intimate. To characterise the relationship as hopeful and possibly en route to problem solving might be a just assessment.

The Nazi invasion in the west and the swift occupation of the three Lowland states produced governments-in-exile in London in very short order. These legitimate states, represented by coalition ministries, immediately reflected a deep and strong current of dual common causes. In a strikingly thorough and swift manner, sharing with their fellow Europeans in free Britain the task of contributing to the downfall of the Axis, powers the two larger Lowland nations organised their small bureaucracies and emigré populations to contribute to the war effort.[4] The normal functioning and operations of a modern parliamentary government were not only drastically reduced for them, with no national population to deal with and no national economy to regulate, but all aspects of governance were substantially reduced. Mobilising the few Belgians and Dutch and their limited resources, including the valuable colonial ones, was no small task, but it was certainly not a time-consuming one for the Lowland Londoners. Much of their own literature in those years and in interviews after the war indicate the importance of this 'free time' and the 'reflective capabilities' in the evolution of both the ideas and processes that resulted in Benelux.[5]

Furthermore, the atmosphere and tone of wartime London with its heavy accentuation on cooperation, 'common cause' and even common values and beliefs amongst the Allies against Fascism appears to have been very influential on the Dutch and Belgian communities. The statesmen, politicians, businessmen and intellectuals who had come across the Channel from the Lowlands to the centre of collective resistance were committed and absolute. In addition to the physical proximity and unavoidable frequency of contact that was largely prescribed in those days between military allies, there developed very quickly in Belgian-Dutch circles a general tendency to utilise the 'leisure and reflective time' to address their bi-national future and perhaps general European peacetime questions of primary significance. The aura of London's optimism about the short and long term future (as expressed in late 1941 and 1942 was not only strongly prevalent amongst the Belgian and Dutch communities, but apparently embraced wholeheartedly by the ministerial and business sectors of Lowlander Britain.[6]

Although there were some general talks about Belgian-Dutch problems and post-war issues before the autumn of 1941, it was only then that two basic and highly critical points of agreement emerged. According to Paul-Henri Spaak, the Belgian Foreign Minister for the Pierlot Government, and his Dutch counterpart, Belco van Kleffens of the Gerbrandy Ministry, there was a consensus that the lessons to be drawn from the inter-war period were absolute and clear-cut. The small northwestern European states would be forced to reject the idea of neutrality as a viable future alternative. Equally important in terms of future international relations, the two men agreed that the post-war period would require a global organisation with expanded and more precise capabilities than the League of Nations. Spaak and van Kleffens asserted their common belief that an international organisation would be required in order to reflect the interests of the small states sufficiently to ensure that Great Power hegemony, control and power would never again be possible. The first of these two ideas concerning neutrality was a revolutionary change in thinking for both states, but particularly for the Belgians who had only recently returned to the 'politics of independence' (neutrality) in 1936. The second point of government consensus was more of a continuity factor, in that both had been ardent League supporters for a variety of reasons but had always viewed that organism centrally as an instrument for the defence of small nations' interests, and as a counterweight to the bigger powers.[7]

In the late autumn of 1941 two central perceptions about the Lowlander place in the post-war Europe and globe were introduced into the normal diplomatic connections. Within months in early 1942, two more novel and eventually intertwined orientations emerged from Lowlander talks that would fundamentally alter the future work of both governments. With probably not only Dutch and Belgian but also British business circles at the centre of these new developments, the notion of the necessity to plan post-war economies in cooperation became so compelling that this idea, but not the accompanying strategy, was embraced by both governmental establishments in London. The argument seemed to be that Europe had definitively outlived the usefulness and validity of economic separatism. In interpreting the past economic rivalry and disorder not simply in the Lowlands but in Europe and beyond, the two ministries-in-exile arrived at the conclusion that there was a need to conquer the menace of economic particularism by a mutual agreement. What was called for was an economic union for the Lowlands via monetary accord and a customs union.[8]

This expression that their common fate should now arise from solidarity and not strife was based on elaborate discussions and debates within the several Lowlander communities in London which had taken place by early 1942. Significantly, these discussions took place within and between public and private entities and businessmen then lobbied their government officials. The élitist nature and base of these early integration concepts is very evident in the relatively few primary sources available.

The businessmen claimed that unregulated economic rivalry would be totally ruinous after the war, particularly for any smaller nations in a revamped world of more massive economies of scale. Each of the two states would depend even more heavily on its exports and on trading in what was viewed as an intensively competitive marketplace. For Belgium and its industrial prowess and The Netherlands with its agrarian and commercial foundations, trade competitivity had to be assured.[9] Amalgamating their relatively small economies in a step-by-step process would require addressing major questions of currency, finance, and investment as a prelude to constructing a customs union with a common external tariff policy for both states.

The cardinal concept of a general customs union appeared first when three businessmen, one Dutch, one Belgian and one Englishman approached Camille Gutt, the Belgian Finance Minister, in late 1941. Gutt transmitted these ideas to Spaak who had a full airing of these radical notions with van Kleffens.[10] Two primary external catalysts for this initial exposure and debate appear to have been the writings of Louis de Brouckère, a major Belgian socialist who wrote in the influential *France* from London, and Marcus van Blankenstein, a Dutch intellectual and journalist whose articles appeared regularly in *Vrij Nederland*. In all of the thinking about economic reconstruction and re-ordering, the attacks on economic nationalism, autarky and tariff wars were extremely vigorous, so much so that the ministerial elements, most particularly Spaak and van Kleffens themselves, were total converts to the customs union scheme by early 1942.[11]

As the new year began, the two governments scheduled negotiating sessions employing the general model of the 1921 Belgian–Luxembourg Economic Union (BLEU) as their basic model.[12] Thus, Belgium and Luxembourg were already economically one and negotiated as such. In these negotiations, the central relationship of the foreign ministers appears to have been acute. Van Kleffens, the ultimate pragmatist, quiet, extremely reserved, even cool, found in Spaak, the animated and verbose rhetoretician, an apparent opposite personality, but a likeable and admirable one. In short, although superficially opposites both recognised that their outward personalities were secondary and relatively inconsequential when compared to their realism as statesmen and their common search for reasonable means to achieve a much coveted common goal. Even in their choice of a Belgian Economics Ministry official, Hubert Ansiaux, the two ministers found the ultimate middle man and trusted liaison whose expertise translated many of their generalities into acceptable specifics through actual negotiation.[13]

The problems were so enormous that a basic decision was made to proceed in a linear fashion to a monetary accord first.[14] Assaulting this most important and yet difficult sector first became a procedural decision that most likely allowed for eventual overall success. Given the original optimism and audacity of these early 1942 talks and their translation into an agreement in the autumn of 1943, the bilateral sessions were important not simply because they bore fruit but because they exposed more disagreement about national economic policy. Therefore their efforts to find an arrangement which would facilitate payments did result in a monetary accord, but it also produced such great obstacles to the broader customs union diplomacy, and so many of them that the negotiators were forced to revise their basic approach and strategy.[15]

The tangible diplomatic success of the 21 October 1943 agreement had given heart to the overall endeavour but apparently insoluble differences were not apparent to both sides. In the context of difficult diplomatic negotiations, the two governments became involved in the more extensive attempt to find common ground in discussions about European-level post-war economic and defence groupings. This occurred at a time when the Europeans-in-exile and even Europeans under Nazi occupation commenced elaborate discussions about regional organisations for the post-war era. Central to the entire extended writings and talks was the idea of federalism.[16] On this issue the Belgians and Dutch found themselves at odds about the future of Europe, particularly whether a Pan-European, federal union or a looser, sub-regional, more functionalist grouping would be best. The Dutch rejected the federalist concept and solution in London; interestingly their compatriots in the Resistance movement in The Netherlands were already the most fervent advocates of surrendering parts or their entire national sovereignty to a trans-national authority for the commonweal. The London Dutch were of an opposite mind primarily because they felt colonial, mercantile and commercial interests would necessitate a clear-cut local power base that insured the survival of the small in a world of tightened states.[17] The London Belgians, sharing the world-level organisational bent of the Dutch, were not attached to the federalist model either, but were active, primarily through Spaak in searching with the French and British for comprehensive post-war western European linkages. In discussions with the British, French and Scandinavian governments, the Belgians inclined toward security and economic arrangements which would allow a federalist orientation.[18]

In these Lowlander discussions, Dutch apprehension about Belgian closeness to Paris became a real issue separating the two in 1943. As the Dutch desire to make the British and then indirectly the Americans the centrepieces of any security and probable economic pact emerged, a critical difference about regionalism and a split about each country's primary choice of European partner divided the two even more. Although these talks contained the seed of later 'Atlanticist' thinking,[19] they also brought out Belgian-Dutch disagreement about the region's institutional structure in peacetime.

With a stalemate threatening the customs union talks at the same time as a schism developed and deepened over the basic concept of western European regional institutions, Spaak and van Kleffens made a momentous decision. All of these differences were to be put aside and they would complete what they could do alone. By November 1943 their orders to their negotiators were to work out what the London governments had the exclusive competence to negotiate. The art of the possible was applied to Belgian-Dutch diplomacy and the area of dispute—what regional solution for western Europe?—put aside for the near future.[20]

One senses that the diplomatic decision was motivated by the thought of grabbing what they might get and putting aside what they might influence eventually but not get in the immediate future. The subsequent invasion of Fortress Europe was not only planned but in a few short months it was launched. The negotiators were instructed to rush to the completion of the customs union work with the Spaakian exhortation of '. . . construct[ing] an agreement to agree hereafter'. The principle that was applied, that is to employ the *loi cadre* or the framework treaty, was interestingly the same as that utilised 12 years later, again by Spaak, in the final preparation of the European Economic Community in the Treaty of Rome.[21] Certain unanswerable, non-negotiable questions meant unresolved problems, but need not have meant failure. Contrary to their original intention to base their union on concrete and precise solutions, the Lowlander governments settled for a statement of general principles which emerged in the summer of 1944. Spaak and van Kleffens convinced their ministries that an outlined set of generalisations would not only be sufficient but also be a compelling priority for the post-war political process at home. If brought back to their liberated peoples as the outlines for their future, not only the logic of cooperation and union would be put forward, but a full popular foundation could be given to what was clearly at that time an élitist conception. In other words, the political élite in London chose swiftly to delineate a basic structure for a new economic bond and rely on their future political capability plus the democratic concept and post-war spirit of collaboration to finish the job. Thus, out of regional differences was to come a Lowlander triumph.

The governmental decision to find agreement in general principle and to leave the finalisation of a union for the future was, in 1944, consistent with a parallel track pursued by the twin national governments.[22] The road to an economic union that was conceived by a small portion of the communities in exile was to include the two societies *in toto*. Therefore, the government's campaign to enhance greater understanding and interaction of all Belgians and Dutch in Britain was meshed with the viewpoint that their respective post-war democratic processes would and should give greater weight and validity to a frontier-breaking economic agreement.

The two small states had found in their war-time relations common ground about the post-war economic imperative. Their London interchanges had produced a formula wherein the reality perceptions about post-war Europe centered on economic reorganisation, not simply for the survival of the small states, but for growth and competitiveness. What had been produced came from a new found understanding achieved through close and frequent contacts about the need for an economic merger. The union of their economies was rationalised in two basic ways. First, there was the idea that in union there was greater strength and, second, in union was the diminution of economically-based national rivalry. Finding that their European regional concepts were not in fact similar, the Belgian and Dutch leadership felt forced to transcend their numerous and growing differences about the exact substance of an economic union and forge a basic instrument of agreement for the future. These leaders were not convinced that a Lowlander post-war *détente* was inevitable and that truly cordial and amiable post-war relations would be automatic because of the war-time common cause.

The Spaak-van Kleffens combination was convinced that it needed to set the post-war agenda at home in a particular fashion. The closer cooperation mode that they advocated was in fact economic amalgamation, but to be completed only through the post-war decisions and consent from below. The two London governments therefore agreed to a goal that would have a popular base. Even in the numerous activities of the London governments commencing in 1942 one observes their attempts to create closer and deeper ties between the Belgians and Dutch. Although most efforts were aimed at the emigré communities, some were efforts to foster closer post-war connections between the two peoples and governments through contacts and discussions with war-time resistance groups. The most interesting and different example of the governmental process of bridge building between peoples was the bi-national government sponsorship of soccer matches between the Belgian and

Dutch armies in exile. What before the war would have been either impossible or at the very least an opening for a contentious bi-national, bi-lingual, bi-cultural confrontation on and off the field was carefully, diplomatically, and successfully staged several times in Britain in 1943–44. Other government sponsored 'people to people' projects were part of a broadening campaign that lobbied the need for and value of popularly based bi-national interchanges and meetings. The previous suspicious, even mistrustful attitudes about their neighbours were not overcome overnight, but the governments' sponsorship and active prodding of public exchanges and contacts became an integral part of a package deal. The restricted circle of statesmen negotiating an economic union became enlarged through efforts to build a community of interest that reached into the more general populace. Limited as it was in scope and achievement in Britain, this broadening of the friendly base after liberation was projected by the Belgian-Dutch leadership to be the route to their post-war economic reorganisation goals.

Wartime London was not therefore a setting in which Belgian and Dutch conflicts of long standing were basically overcome. Some consensus about the meanings of the historical past, especially about neutrality and economic nationalism and shared perspectives about their general post-war economic needs did in combination forge such a strong bond that a revolutionary change could be initiated. A perceptive and innovative diplomacy, a willingness both to proscribe a radical economic reorientation and to subject that change to a democratic debate were translated into a realist economic statecraft.

Notes

1. Amry Vandenbosch, *Dutch Foreign Policy since 1815* (The Hague, M. Nijhoff, 1959); Jame K. Miller, *Belgian Foreign Policy Between the Wars* (New York, Bookman Associates, 1951); Jonathan Helmreich, *Belgium and Europe* (The Hague, Mouton, 1976), and the elaboration of specifics in Ch. de Visscher and F. van Laugenhove (ed.), *Documents Diplomatiques Belges, 1920–40* (Bruxelles, Palais des Academies, 1966); L. de Jong, *Het Koninkrijk der Nederlanden in de Tweede Wereldoorlog*, deel 9 (*Londen*) (The Hague, M. Nijhoff, 1979). On the economic problems, see in particular P.W. Klein, 'Depression and Policy in the Thirties,' *Acta Historiae Neerlandica*, 5, pp. 123–158.
2. Frank E. Huggett *Modern Belgium* (London, F. Praeger, 1969), p. 247.
3. E.H. Kossmann, *The Low Countries, 1780–1940* (London, Oxford, 1978), pp. 659–667.
4. See the early editions of *Memo from Belgium* for the Belgians and the section on the Dutch in Walter Lipgens (ed.) *Documents on the History of the European Integration: Plans for European Union in Great Britain and in Exile, 1939–1945*

(Berlin, De Gruyter, 1986).
5. See Paul-Henri Spaak, interview, 9 August 1967 and Camille Gutt, interview, 2 August 1967. Also Herman Balthazar and José Gotovitch (ed.) *Camille Huysmans in London* (Antwerp, Standaard Wetenschappelijken U, 1978).
6. Paul-F. Smets, *La pensée européenne et atlantique de Paul-Henri Spaak (1942–72)* (Bruxelles, Goemaere, 1980), I, documents 5 and 6.
7. Paul-Henri Spaak, *Combats Inachevés*, I (Paris, Fayard, 1969), I, pp. 136–148.
8. Camille Gutt, *La Belgique au carrefour 1940–44* (Paris, Fayard, 1971).
9. See Balthazar and Gotovitch, op. cit., and Camille Gutt, interview, 2 August 1967.
10. Camille Gutt, *La Belgique au carrefour 1940–44*, op. cit., and Paul-Henri Spaak, interview, 9 August 1967.
11. *France*, 23 October 1943.
12. See James Meade, *Negotiations for Benelux: an annotated chronicle, 1943–56* (Princeton, Princeton University Press, 1957).
13. Paul-Henri Spaak, interview, 9 August 1967.
14. James Meade et al., *Case Studies in European Economic Union: The Mechanics of Integration* (London, Oxford, 1962).
15. Paul-Henri Spaak, interview, 9 August 1967 and Spaak, I, pp. 146–153.
16. See Lipgens, *Documents*, op. cit., and his sections on the Belgians.
17. Van Kleffens in *The Times*, 25 March 1943.
18. See Lipgens, op. cit., *Documents*, especially pp. 415–449 which includes the 'Ajax'-van Cauwelaert debate on federalism.
19. Van Kleffens in *The Times*, 30 March 1942.
20. Paul-Henri Spaak, interview, 9 August 1967. *Customs Convention Between the Netherlands and the Economic Union of Belgium and Luxembourg in London, 5 September 1944 with 1947 Protocol amendments* (London, HMSO, 1947).
21. Pierre-Henri Laurent, 'Paul-Henri Spaak and the Diplomatic Origins of the Common Market, 1955–56', *Political Science Quarterly*, Vol. 75 (1970), and 'The Diplomacy of the Rowe Treaties, 1956–57', *Journal of Contemporary History*, 7.
22. Paul-Henri Spaak, interview, 9 August 1967; *Memo from Belgium*, IV, no. 3, 22 January 1944; IV, no. 38, 23 September 1944, and Smets, I, documents 7 and 8.

10 Political Catholicism, European unity and the rise of Christian Democracy

Michael Burgess

One of the most enduring features of Christian Democracy in post-war Western Europe has been its avid commitment to European integration. Today the European Peoples Party (EPP) in the European Community may still be 'more a federation of parties than a unified party' but Christian Democracy retains its identity as an important and distinctive political ideology dedicated to the goal of a federal Europe.[1] This chapter seeks to account for the emergence of Christian Democracy as a significant political force during and after the Second World War and to explain its strong ideological attachment to a particular conception of Europe. But our analysis of these two separate, if interrelated, issues cannot ignore the development of political Catholicism which both inspired and was subsequently superseded by Christian Democracy. Indeed, the title of this chapter suggests connecting links between these two phenomena and conveys a sense of transition from narrow to broad political values. We will focus our initial attention upon the gradual shift from political Catholicism to Christian Democracy.

Broadly speaking the emergence of political Catholicism can be explained in terms of the defensive response and reaction of the Catholic world to three main historical challenges: the Protestant Reformation, the French Revolution and the industrial revolution. The repercussions of these successive challenges to the hegemony of the Catholic universalist tradition from the fifteenth century have continued to shape European politics and government until the present day. In terms of cumulative social cleavages and the evolution of European party systems, the pioneering work of S.M. Lipset and S. Rokkan has ably demonstrated this.[2] Today the overall impact of this evolution in western Europe can be witnessed in three general patterns of religious balance: the mainly Roman Catholic countries, those with approximate Catholic and Protestant parity, and countries which are largely Protestant.[3] Political Catholicism can therefore be historically located and identified with both the resistance and accommodation of the Roman Catholic Church to these three great forces of change.

By the late nineteenth century, political Catholicism had developed unevenly in different countries at different times. Where the Reformation had been successful, as in Germany, the politics and policies of Catholicism were compelled to take account of the facts of Protestant power. Their very survival as a force unaccustomed to minority status depended upon their ability to adjust to this new reality. In Germany the Catholic *Zentrum* epitomised this dilemma.[4] To survive it had to perform a very delicate balancing act. Its minority position in a Protestant dominated country combined with the awkward social and economic heterogeneity of the Catholic population imposed upon it a chameleon-like strategy in Bismarck's Second *Reich*. Such Catholic confessional political parties seeking to defend their religious autonomy found it expedient to liberalise their beliefs and policies without actually abandoning their fundamentally universalist and exclusive doctrines. Religious toleration was the recipe for survival. But the Catholic parties were not passive victims of historical change. They used their accommodative skills to resist the inexorable encroachments of the secular state on private and spiritual freedoms and, as G. Almond observed: 'out of these struggles in the Protestant areas there developed a form of Catholicism which had adjusted itself institutionally and in part spiritually to the great revolutions of Western culture.'[5]

Political Catholicism in the mainly Catholic areas stood in stark contrast to the expedient liberalisation just described. Here—in Italy, France, Austria, Spain and Portugal—a siege mentality borne of successful counter-revolution prevailed. The Catholic Church set its face resolutely and with little compromise against the contemporary economic, social and political challenges which confronted it. Concessions, when yielded, were given only grudgingly. Almond claimed that in these areas the Church persisted in its identification with medievalism: 'throughout the nineteenth century the greater part of the Church identified itself with Catholic authoritarian dynasties and with the aristocracies in their efforts to suppress the freedoms won by the middle and lower classes.'[6] It did so, as he remarked, with disastrous consequences for the position of the Church, as it first lost its hold upon the emerging commercial, industrial and professional middle classes and then found its spiritual grip upon the working classes loosened to the point where secure support could be guaranteed only in those pockets which 'had been isolated from the great historical currents of the period'.[7]

Two main strategies emerged as the Catholic Church struggled to come to terms with this loss of influence. First the Church resorted to the appeal of Catholic romanticism and historicism. It attempted to regain some of the lost ground by stressing the aesthetic and traditional aspects of the faith. Second there grew up a separate distinctive strand of liberal Catholicism which sought to detach the Church from its debilitating alliance with the Conservative forces of continuity epitomised by monarchy and aristocracy. It championed political liberalisation and strove to widen the basis of Catholic appeal by meeting the growing demands of the industrialised working classes for economic and social reform. This movement which was barely tolerated during the latter part of the papacy of Pius IX (1846–78) suddenly found a new impetus under his successor Leo XIII (1878–1903). In a series of encyclicals—*Immortale Dei* (1885), *Libertas* (1888), *Rerum Novarum* (1891) and *Au Milieu des Sollicitudes* (1891)—he instituted a radical reappraisal of Catholic policy which provided an authoritative basis for the liberalisation of the position of the Church. Materialism, socialism and secularism were still condemned and political liberalism was sanctioned rather than favoured, but the Church was no longer hostile to the progressive forces of liberal and social reformism. Indeed Leo XIII encouraged Catholics to exert pressures on governments to endorse legislation with the purpose of alleviating economic and social distress. And the tide of events at last ran agreeably for the burgeoning Catholic social movement which had struggled in a previously bleak climate to promote workers' self-help and trade unions.[8]

The principle of the indifference of the Church to forms of government as long as Church interests were protected was put into practice by Leo XIII when he called upon French Catholics to rally to the Third Republic. Both *Au Milieu des Sollicitudes* (1891) and *Inter Innumeras* (1892), addressed specifically to the French, declared all established governments to be legitimate and promoted a union of all political parties behind the Republic. In 1893, Count Albert de Mun, a leader of the Catholic social movement who supported social welfarism as a means to undermine socialism, formed a parliamentary group of 35 *Ralliement* deputies who formally accepted the Republic. In Germany, as we have seen, an important Catholic political party already existed, and in Italy a number of Catholic social and political movements sprouted in the inhospitable climate of *Non Expedite* (1867) which instructed Catholics to boycott the liberal democratic state.[9]

It is important to note that the reformist zeal of the papacy of Leo XIII did not give formal Church approval to democratic movements. As Almond has emphasised, the 'liberal' encyclicals of the late nineteenth century had merely made it possible for Catholics as individuals to reconcile their faith with democratic aspirations.[10] But this short survey of political Catholicism and its predicament nonetheless serves to highlight the ineluctable pressure for democratisation in the economic social and political spheres of Catholic policy. At the dawn of the twentieth century the origins of Christian Democracy were well-established. In Italy the phrase 'Christian Democracy' was commonly used to describe the progressive wing of the Catholic political and social movements and it was endorsed by Leo XIII in the encyclical *Graves de Communi* in 1901. In France its development was 'slow and uneven', but 'some progress was made towards encouraging Catholics to accept the Republic, face up to their social responsibilities, and participate, albeit tentatively, in the democratic process'.[11]

Before we look at the emergence of Christian Democracy as a major political force during and after the Second World War it is important to underline the crucial distinction between political Catholicism and Christian Democracy. One leading scholar of Christian Democracy, R.E.M. Irving, alluded to 'progressive democratic Catholics' as 'potential Christian Democrats' and argued that up until 1914 it was difficult for Catholics to be committed liberal democrats:

> The authoritarian structure of the Church, its resentment at the loss of its temporal possessions, its hankering after the *ancien régime*, and its resultant uneasy relationship with Republican France and Liberal Italy, all militated against it accepting the basic *political* tenet of Christian Democracy, namely that Catholics should involve themselves fully in all aspects of the democratic process.[12]

But the economic and social democratisation of the Catholic world proceeded apace. In the years between *Rerum Novarum* and the end of the First World War the Catholic trade union movement spread across France, Germany, Italy, Belgium and the Netherlands. Together with the peasants' associations the Catholic trade unions sparked the left wing of the various Christian movements into existence and, supported by a militant group of Catholic clergymen and intellectuals, they furnished the basis of a distinctive Christian Democracy in this period.

The impact of the First World War produced yet another shift in Vatican policy. Catholic democratic parties were at last permitted a formal existence. In Italy the first mass-based Christian Democratic party, the *Partito Popolare Italiano* (PPI) was launched in January 1919 by Don Luigi Sturzo. Between 1919 and 1926, when it was suppressed by Mussolini, the PPI succeeded in becoming a broadly based centre party whose autonomist Catholicism, based upon freedom from Vatican control, enabled it to act as conciliator between the antagonistic social classes of Italy. In Germany the *Zentrum* participated in the parliamentary democracy of the Weimar Republic without ever being wholly committed to the basic tenets of liberal democracy. As Irving has observed, there was no such thing as Christian Democracy in Germany before the Second World War 'in the sense of a substantial political movement committed to Christian and democratic principles'.[13] However, it is worth recognising the existence of joint Protestant-Catholic movements as active German affiliates of the expanding Christian trade unions in the inter-war years. In France the majority of practising Catholics continued to support conservative and monarchist movements. The bitterness of the continuing conflict between Catholics and Republicans ensured that the emergence of Christian Democracy in France would be both pedestrian and puny. However, the *Parti Démocratie Populaire* (PDP) was formally established as a national Christian Democratic political party in January 1924 and survived as a small parliamentary group of up to nineteen deputies in the French Assembly until the Nazi occupation of 1940. Moreover, the *Jeune République*, originally founded in 1912, was revived after the First World War and represented the left wing of the Christian Democratic movement in France.[14]

Clearly, in the inter-war years Christian Democracy remained very much a minority feature of the overall Catholic political tradition. But if the Belgian, Dutch, Austrian and German Catholic parties were largely under the control of conservative influences it was nonetheless evident that 'in each one a Christian Democratic wing was in active existence during the period before the outbreak of World War II'.[15] And both the *Partito Popolare Italiano* and the *Parti Démocratie Populaire* already displayed political ideas and principles palpably characteristic of their respective post-war Christian Democratic successors—the *Democrazia Cristiana* (DC) and the *Mouvement Républicain Populaire* (MRP). The ideas were broad and the principles were vague. They included the commitment to liberal democracy and human rights, economic and social reform, a distinct emphasis upon morals and religion and a foreign policy of benevolent internationalism. Roman Catholic doctrine and values remained the ideological core of this body of thought but it was no longer restricted to traditional political Catholicism. The specifically Christian Democratic appeal resided in its claim and purpose to represent Christian values in politics rather than narrow Catholic interests and this furnished the rationale for its sense of commitment to class reconciliation as part of the overall attempt to bridge conventional social and political divisions.

But Christian Democracy, we are reminded, was a minority element of European Catholicism during the inter-war years. How, then, can we account for its sudden and dramatic emergence as a major—and in some countries a dominant—political force immediately after the Second World War? The context of inter-war European politics together with the war experience itself are central to our explanation. Although depicted essentially as a post-war phenomenon, the success of Christian Democracy can be explained only by reference to what occurred both before and during the Second World War. Political scientists have tended to acknowledge the importance of this consideration without actually explaining it.

Let us begin with the broad scenario of European politics in the 1930s. Europe at this time was dominated by the rise of Fascist movements in some countries, notably Italy and Germany, and authoritarian governments in others, especially Austria, Portugal and Spain. What was the official response of the Catholic Church to these developments? Given the Catholic authoritarian tradition which we have already emphasised in this chapter it comes as little surprise to learn that the majority of the Catholic populations of Europe were quite susceptible to authoritarian appeals. The papal encyclicals of Leo XIII had to some extent been reversed by his successor, Pius X (1903–1914), and had in any case been somewhat expediential in their attempts to turn back the late nineteenth century tide of liberalism and socialism. Catholics, as Irving concluded so succinctly, could be 'good social workers, but not good democrats'. Almond too wrote in 1948:

> there can be little doubt that the dominant attitude of European Catholicism before the outbreak of World War II was distrustful of democracy, and favoured the clerical-authoritarianism of Portugal, Spain, Austria and later that of Vichy France. At its extreme right, Catholicism recognised the virtues, and minimised the vices, of the totalitarian regimes of Germany and Italy.[16]

But what was the reaction and response of Irving's 'progressive democratic Catholics' — the 'potential Christian Democrats'? In the face of overwhelming ideological and military odds the minority groups of progressive Catholic intellectuals, middle classes and trade unionists clung tenaciously to their democratic and reformist beliefs and rallied to the support of regimes threatened directly from both extremes of right and left in the polarised politics of Europe in the 1930s. And when European military resistance to the Nazis collapsed in 1940 the majority of these small groups inevitably found their way into the ubiquitous liberation movements which furnished in the main an intellectual resistance to totalitarianism during 1940–45.[17]

Even the Vatican hierarchy and traditional Catholic conservatives, it should be noted, had become increasingly alienated from the Fascist, Nazi and collaborationist regimes by the time of the military turning-point of the war in 1943. The violence of Nazi anti-clericalism and the widespread attack of National Socialism upon traditional morality had always stood in the way of any genuine and effective reconciliation with this particular version of the extreme right, and the violent excesses of the German occupation authorities had finally put paid to official Catholic acquiescence. Catholic patriotism, in itself an historical irony, in the occupied countries eventually resulted in a general opposition and moral resistance to the Nazis among all elements of the Catholic populations. Such was the bitter harvest reaped by the Nazis that virtually all anti-democratic elements within the Church had reversed their positions and looked favourably upon a post-war liberal democratic restoration. But how did the Catholic Church become such a wholehearted advocate of democracy and the sponsor of aconfessional, Christian political movements in the immediate aftermath of the Second World War?

Almond's answer was both simple and unequivocal. The Church saw its new threat as the Soviet Union. In these radically changed circumstances it was hurriedly prepared to support the progressive Catholic resistance movements and 'with the great weight of its influence mobilised practically the whole of Western European Catholicism behind their leadership'. And in the chaos of post-war Europe 'the Church stood as the only ubiquitous non-Communist and non-Nazi institution'. Consequently to the Church-backed Christian movements there flocked 'practically all that part of Western Europe which was neither Marxist nor "liberal" in the classic meaning of that term'.[18] Most noteworthy among these emergent Christian movements was the merging of the Catholic and Protestant elements of Germany in the *Christlich-Demokratische Union* (CDU). The foundation for this confessional political merger had been laid, as we observed earlier, in the German Christian trade union movement which included both Protestant and Catholic workers. But it had also been entrenched in the wartime resistance experience of members of the Protestant and Catholic clergy and laity. J.D. Wilkinson's emphasis upon the moral, spiritual and intellectual nature of the European Resistance has stressed the essentially Christian inspiration that underlay much of the German Resistance. Both the *Kreisau* Circle and the *Weisse Rose* movement found a basis in Christian teachings. In 1942 Moltke, organiser of the *Kreisau* Circle, wrote to his British friend, Lionel Curtis:

> 'The most important development is the spiritual awakening which is starting up, coupled as it is with the preparedness to be killed, if need be. The backbone of this movement is to be found in both the Christian confessions, Protestant as well as Catholic . . . We are trying to build on this foundation'.[19]

In Italy, *Democrazia Cristiana* (DC) was founded in 1943. At its outset it combined several diverse groups among which the ex-*Popolari* elements were particularly prominent. Alcide De Gasperi, who had taken over the secretaryship of the PPI from Don Sturzo in 1923, gradually came to dominate the DC by virtue of his ability to harmonise the personal and ideological conflicts within the party. And in the early post-war years from December 1945 to May 1948 the first four ministries of De Gasperi had one consistent theme: the development and application of a policy of anti-communism, both nationally and internationally.[20] The DC's subsequent reputation as a party avowedly committed to European integration grew only out of practical considerations. De Gasperi and the DC were, in effect, forced to think out their position and to commit themselves to 'Little Europe' as a result of the development of the cold war.[21] As F.R. Willis observed, in 1943 De Gasperi had not yet come to the idea of uniting Europe into a political unit and his views on economic integration had not advanced beyond the freeing of trade.[22]

In conjunction with Pope Pius XII, De Gasperi's vehement anti-communism compelled him to choose between the new liberal democratic regimes of western Europe and the atheistic Marxist-Leninist states of the Soviet Union and eastern Europe. It was Piero Malvestiti who was one of the earliest proponents of European integration within the DC. Malvestiti's own programme, dating from 1942–43, stood out in its open advocacy of a 'Federation of the European States governed by a system of liberty'. De Gasperi did not accept the economic and political integration of the non-Communist European states until much later. When he did, however, he fully absorbed Malvestiti's ideas and, as Willis remarked, he fought for them so strongly that he himself came to be regarded as their original sponsor in Italy.[23] Before we look more closely at how Christian Democracy evolved a strong ideological attachment to the goal of a federal Europe it is worth underlining the essentially chameleon-like qualities of the Italian DC during the early post-war years. Irving noted that it was perfectly natural for the DC to want to emphasise its transitional links with the important Christian Democratic parties of France, West Germany, Belgium and the Netherlands, but that it should not be assumed that 'Catholicism as such was a major motive for the DC'. On the contrary it always advocated a Europe to include Protestant, democratic countries such as the United Kingdom, Norway and Denmark. It was at a personal level that Catholicism 'helped to oil the machinery of cooperation and increase the Christian Democrats' enthusiasm for integration'—an assertion corroborated by the pioneering exploits of Adenauer, Schuman and De Gasperi, all devout Catholics.[24]

Given the peculiar circumstances of the emergence of Christian Democracy during and after the Second World War it should come as no surprise to learn that its ideological coherence has always been in question. Almond, in 1948, claimed that while there was a common body of doctrine to which all Catholic political theory referred, this was stated in so general a form as to permit a variety of interpretations:

> It is impossible to treat the political theory of contemporary Christian Democracy as one would treat the political theory of a disciplined and coordinated movement such as Stalinism. There are contradictory and conflicting tendencies, within each national movement, and significant differences between national movements with regard both to doctrine and national interests.[25]

In 1976 G. Pridham acknowledged that Christian Democracy was 'not comparable to Communism or Socialism since it does not offer an integrated body of political thought or interpretation'.[26] While observing that this broad synthesis 'does not amount to a sufficiently precise corpus of doctrine for it to be appropriate to refer to Christian Democratic ideology', Irving nonetheless conceded, in 1979, that there were 'certain common ideas and principles which amount to a solid corpus of Christian Democratic theory'.[27] In the light of our brief historical analysis of Christian Democracy, in particular its emergence from and relationship to political Catholicism, what lies at the root of its peculiar conception of European integration? Why, indeed, did it develop such a strong ideological attachment to the values and the goal of a federal Europe? In the rest of this chapter we will concentrate upon this dimension of Christian Democracy.

Clearly anti-Fascism and anti-communism provided the initial negative moral force which drove Christian Democratic parties and movements to champion the European cause. The resistance experience also had a crucial impact upon the Christian Democratic belief in the need for a new kind of Europe. Its effects were many-sided. In France, for example, the Resistance paved the way for the emergence of Christian Democracy as a significant political force in two important ways: it showed that Catholics could cooperate with Republicans, and it provided the MRP with an élite of leaders.[28] In Italy association with the Resistance became the obvious ticket to political respectability. Both the DC and the PCI could boast of their respective roles in the Resistance and this in a sense accounted for the persistence of the anti-Fascist motive in Italy. Anti-Fascism in particular offered 'the most straightforward launching position for a break with the past', seeing that Christian Democracy claimed to represent 'a movement for moral and political renewal'.[29] Unsullied by the social, economic and political bankruptcy associated with the traditional conservative parties of the inter-war years and yet offering only a vague set of alternative 'programmatic' ideas and principles based largely upon old values, Christian Democracy was ideally suited to filling the post-war political vacuum on the Right.

We began this chapter by referring to the European People's Party (EPP) in the European Community, which is dominated by the Christian Democratic parties of the member states. Here Christian Democracy has been elevated to the supranational level. Let us look closely at the core elements of this distinctive set of ideas about Europe.

The party statutes are remarkably lucid about the future of Europe but we also need to probe into their ideological and philosophical origins and assumptions if we are more fully to understand what amounts to an organic view of European society. Moreover, the Christian conception of Europe is not restricted to the European Community alone. As the EPP Group Secretariat put it, 'we are only the onset for Europe . . . those people which are at present separated from us by military force also belong to Europe . . . the final aim of any European policy worthy of the name must be to achieve the peaceful reunification of Europe.'[30] In such terms is the military reality of 1945 clearly repudiated and the underlying social, economic and cultural identity of European history asserted in the face of political division.

The current political divide is to be overcome in a fashion boldly stated in the overriding *raison d'être* of the party's statute: 'We are firmly committed to the final political objective of European unification, that is the transformation of the European Union into a unique European Federation'. But the essentially Christian-based nature of this goal transcends even Europe and searches for peace, freedom and justice via movement towards a world order which is grounded in fundamental principles characteristically Christian Democratic: pluralism, personalism, solidarism and subsidiarity. These principles, taken together, yield a particular brand of European federalism whose ideological roots lie deep within Catholic social theory. Without wishing to enter the now somewhat sterile debate about whether or not these Christian Democratic principles amount to a solid, distinctive political ideology, it is clear that they underscore certain political and philosophical ideas which, if sometimes wide-ranging and imprecise, are none the less sufficiently developed to have an individual identity. In his classic work on *Christian Democracy in Western Europe, 1820–1953*, M.P. Fogarty observed that the essence of Christian Democracy was its catholicity: Christian Democrats were 'trying to create a broad synthesis incorporating and bringing into perspective elements which tend . . . to be one-sidedly emphasised in the traditions of conservatism or liberalism or socialism; together with certain other federalist or pluralist ideas which are the characteristic contribution of the Christian social movement itself. It is this catholic, synthetic view which makes the Christian Democratic parties . . . tend to appear at or about the centre of the political stage'.[31]

Given that European Christian Democracy may be suspect from the standpoint of its ideological promiscuity, what implications do these common ideas and principles have in terms of European integration? Elevated to the international and supranational levels, what is specific to the Christian Democratic conception of 'closer union'? The Christian Democratic notion of a federal Europe is rooted in a peculiarly Catholic view of organic society given particular ecclesiastical authority in the papal encyclicals of *Rerum Novarum* (1891), *Quadragesimo Anno* (1931) and *Pacem in Terris* (1963).[32] Together these doctrinal pronouncements constitute a philosophy of man and society in which federalism is located as a central organising principle of society ranging from association between individuals to that between distinct social groups. In this view association is the first principle of federalism. It extends beyond federation between states to become a basic concept of social life and in consequence of man himself. Hence the Christian Democratic goal of a federal Europe suggests that the federal principle thus conceived must be firmly woven into the institutional fabric of the European Community.

Personalism, solidarism and subsidiarity are each bound up with the Christian concept of man and they coalesce in the pluralist form of political organisation. The personalist doctrine, arising out of Catholic principles of divine and natural law, came in the twentieth century to be linked with democratic values which rejected the liberal theory of individualism. Attacking the 'atomisation' alleged to be implicit in liberal individualism, it stressed instead the idea of man as a spiritual being capable of initiative, decision and responsibility with a personal life which exceeded in value all the material universe. Thus the organisation of social, economic and political life must be structured so that man may freely develop as a person, both spiritually and morally. Solidarism, or mutualism as it is sometimes called, was conceived as the democratic and Christian alternative to Socialism and Fascism on the one hand and liberal individualism on the other. It suggests that coordination both in society and in the political system should be achieved by individual and group acquiescence on the basis of a mutual recognition of the interdependence of human life. Both personalism and solidarism imply coordination and acquiescence in the 'common good'; man is a social being who seeks a human order in which the various dimensions of his personality are firmly integrated into society while retaining their vitality and initiative.[33]

Subsidiarity fits logically into this scheme of things. It is a principle of natural justice concerning primarily social relationships which must be protected against the encroachment of the modern state. Pope Pius XI provided the clearest explanation of the idea in *Quadragesimo Anno*:

> It is a fundamental principle of social philosophy, fixed and unchangeable, that one should not withdraw from individuals and commit to the community what they can accomplish by their own enterprise and industry. So, too it is an injustice and at the same time a grave evil and a disturbance of right order, to transfer to the larger and higher collectivity functions which can be performed and provided for by lesser and subordinate bodies. In as much as every social activity should, by its very nature, prove a help to members of the body social, it should never destroy or absorb them.[34]

The Christian Democratic conception of federalism demands that this principle be applied to the entire social order. It regards excessive state interference in the social domain as an offence against natural justice which can lead only to the stunting of men's personal lives by denuding them of their responsibilities and inhibiting their spiritual expansion. In *Pacem in Terris*, however, this principle was elevated to the discussion of international relations and world order. The Catholic conception of the world community, having as its fundamental objective 'the recognition, respect, safeguarding and promotion of the rights of the human person', requires that modern states acknowledge their interdependence in solving major problems. The principles of subsidiarity applied to relations between the world community and modern states is expressed thus:

> The public authority of the world community is not intended to limit the sphere of action of the public authority of the individual political community, much less take its place. On the contrary, its purpose is to create, on a world basis, an environment in which the public authorities of each political community, its citizens and intermediate associations, can carry out their tasks, fulfil their duties and exercise their rights with greater security.[35]

It is clear from our brief examination of the political ideas of Christian Democracy that they predispose towards an essentially pluralist approach to power and authority. Man is a member of certain natural groups—the family, the profession, the commune, the region—which are natural law entities whose autonomy should be protected by the state. Since the main danger in modern society is defined as the development of an all-powerful state, Christian Democracy favours the dispersion of power both territorially and functionally. The idea of federation thus emerges as a political order which seeks to accommodate the greatest possible number of communities and societies, primary and intermediate, without destroying them. It is a living, pluralist, organic order which builds itself from the ground upwards, constructing its tiers of authority and decision-making according to the principle of subsidiarity.

We can see from this short résumé of Christian Democratic social and political thought that the concept of federalism is both multi-dimensional and organic. It is rooted in Catholic social theory which gives it a profoundly unique and distinctive character. In order for these basic social values, beliefs and perceptions to be promoted, sustained and preserved in the context of European integration, then, it is hardly surprising to discover that the EPP's own particular interpretation of European integration is categorically federal. A European federation is the only answer to Europe's problems. Only a European federal state can logically satisfy the requirements of the social order described above.

We have now traced the historical and ideological development of Christian Democracy from its narrow base in political Catholicism to its wider, chameleon-like synthetic appeal characterised by 'programmatic' diversity. If it is inappropriate to refer to Christian Democratic ideology as having a coherent view of politics based on a precise programme and objectives it is nonetheless clear that it does have a particular conception of Europe. Neither the Christian Democratic parties nor the movements have historically expressed exclusive and logically complete philosophical systems. They have never become *Weltanschauungsparteien* in the sense of Fascist or Communist parties. The 'closed universe' of political Catholicism would have been suicidal in the post-war world. This chapter demonstrates that Christian Democracy has emerged and survived precisely because of its concessions of principle and its overall conciliatory tendencies. Christian Democracy has been accommodation of convenience. But if its rise and continued resilience has been due largely to ideological expediency this is probably the price which every political movement or party has had to pay in western Europe since 1945.

Notes

1. See R.E.M. Irving, *The Christian Democratic Parties of Western Europe*, (London, Allen and Unwin, 1979), p. 246. For detailed discussion of the European federalist ideas in Christian Democracy, see M. Burgess, *Federalism and European Union: Political Ideas, Influences and Strategies in the European Community, 1972–1987*, (London, Routledge, 1989), Ch. 5, PP. 144–152.
2. S.M. Lipset and S. Rokkan (eds), *Party Systems and Voter Alignments: Cross-National Perspectives*, (London, Collier-Macmillan, 1967).
3. See G. Smith, *Politics of Western Europe*, (London, Heinemann, 1976), pp. 17–24.
4. See Irving, *Christian Democratic Parties*, op. cit., pp. 10–19.
5. G. Almond, 'The Political Ideas of Christian Democracy', in *Journal of Politics*, Vol. 10 (November 1948), p. 736.
6. Ibid., p. 736.
7. Ibid., p. 737.
8. Irving, *Christian Democratic Parties*, op. cit., p. 24.
9. Ibid., pp. 1–28.
10. Almond, 'Political Ideas', op. cit., p. 744.
11. Irving, *Christian Democratic Parties*, op. cit., pp. 19 and 26.
12. Ibid.,.p. 28.
13. Ibid., p. 18. See also G. Pridham, *Christian Democracy in Western Germany*, (London, Croom Helm, 1977).
14. For a detailed discussion of Christian Democracy in France, see R.E.M. Irving, *Christian Democracy in France*, (London, Allen and Unwin, 1973).
15. Almond, 'Political Ideas', op. cit., po. 743–744.
16. Ibid., p. 746.
17. For this view of the Resistance, see J.D. Wilkinson, *The Intellectual Resistance in Europe*, (Cambridge, Mass., Harvard University Press, 1981).
18. Almond, 'Political Ideas', op. cit., pp. 748–749.
19. Quoted in Wilkinson, *Intellectual Resistance*, op. cit., pp. 122–123.
20. See F.R. Willis, *Italy Chooses Europe*, (New York, Oxford University Press, 1971), p. 257.

21. See R.E.M. Irving, 'Italy's Christian Democrats and European Integration', *International Affairs*, Vol. 52, p. 404.
22. Willis, *Italy Chooses Europe*, op. cit., p. 255.
23. Ibid., p. 256.
24. Irving, 'Italy's Christian Democrats', op. cit., p. 405.
25. Almond, 'Political Ideas', op. cit., p. 752.
26. G. Pridham, 'Christian Democracy in Italy and West Germany: A Comparative Analysis' in M. Kolinsky and W. Paterson (eds), *Social and Political Movements in Western Europe*, (London, Croom Helm, 1976), Ch. 6, p. 147.
27. Irving, *Christian Democratic Parties*, op. cit., pp. 29 and 56.
28. Ibid., p. 218.
29. Pridham, 'Christian Democracy in Italy and West Germany', op. cit., p. 149.
30. *Europe: The Challenge – The Principles, Achievements and Objectives of the EPP Group from 1979 to 1984*, General Secretariat of the EPP Group, European Parliament, December 1985, p. 6.
31. M. Fogarty, *Christian Democracy in Western Europe, 1820–1953*, (London, Routledge and Kegan Paul, 1957), Preface, p. xiv.
32. See A. Freemantle (ed.), *The Papal Encyclicals in their Historical Context*, (London, Mentor-Omega, 1963).
33. On personalism see Fogarty, *Christian Democracy*, op. cit., pp. 27–40 and F. Kinsky, 'Personalism and Federalism', *Publius*, Vol. 9 (1979), pp. 131–156.
34. See Freemantle (ed.), *Papal Encyclicals*, op. cit., p. 342.
35. Ibid., p. 420.

11 British ideas of European unity and regional confederation in the context of Anglo-Soviet relations, 1941–45

David Weigall

It was inevitable that the collapse of France together with that of Belgium, the Netherlands, Denmark and Norway between 9 April and 22 June 1940 should divert the course of the debate which had figured so prominently in the numerous publications of the Federal Union movement. Though the idea of European federation remained on the agenda of British political discussion, at no time subsequently has it reassumed the prominence it had in 1939–40. Many people who had given serious consideration to and supported the idea of European federation now pinned their hopes on Anglo-American union, as the British Government did on United States military assistance. The immediate future for Great Britain was inescapably now linked with American policy and, after Hitler's invasion of Russia in June 1941, with that of the Soviet Union.[1]

At the same time, the events of 1940 fortified British national pride so that the widespread disenchantment with the idea of the nation state and the conviction that nationalism was bankrupt, which were common on the Continent, especially in Resistance circles, were in no way broadly shared by people on this side of the Channel. Federal Union's plans were seen (to the extent that they were appreciated) as something for the longer term. At the official level their ideas had never been seen, in any case, as having great relevance for the problems of post-war reconstruction. Illustrative of this was the attitude of R.A. Butler. When, as Parliamentary Under-Secretary of State for Foreign Affairs, he had requested a paper on Federal Union, it was not in the belief that this movement had a great contribution to make but rather, as he dismissively put it, because 'we can't have the British people chasing will o'the wisps every twenty years'.[2] As far as public opinion as a whole in the country can be assessed, it was either unconcerned about European union or opposed to British participation in such a union.

It was furthermore assumed in Britain, in the years under consideration, that she would maintain a position of equality in world affairs with the United

States and the Soviet Union after the war. Internationalist thought in this country tended to concentrate on the problems of a new world order under the leadership of the 'Big Three' or, in Roosevelt's formulation, the 'Four Policemen'—the United States, the Soviet Union, Great Britain and China—especially in the context of British relations with the United States and the Commonwealth. At all events there was clear official recognition that the attitudes of the emergent superpowers would be crucial. Such emphasis as there was on Europe tended to be on the economic and practical administrative aspects rather than the idealistic.

Winston Churchill said in 1942 that no planning for the future 'should divert our thoughts or our combined energies from the task of saving the nation'. What, then are we to make of his recurrent musings over the idea of European union? To what extent, if any, did these reflect Foreign Office notions? Preoccupied as Churchill was with winning the war, is it appropriate to see them as more than rhetorical and sometimes perhaps tactical too? If, for instance, the idea of a democratic united Europe was advanced as a propagandist ploy in contrast to Hitler's New Order, this could well have been beneficial. But, beyond that, was there anything consistent or coherent here? Sir Alexander Cadogan, the Permanent Under-Secretary at the Foreign Office between 1938 and 1946 was not alone in considering some of Churchill's ideas on international organisation misguided and frivolous. One of the problems faced by the Foreign Office was how to handle the Prime Minister's vague hankering after a 'United States of Europe'—something which dated back to the inter-war years.

Britain's dramatic offer of union with France in June 1940 was not an affirmation of federalistic faith. It was in fact little more than a last desperate effort to keep France in the war against Nazi Germany, a move to forestall a French request for a separate armistice, and to prevent the French navy falling into German hands. It emphatically did not embody any long-term official aspiration towards European unity.[3] At this time in any case, in Churchill's view, the forging of an effective partnership with the United States was the only reliable means of defeating Germany. However, the idea of some form of European unity, either Pan-European or involving regional groupings continued to be discussed. In the years 1941–45 they interacted with the formulation of British foreign policy in the following ways: in the definition of war aims, in contacts with the European governments-in-exile in London, in planning for the post-war order and, towards the end of the war, in the debate over the formation of a Western European Bloc.[4]

The question this paper attempts concisely to consider is how such ideas of European grouping, both Pan-European and regional, and their official reception, were conditioned by the demands of British relations with the Soviet Union in the period of common war effort between 1941 and 1945.

Eastern European federations

British official attitudes towards the Soviet Union after the launching of Operation Barbarossa on 22 June 1941 were primarily determined by military rather than ideological considerations. Hardly ever can two powers have become allies in less amicable circumstances.[5] The background of Anglo-Soviet hostility and distrust had further darkened with the Molotov-Ribbentrop Pact and the Soviet invasion of Finland. The latter had even led the British government to toy with the idea of declaring war on the Soviet Union as well as Germany. Yet, after Hitler's invasion of the Soviet Union, Churchill at once spoke over the radio pledging aid to Stalin and appealing to the other Allies to follow the same course. As regards the states of eastern Europe, he adopted the policy of making them adjust themselves to the interests of the Soviet Union rather than encouraging them to press for clarification of Soviet long-term ambitions in their area.

Of immediate importance here were the Polish-Czechoslovak Agreement, made public on 23 January 1941, and the Greek-Yugoslav Agreement on the constitution of a Balkan Union, 15 January.[6] It very soon became obvious that a policy of Anglo-Soviet friendship was not going to be compatible with British encouragement of federations or confederations in eastern and central Europe. As Geoffrey Wilson, in the Northern Department pointed out in 1942:

> There is little evidence that the Soviet Union will be prepared to agree to federations in Eastern Europe after the war. The reason for this attitude is their fear lest such federations might be directed against themselves. Thus, when the Anglo-Soviet Treaty was under discussion in April, a draft was sent to Moscow in which the idea of federation figured fairly prominently. The Moscow counter-draft omitted federation altogether and on being questioned on this Molotov said that 'the Soviet Government had certain information to show that some federations might be directed against the Soviet Union'. During the negotiations in London he only consented to the inclusion of the federation idea in the draft on condition that a clause was added to the effect that any such federations should be 'on the basis of friendly relations towards the USSR and Great Britain'. Her dislike of them must therefore be based on the fear that they will prevent her 'getting into Europe', or a fear that they will be used by other powers against her interests, in much the way that Finland was used by Germany.

Wilson concluded that if the British Government irritated the Soviet Union by supporting such federations, 'the Russian tendency will be to oppose our plans not only in Eastern Europe but in Western Europe as well'.

The sustained Soviet policy of dissuasion over a Czech-Polish confederation, as Piotr Wandycz has shown, consisted of territorial claims on Poland, the exploitation of continuing Czech-Polish differences (particularly the dispute over Teschen) and the mobilisation of public opinion in western countries against the idea of 'reactionary federations', which were also perceived as an anti-Soviet *cordon sanitaire*.[7] There was also a degree of Foreign Office suspicion of Polish intentions. Harry Hopkins noted in March 1943: 'Eden [British Foreign Secretary] said to Roosevelt Sikorski was forever meeting with the small states of the Balkans promoting Polish ambitions'. Sikorski, the Polish General, and leader of the 'London Poles' had in fact advanced the idea of sub-federations within a federal union of all Europe.

In 1942, on Sikorski's initiative, Foreign Ministers of the Allied governments in London began to hold regular meetings to prepare for the post-war unity of Europe. He had among other things proposed that a declaration of post-war solidarity should be made by the Governments of Poland, Norway, the Netherlands, Belgium, Luxembourg, Czechoslovakia, Greece and Yugoslavia. Eden had expressed conspicuous lack of enthusiasm, questioning the wisdom of setting up committees on which the great Allied powers were not represented. He also argued that the Soviet Union might well diagnose in this Eight-Power Declaration an anti-Soviet intent for which Britain would be held responsible, thereby straining Anglo-Soviet relations.

Was Britain now to reconcile support for a Polish-Czech agreement with harmonious relations with the Soviet Union? This difficulty was discernibly sidestepped by Churchill in his broadcast of 21 March 1943 in which he envisaged the creation of a world council based on regional councils for Europe, America and the Pacific. Europe was to be composed, he said, of states and confederations, among which he mentioned Balkan and Danubian federations. Neither Poland nor Czechoslovakia were to be assigned to them but were 'to stand together in friendly relations to Russia'.

On 26 April 1943, after the uncovering of the Katyn Forest Massacre by the Germans, Molotov announced the severing of diplomatic relations between the Soviet Union and the 'London Poles'. The Czechs, resolved to give priority to an understanding with the Soviet Union, dropped their negotiations with the Poles. The publication 'The War and the Working Class' (Moscow, 1943) made the Soviet position unequivocally clear.[8] The establishment of eastern European federations, it said, could be framed, 'but only by renouncing the necessity for friendship and collaboration between the USSR and the Allies in the post-war period, only if the renunciation of the Anglo-Soviet Treaty [the 20 year agreement signed in 1942] is considered'.

As late as the Moscow Conferences of October 1943, however, Eden submitted a proposal for confederations with particular reference to the Danubian area. Cordell Hull, the American Secretary of State, refused to go along with this, stating that general principles of world-wide application had to be agreed before discussing specific areas. Molotov denounced the idea of planning such federations as 'harmful not only to the interests of the small states but also to the general question of European stability'. Eden did not press the issue, while Cordell Hull contented himself with the observation that the United States consistently upheld the rights of small nations provided 'they did not affect the larger questions of peace and security'. On 12 December 1943 a Czech-Soviet alliance was concluded, duly sealing the fate of the idea of Czech-Polish confederation.[9]

The Poles had believed that it would be possible to create such a confederation in spite of Russian opposition. They had assumed that Great Britain and the United States would give their fullest support to the confederative plan. After a while the Foreign Secretary seems to have come to see the Czech-Soviet agreement as a hopeful step. The fact that Soviet relations with what Eden described as a 'petit bourgeois' country appeared so satisfactory led him to believe that the Soviet Union had no desire to impose communist regimes on Central and Eastern Europe.[10] He considered the treaty could serve as a model for post-war understandings with Austria and Hungary. His attitude towards Poland was markedly less sympathetic:

> Large numbers of Poles have unfortunately pinned their faith on British and American support against the territorial and strategic demands which Russia will make of Poland. It would be fatal not only to Anglo-Soviet relations and therefore to the future prospects of peace in Europe, but also to Poland herself if we encouraged the Poles to rely upon such support instead of staking everything upon achieving good relations with Russia.

During 1943 the idea of Balkan federation also died, a victim of the needs of Anglo-Soviet relations and of its own intrinsic unfeasibility. By the end of 1945 the Foreign Office had effectively abandoned the idea of federations or confederations in Eastern Europe.

The 'United States of Europe' and the post-war organisation of peace

In the autumn of 1942 Churchill heard for the first time of President Roosevelt's notion of 'Four World Policemen' as the proposed guarantors of peace in the post-war world. The Prime Minister sent a minute to Eden saying that he considered the idea too 'simple'. He added that he hoped that 'the European family [might] act unitedly as one under a Council of Europe'. In 1941 at Ditchley he had gone so far as to say that there must be a 'United States of Europe' and that he believed that it should be built by the British: 'If the Russians built it there would be communism and squalor; if the Germans built it there would be tyranny and brute force.' John Colville, the

Prime Minister's Assistant Private Secretary at the time, records: 'He spoke of the European Federation that was to come "with their Diet of Worms", and shuddered at the prospect of the intricate economic and currency problems. He felt that while Britain might be the builder and Britain might live in the house she would always preserve her liberty of choice and would be the natural undisputed link with the Americans and the Commonwealth.'[11]

From the spring of 1942 onwards the Soviet Union protested against any idea of European federation or confederation, Pan-European or regional, in terms exactly reminiscent of Stalin's response to the Briand Plan in 1930.[12] Such proposals, she claimed, laid the basis for a 'bourgeois anti-Soviet interventionist movement'. At the same time the Soviet Embassy in London brought pressure to bear on politicians in exile, stressing that it was quite illogical for them to be fighting for the recovery of national independence on the one hand and yet be willing to abandon this to some form of post-war union on the other.

The important point is that the United States, in all essentials, was to accede to this view that a regional European grouping was undesirable. When, in March 1943, William C. Bullitt, the former US Ambassador to the Soviet Union, showed Roosevelt a document of Allied war aims which had been discussed at the New York Congress of Count Coudenhove-Kalergi's Pan-Europa Movement—which spoke of a 'federal organisation for Europe' —the President rejected this with the remark that such federalist proposals would prejudice the understanding between the Soviet Union and the United States.

The turning-point as far as the future of a world organisation was concerned came, as the late Walter Lipgens noted, in the months of March to July 1943 when the United States swung round to accepting the Soviet viewpoint, though from different motives. Cordell Hull feared that a truly international world organisation could be crucially weakened if it was constructed on a basis of continental unions as had been suggested by the Advisory Committee chaired by Sumner Welles. He was also apprehensive that such unions would set up barriers against United States exports.

Several days after Churchill's broadcast of 21 March 1943, to which reference was made earlier, Roosevelt and Welles told Eden that 'the real decisions should be made by the United States, Great Britain, Russia and China, who would be the powers for many years to come and who would have to police the world'. Having failed to support Eden's tentative plea for federations, made at the Moscow Conference, Cordell Hull had secured acceptance by the Soviet Union of his Four-Power Declaration which called for 'a general international organisation based on the principle of the sovereign equality of all peace-loving states' while making the 'Big Four' responsible for security pending the establishment of such a body and for organising agreement on the regulation of armaments in the post-war period.

At the Tehran Conference in November 1943, Churchill tried to persuade Stalin to agree to a Danubian federation, but Roosevelt supported the Soviet leader in refusing to entertain such an idea. Both the United States and the Soviet Union were at one in wishing to prevent the European countries from forming a continental association or union which would have given Europe as such an independent weight in the balance of global forces.

The significant difference of approach between Churchill and the Foreign Office should be stressed. The latter considered the cooperation of the Great Powers to be imperative and argued that the United States would not participate unless there was a genuinely world-wide internationalist system for the preservation of peace. Churchill accepted this, but was also keenly concerned to see the importance of Europe re-established in the balance of world power, while at the same time maintaining close Anglo-American collaboration.

This difference was plainly signalled in the Prime Minister's so-called 'Morning Thoughts' of 30 January 1943, in which he had mentioned as part of the world organisation an 'Instrument of European Government'. These thoughts were received with considerable consternation by the Foreign Office. Gladwyn Jebb, who had drafted the 'United Nations Plan' for Eden, let it be known that 'the only hopeful feature was that where the Prime Minister's proposals were vague, they were, like the Atlantic Charter, capable of being adapted to almost any scheme for a world system that might be approved by the Cabinet, and where they were specific were so impracticable as hardly to merit serious consideration'.[13]

Churchill's view was that one had to prepare for the obvious possibility that after the war the victors would become divided among themselves. In the latter stages of the war he came to regard this as a certainty, as we shall see. Traditional power politics would again triumph over internationalist good intention and the Soviet Union would pose a major threat to European security. Such thinking, however, was far more in tune with that of the Chiefs of Staff than that of the Foreign Office.

Another illustration of this divergence between the attitude of the Prime Minister and that of the Foreign Office is their contrasting evaluation of Count Coudenhove-Kalergi's movement. Churchill sent a goodwill message to him for his New York Congress in March 1943 and let it be known that he thought the Count's ideas had much to recommend them. The Foreign Office suspected that much of their attraction for him lay in their anti-Soviet emphasis. In 'Pan-Europa', the original manifesto of his movement, published in 1923, Coudenhove had written: 'History gives Europe the following alternative: either to overcome all national hostilities and consolidate in a federal union, or sooner or later succumb to a Russian conquest'. While Churchill sent his best wishes, the Foreign Office, unknown to the Prime Minister, instructed the British Embassy in Washington 'to administer a douche of cold water in the appropriate official quarters' and to let it be known in the United States that 'he [Coudenhove] had been known to us for a long time as a well-intentioned crank'.[14]

When Churchill went to Washington in May 1943 he put forward the proposal that the United States, Great Britain and the Soviet Union should form the Supreme World Council to which there should be three subordinate regional councils, one for Europe, one for the Americas and one for the Pacific. Each of the European states should appoint a representative to a European regional council. At the same time there was to be a 'fraternal association' between Great Britain and the United States. This would encompass common citizenship, the sharing of military bases, the continuation of the Combined Staff and a harmonised foreign policy. Again one notes the Foreign Office's anxiety to avoid offending Soviet susceptibilities, since they also suggested that such a plan would lead, sooner or later, to renewed German domination of Europe. Eden held that, in any case, contentious European issues should not be raised in any scheme for world organisation. It would be more practical to work through a United Nations Commission for Europe (UNCE).

UNCE appears to have been the Foreign Office's concession to Churchill with his ill-defined but recurrent ideas about European unity.[15] He was still reiterating such views as late as May 1944 when the Dominion Prime Ministers sided with Eden over his 'United Nations Plan for Organising Peace'.[16] They took the view that regional councils would make the effective working of the Commonwealth in world affairs more difficult, while the Foreign Office again stressed that a regional grouping would be seen as a hostile entity by Moscow. Churchill withdrew his paper, but asked the Foreign Office to reconsider their plan with a view to making a case for regional organisation, keeping in mind the ultimate possibility of a 'United States of Europe'.

The modest ambitions of UNCE are revealed in the Cabinet discussions of July 1944 when Eden described the proposal as 'a projection into the peace of the European Advisory Commission' and as reinforcing the Anglo-Soviet Treaty and forming a bridge between eastern and western Europe. It was designed primarily for 'clearing up the war' and would not necessarily continue after it was over. The Cabinet accepted these recommendations on 4 August. At the Moscow Conference two months later the UNCE project was supplanted by the setting up of a European Advisory Commission which was intended as a mechanism for winding up the war.

The idea of a western European bloc

In July 1943 Eden commented: 'Europe expects us to have a European policy of our own and to state it. That policy must aim at the restoration of the independence of the smaller European Allies and the greatness of France.' A growing number of influential figures warned that, while regionalism might be rejected as a solution to the problems of the post-war world, Britain would have to come to terms with a changed global distribution of power. This must necessarily lead her to reassess her relationship with the Continent. In official thinking, two ideas commanded most attention in this respect in the closing stages of the war: one was an alliance with France, the other was the concept of a western European bloc.

In spite of the vacillations of British European policy, her leaders worked consistently to secure the restoration of France. Alfred Duff Cooper, then serving as Representative to the French Committee of National Liberation and a strong proponent of a post-war Anglo-French understanding, was also among those who argued that Britain should not place all her faith in a global international organisation. He wanted Britain and France to form the nucleus of a grouping which would include Belgium, the Netherlands, Norway and Denmark and later perhaps Sweden, Portugal, Spain and Italy. In this grouping there would be progress towards integration in defence and economics. This constellation of powers should be designed for defence against Germany, but it would also form the basis for security against the Soviet Union should this be necessary. '. . . Two world wars,' Duff Cooper wrote, 'should have sufficed to convince us that the safety of the British Empire should be based on more solid foundations than kind words and scraps of paper can provide.' He received a dispiriting reply on 25 July 1944, signed in Eden's absence by Gladwyn Jebb. Its substance was that Britain's post-war policy should be based on the alliance with the Soviet Union and the United Nations organisation and that to pursue such an idea as Duff Cooper had suggested might alienate the Soviet Union and divide Europe into two armed camps. This provoked Duff Cooper to reply that Eden was putting forward the same arguments as the appeasers before 1939, commenting: 'this specious fallacy paralysed our foreign policy, for rather than risk doing the wrong thing, we preferred to do nothing'. He went on to ask whether Britain could

> allow the formulation of our European policy to wait upon the *ukases* of the Kremlin or the votes of the American Senate. We shall emerge from the war with greater honours than any other country . . . the only country that took up arms of its own will at the beginning and remained undefeated until the end. The leadership of Europe will await us, but we may miss the opportunity of acquiring it

if we hesitate to adopt a positive foreign policy through fear of incurring the suspicion of Russia on the one hand, or the disappointment of America on the other.[17]

In 1944, at Eden's invitation Paul-Henri Spaak, the Belgian Foreign Minister, drew up and submitted to the Foreign Office a memorandum. 'The Organisation of Cooperation between Great Britain and Belgium within the Framework of a West European Regional Entente', which covered military, political and economic affairs. However rumours and press reports of a kind that were liable to excite Soviet suspicions soon circulated and Churchill wrote defensively to Stalin on 23 November 1944 to say that he had not yet considered the matter of a western bloc. Sir Archibald Clark Kerr, the Ambassador in Moscow, was instructed to tell Molotov that there was no truth in the reports that the British were intending to organise a closely-integrated western European system as a counterpoise to the Soviet Union and the United States. The world organisation of peace and the Anglo-Soviet Alliance had to take precedence, although it might be desirable additionally to organise a system of regional defence in western Europe against Germany.

As we have seen, Eden and the Foreign Office had been sceptical about Churchill's earlier ideas on Europe, regarding them as impracticable and incompatible with the policy of working to construct an effective global organisation to preserve peace. In the summer of 1944, though, we find the Prime Minister himself expressing strong objections to the idea of a western European bloc. At this time the Chiefs of Staff, whose views were far more in line with Churchill's than those of the Foreign Office, let the Foreign Office know that a western European coalition would not provide a strong enough defence 'without the incorporation at a later date of all or part of Germany'.[18]

As early as the Tehran Conference, Churchill was becoming apprehensively preoccupied by the prospect of post-war Soviet preponderance over Europe.[19] He commented at this time to Harold Macmillan: 'Germany is finished, though it may take some time to clear up the mess. The real problem now is Russia. I can't get the Americans to see it.' Combined with his inveterate anti-communism, this fear of Soviet expansionism had come to eclipse his fear of revived German might. As his doctor recorded in his diary in August 1944: 'Winston never talks of Hitler these days; he is always harping on the dangers of communism. He dreams of the Red Army spreading like a cancer from one country to another. It has become an obsession and he seems to think of little else.'[20] By this time it was obvious that any ideas of eastern European federation were unrealisable except under the aegis of the Soviet Union and that Soviet military power would have major political consequences in Eastern and Central Europe. While all plans and proposals for a European grouping or groupings were discussed in terms of the containment of post-war Germany, the question which haunted Churchill was whether such proposals, if they materialised, would be able to contain the Soviet Union. Over this he was very melancholy, describing the countries of Western Europe as 'nothing but hopeless weakness'.[21] In particular, he regarded the smaller states as 'liabilities rather than assets'.[22]

This overriding fear led Churchill to propose the Balkan 'percentages deal' to Stalin in Moscow in October 1944. In his view Britain would not be able to rely on her own strength or that of a consolidated and friendly Europe for her defence in the post-war world. In future the United States rather than a reorganised Europe would have to counterbalance Soviet power. At the same time, as we have seen, the United States had rejected a regionalist solution for the preservation of peace. W.H. McNeil has suggested that this turnabout in Churchill's approach dates from the summer of 1943.[23] However, Churchill was still to be found advocating European regionalist ideas as late as May 1944 in his paper to the Dominion Prime Ministers. The implications of this emphasis on the imperative of a close transatlantic understanding for the post-war world initially aroused some apprehension in the United States — illustrated by Harry Hopkins' warning that 'the United States should not be manoeuvred into a position where Great Britain had us lined up with them as a bloc against Russia to implement England's European policy'.

In these various ways, therefore, the evolution of a consistent and constructive British policy for Europe was frustrated by, among other things, the incipient global struggle between east and west. As H.B. Ryan has recently pointed out, 'the Russian threat is clear but never admitted in the Foreign Office papers on the subject, whereas Churchill is characteristically explicit on the question'.[24] On the one hand there was the fear that support for ideas of Pan-European or eastern European federation or a western regional bloc would help to destroy any prospect of enduring post-war cooperation with the Soviet Union and would increase distrust in a relationship already fraught with such questions as the timing of the Second Front. On the other hand, towards the end of the war there was Churchill's perception, shared by the Chiefs of Staff, that such groupings as were envisaged would be quite incapable of providing security against a future Soviet threat. There was, additionally, some official concern that a western European grouping might invite renewed German domination—that Germany would emerge as the natural leader in such a bloc.

The concessions made during the war years by the United States and Great Britain in the hope of securing post-war cooperation with the Soviet Union became reasons why that cooperation was subsequently to elude the powers and why the idea of global international peace-keeping faded before the reality of a world divided into spheres of influence. The debate over the European idea between 1941 and 1945 is part of that story.

Notes

1. Walter Lipgens (ed.) *Documents on the History of European Integration*, Vol. II (Berlin, Walter de Gruyter, 1986), Vol. II, pp. 156–205.
2. C-26040/267/62, 19 February 1940.
3. Avi Shlaim, 'Prelude to Downfall: The British Offer of Union to France, June 1940', *Journal of Contemporary History*, Vol. 9 (1974).
4. Avi Shlaim, *Britain and the Origins of European Unity 1940–1951*, (University of Reading, The Graduate School of Contemporary European Studies, 1978).
5. See particularly, Victor Rothwell, *Britain and the Cold War 1941–1947* (London, Jonathan Cape, 1982), Chapter 2.
6. The proposal had originally been put forward in the Polish-Czechoslovak Declaration of 11 November 1940. The two governments, this stated, 'are determined, on the conclusion of the war, to enter as independent and sovereign states into a closer political and economic association, which would become the basis of a new order in central Europe, and a guarantee of its stability. Moreover, both governments express the hope that in this cooperation, based on respect for the freedom of nations, the principles of democracy and the dignity of man, they will also be joined by other countries in that part of the European Continent'.
7. See Piotr S. Wandycz – *Czechoslovak-Polish Confederation and the Great Powers 1940–43* (Indiana University Publications, Slavic and East European Series Vol. III, 1956).
8. Quoted in *The Times*, 19 August 1943.
9. As early as 10 November 1941 Beneš had stated: 'The active participation of Soviet Russia in the establishment of European equilibrium must, of course, find expression first of all in an agreement between the Soviets and the Czechoslovak-Polish Confederation'. This was on the eve of the Declaration (see: note 6), C13398/216/12.

   In an article in *The Sunday Times* 11 January 1942 the acting Polish Foreign Minister, Raczynski, stated that the Confederation would become 'a centre of attraction for other nations occupying the strip of Europe from north to south— from Lithuania through Poland and Czechoslovakia to Hungary and the Balkan group of states'. This provoked a prompt attack from Alexander Bogomolov, Soviet Ambassador to the Polish government-in-exile on the grounds that Lithuania was part of the Soviet Union. (See A. Polonsky, *The Great Powers and the Polish Question 1941–1945* (London, London School of Economics, 1976), pp. 100–101.) On 12 September 1942, we find Beneš informing Bogomolov that the Czechs would not press the idea of a confederation with Poland 'in the face of Soviet opposition' (C9156/151/12). A conversation between Beneš and a senior Polish official in August 1943 is recorded in which Beneš is reported as saying: 'No power on earth will be able to detach Czechoslovakia from this collaboration with Russia. We have lost confidence in the Western countries after what happened in Munich. The Czechoslovak people have no confidence in France, Britain or America. We do not want to be regarded as a western European nation. We are more closely bound up with the east.' (C10484/525/12).

10. Martin Kitchen, *British Policy Towards the Soviet Union During the Second World War* (London, Macmillan, 1986), pp. 201–202.
11. Quoted in Shlaim, *Britain and the Origins of European Unity*, op. cit., p. 28.
12. For an interesting discussion of communist responses to the idea of European unification in the inter-war period see Renate Monteleone, 'Le Ragioni Teoriche Del Rifiuto Della Parola D'Ordine Degli Stati Uniti D'Europa Nel Movimento Communista Internazionale', in Sergio Pistone (ed.), *L'Idea Dell'Unificazione Europea Dalla Prima Alla Seconda Guerra Mondiale* (Turin, Fondazione Luigi Einaudi, 1975), pp. 77–95.
13. *The Memoirs of Lord Gladwyn* (London, Weidenfeld and Nicolson, 1972), p. 122.
14. C696/696/62, 2 January 1943 and C1006/696/62, 22 January 1943.
15. Shlaim, *Britain and the Origins of European Unity*, op. cit., p. 52.
16. See Sir Llewellyn Woodward, *British Foreign Policy in the Second World War*, (London, HMSO, 1976), Vol. V, pp. 116–126.
17. John Charmley, *Duff Cooper* (London, Weidenfeld and Nicolson, 1986), pp. 184–188.
18. Woodward, *British Foreign Policy in the Second World War*, op. cit., Vol. VI, p. 190.
19. Quoted in John W. Wheeler-Bennett and Anthony Nicholls, *The Semblance of Peace* (London, Macmillan, 1974), p. 290.
20. Lord Moran, *Winston Churchill: The Struggle for Survival 1940–1965* (London, Constable, 1966), p. 173.
21. U/8473/G December 1944.
22. Woodward, *British Foreign Policy in the Second World War*, op. cit., Vol. V, p. 193.
23. W.M. McNeill, *America, Britain and Russia: Their Co-operation and Conflict, 1941–1946* (London, Oxford University Press, 1953), p. 323.
24. Henry Butterfield Ryan, *The Vision of Anglo-America: The US–UK Alliance and the Emerging Cold War 1943–1946* (Cambridge, Cambridge University Press, 1987), p. 14.

12 The wartime national fronts in eastern Europe: ideal and reality

Ben Fowkes

In this paper I want to examine three main themes within the general area of the national front policy pursued by Communist parties in eastern Europe during and after the Second World War. They are:

1. The development of the popular front of the 1930s into the national front of the 1940s.
2. Variations in the application of the National Front in wartime conditions.
3. The character of National Fronts as they emerged as ruling coalitions after the Allied victory in the Second World War.

Early stages of the National Front in eastern Europe

The national front originated as a continuation and development of the popular front strategy implemented between 1935 and 1939 by the Communist International, originating at its Seventh Congress. But when did it start and how did it differ from the popular front? These questions are less easy to answer than at first appears. The national front as proposed was intended to be as broad a front as possible, comprising all those components of a given nation which were prepared to fight against Fascism, but so was the popular front. After all, the popular front (unlike the united front of the 1920s) was intended to include part of the bourgeoisie. If we look for a formal announcement by the Comintern of the change from popular front to national front, we look in vain. We have to rely on the hints at a new policy which began to emerge after the Munich crisis of 1938. The reaction of the Comintern to the Munich débâcle was to claim that only the Communist party could lead the national struggle. As an editorial published in February 1939 in *Die Kommunistische Internationale* [*KI*] put it: 'only the working class can

169

take over the leadership of the nation'.[1] Yet the same issue of the Comintern's journal proclaims on another page 'The Popular Front is not dead'. The apparent contradiction is resolved by the distinction between a country like France, which was still independent, and where the term 'popular front' applies, and countries like Czechoslovakia and Austria, which had lost their national independence, and needed a 'national united front' to restore it.

The term 'national front' began to be used in this new sense in *KI* early in 1939. An editorial of 20 January 1939 referred to 'the expansion of the popular front into a genuinely national front against the Fascist aggressors',[2] and in March 1939 Manuilsky reported to the Eighteenth Congress of the Soviet Communist Party that: 'These five years [1934 to 1939] have brought the formation of the Popular Front in France . . . and the formation and extension of the National Front in a series of colonial and dependent countries.'[3] The application of the national front was thus explicitly limited to 'colonial and dependent countries'. Czechoslovakia was now regarded as one of the latter. In fact it was in Czechoslovakia alone that the national front policy was effectively carried out before the Second World War, in the period between March and September 1939. The aim of the Communist Party of Czechoslovakia (KSC) at this time was the restoration of the Czechoslovak republic, in cooperation with all classes or groups, including the bourgeoisie and parties of the Right, which were prepared to resist Fascism. The National Front would be set up from 'from above' and 'from below', but agreements 'from above' did not mean the KSC's subordination to its allies. In fact the KSC's Guidelines of June 1939 implied a claim for hegemony within the alliance: 'Dr Beneš cannot be at the head of the national liberation movement . . . A united nation cannot be led to a second liberation by Dr Beneš and his friends but only by the KSC headed by Klement Gottwald.'[4]

The National Front, first edition, did not last long. The Nazi-Soviet Pact and the consequent change in Soviet and Comintern policy in September 1939 meant that the Second World War was now characterised as 'imperialist on both sides' and 'unjust': Communist parties were required to be neutral in the struggle between rival imperialist powers. The National Front disappears from Comintern and KSC documents, to be replaced again by a popular front, defined now as the 'front of workers, peasants and intellectuals under the leadership of the Communist party': not a popular front against Fascism but a popular front against imperialist war, with the aim of socialist revolution.[5] Not until mid-1941 was the National Front again referred to.

What put the National Front back on the agenda was the German invasion of the Soviet Union on 22 June 1941. This event seemed to have altered everything at a single stroke. Yet it did have a precursor: the coup of March 1941 in Yugoslavia against Prince Paul's pro-Axis policy and the establishment there of a government of resistance to Nazism. Stalin's encouragement of this movement seemed to signify the end of the Nazi-Soviet pact and the top Comintern officials drew the appropriate conclusions. Hence on 17 May 1941 new guidelines were issued for the KSC by its exiled leadership in Moscow under Gottwald: 'The tactical task is to create the broadest popular front of national resistance. The situation now demands a change in the relation between our own resistance movement and the so-called Benešites. The latest Balkan events . . . have created conditions for the creation of a united camp of resistance at home, under our leadership, which will stand firm against German imperialism and the compromising . . . bourgeoisie . . . Recognition of the class struggle is not a condition [for the alliance].'[6] In the same month, the Central Committee of the Communist Party of Yugoslavia (KPJ) declared its readiness 'to unite with groups from the dissolved bourgeois political parties which are ready to fight the occupiers . . . under the leadership of the KPJ.[7] This was halfway towards a national front, although it was still to be an assemblage of groups under Communist party leadership rather than an alliance of parties. Not until the fateful day of 22 June 1941 and the invasion of the Soviet Union by Hitler's army was a thorough and complete strategic reorientation made in Moscow.

The wartime application of the national front strategy

The national front strategy, and its link with the preceding popular front, was presented by the Austrian Communist and Comintern functionary, Ernst Fischer, writing in *KI* in October 1942: 'The popular front has risen like a phoenix from the ashes in the form of the national front . . . At the present time . . . people of all possible parties, religions and world views have joined in a great national front of peoples against the Fascist oppressors and the native quislings'.[8] This was the view from Moscow. The reality was somewhat different. The 'great national front of peoples' was most of the time, a front of the Communist party with itself. Either suitable alliance partners were lacking; or the would-be partners rejected the advances of the Comintern; or the allies were insignificant in numbers or political weight. In only one case, Czechoslovakia, could a broad national front of the type referred to by Fischer be achieved.[9] There was also one sphere of activity where national front policies could hope to gain broad support: the nationality question. The recognition of the right of national self-determination was central to the post-1941 National Front (unlike the popular front, which, for example, rejected Slovak claims). Wherever there were national minorities, Communist parties took up their demand (the Sudeten Germans are a special case, but even here the KSC tried at first to resist the idea of expulsion). Thus the Communist Party of Slovakia (KSS) called for Slovak autonomy jointly with the Slovak Democrats; the KPJ programme included federal autonomy for all the Yugoslav nationalities, including the Macedonians whose claims were not recognised by any other Yugoslav party; the Romanian Communist Party was allied with a Federation of Hungarian Workers in Romania, which claimed to represent the Hungarian minority; the Polish Communists alone accepted Poland's new eastern frontier, and thereby the national claims of Ruthenes and Lithuanians. But the nationality question was the exception. In all other spheres, and in all countries except Czechoslovakia, the national front idea met with insuperable problems. I shall try to illustrate these points by looking at three main examples, starting with Yugoslavia.

In the case of the Yugoslavian National Front, military priorities were in the forefront from the beginning; the instructions of the Comintern (in a telegram from 'Grandfather', i.e. Dimitrov) were to 'develop a movement under the slogan of a united national front . . . of struggle against the German and Italian fascist brigands',[10] and to 'organise partisan detachments and start a partisan war'. These partisans could hardly be other than Communists, but the General Staff guidelines of August 1941 at least paid lip service to the national front idea by describing the partisan detachments as 'not the fighting formation of any political party or group—in the concrete case, not the Communist party—but fighting detachments of the nations of Yugoslavia, in which all patriots must fight without regard to their political convictions . . . The political line of the partisan detachments is the formation of an anti-Fascist national liberation front of all the nations of Yugoslavia irrespective of political or religious conviction.[11]

There were other resistance forces in Yugoslavia in 1941 with which, on the face of it, the Communists could have cooperated. In Serbia there were the *četniks* or Draža Mihailović; in Slovenia there was the Slovene Legion. But there were two stumbling blocks: the insistence of the KPJ on non-recognition of the government in exile and the question of when to start the actual fighting—the Communists said immediately, whereas both the *četniks* and the Slovene Legion favoured making gradual preparations for a struggle, which would be taken up 'at the appropriate moment'.[12] Behind these questions lay rival claims to the leadership of the liberation movement: Tito and the KPJ would not compromise on this, despite pressure from Moscow. After the break with Mihailović they decided to set up five 'proletarian shock brigades'. These units had political commissars, hammer and sickle flags and were under Communist command. All this was incompatible with the national front as the Comintern understood it, and a telegram of 5 March 1942 from Dimitrov asked plaintively 'Why did you need to form a special proletarian brigade? Surely the immediate task is to unite all anti-Nazi currents . . . Are there really no other Yugoslav patriots—apart from

Communists—with whom you could join in a common struggle against the invaders?[13] The answer to this question, the KPJ claimed, was simply, no. Further attempts were made by Moscow to enforce a national front in Yugoslavia. In November 1942, on receipt of a telegram from Tito informing him of his intention to set up 'a kind of government', to be called the National Liberation Committee of Yugoslavia, Dimitrov replied: 'You must not fail to give the committee an all-national Yugoslav and an all-party anti-Fascist character . . .. Do not look upon the committee as a kind of government . . . Do not place it in opposition to the Yugoslav government in London. Do not put forward the slogan of a republic.' These instructions were unwelcome to Tito, and he obeyed them only in part. The 'National Liberation Committee', renamed the 'Anti-Fascist Council of the People's Liberation of Yugoslavia' (AVNOJ), was not described as a government in November 1942, but it functioned as one and no other political party entered it. A handful of non-communists were present, but they only represented themselves.

The relation between these non-communist individuals and the National Liberation Front is made clear by a document from Slovenia, a declaration of 1 March 1943 'on establishing the unified political organisation of the Liberation Front in Slovenia under the leadership of the Communist party.' Leaders of the Slovene *Sokols* (a patriotic sporting organisation) and the Christian Socialists announced their participation in the Slovene Liberation Front, but accepted the 'vanguard role of the KPS [Communist Party of Slovenia]' and renounced any intention of forming their own separate party organisation 'because they do not feel the need for it, as their aims in fundamental questions are identical with the aims of the KPS'.[14] The domination of the KPJ extended right down to the local level of civil administration. The People's Liberation Committees were run by Communists 'or people closely connected with the party in one way or another'.[15]

Even when it was clear that Tito and the Communist partisans were on the way to securing victory by themselves, Stalin still considered the policy valid for Yugoslavia; hence the decision of the second session of the AVNOJ in November 1943 to set itself up as the government of liberated Yugoslavia was greeted with fury in Moscow. 'The boss is extremely angry' said Manuilsky; Stalin is reported to have called it 'a stab in the back for the Soviet Union.[16] Soviet and western pressure together forced Tito to make an agreement with Ivo Šubašić, the prime minister of the exiled royal government of Yugoslavia in June 1944 and then to include two other bourgeois politicians (Milan Grol of the Serbian Democratic Party, and Juraj Šutej of the Croat Peasant Party) in the Provisional Government set up on 7 March 1945. Thus a national front of a kind was enforced from outside; but with very little result, since the KPJ made it clear from the start that they regarded them as 'former party leaders without influence among the people'.[17]

In Yugoslavia, then, a national front hardly existed; or at most was a national front from below, with the entry of individuals who had both abandoned their former parties and changed their political convictions.

In Poland it was the same, but for different reasons. There was no communist party in Poland at the opening of the Second World War. The Communist Party of Poland (KPP) had been dissolved by Stalin in 1938 and many of its leaders liquidated; moreover, the surviving Polish Communists had been forbidden to set up their party again without the explicit permission of the Executive Committee of the Communist International. In February 1941 some Polish Communists advocated the establishment of a Polish Soviet Republic as part of the Soviet Union, but this was not a popular slogan under the circumstances of the time.[18] The invasion of the Soviet Union in June 1941 transformed the situation and created the conditions for a national front policy, in Poland, as it did elsewhere. On 30 July 1941 the Polish émigré government under General Sikorski made an alliance with the Soviet Union and the threat which German occupation policies in Poland presented to all groups of Polish society meant that conditions on the ground favoured a common resistance to the Nazis.

When a communist party was set up again in Poland, on 5 January 1942, in occupied Warsaw, it was under the different title of the Polish Workers' Party (PPR). This change of name was intended to ease the way to a national front by sidestepping the hostility felt towards communism by most Poles at the time. The manoeuvre was quite transparent and did not deceive any of the other political groups. The PPR proposed to the Political Consultative Committee, the underground parliament of the Polish resistance, that a national front be set up. The proposals were rejected. The non-Communists objected to the PPR, not so much for its social radicalism (after all, the left socialists themselves analysed the war as an imperialist war leading inevitably to socialist revolution) as for being the instrument of a foreign power. Even the left socialists saw the PPR as 'lacking political independence' and 'subservient to foreign influences'. Another vital issue was Poland's eastern border. The PPR was the sole party to accept the new eastern frontiers drawn by Stalin in 1939. The London Poles, on the other hand, assumed that the war would end with the exclusive victory of the western powers, who would re-establish Poland with its old borders.

The PPR therefore had no hope of securing any allies of any political significance; the only basis for a national front in Poland was a struggle, under the political leadership of the party, against both the German occupier and the London-oriented underground.[19] This narrowing of the national front was, however, delayed by external factors. Stalin's foreign policy of alliance with the west implied, if possible, an alliance with the London Poles. Not until April 1943 was there a breach between the two, followed by the ending of diplomatic relations. Hence there is a clear distinction between the PPR's line in March 1943 and its line in November 1943. The March 1943 programme of the PPR advances the conception of a broad national front, 'excluding only traitors and capitulators' and covering a spectrum 'from the bourgeois-conservatives to the communists',[20] whereas the Proclamation of November 1943, 'What we are fighting for', denies the legitimacy of the government-in-exile, asserts the impossibility of restoring the pre-war bourgeois régime, defines the future government as one of 'People's Democracy' and lists some far-reaching socio-economic demands such as the nationalisation of large-scale industry, banks and means of transport, the control of production by factory committees and the 'transition to the socialist order made by the working class within the framework of the democratic state'.[21]

Neither the Polish Socialist Workers' Party (RPPS), the left Socialists nor the People's Party (SL) would cooperate with the PPR on this basis or any other, so the only way of even approaching a national front was to secure the support of a number of individuals, such as Osóbka-Morawski from the RPPS, and some members of the Peasant Battalions associated with the SL. Hence the National Council of the Homeland [KRN] was founded on 31 December 1943 with, as Gomułka himself later admitted, 'the relatively slim participation of other groups . . . The chief decisive and genuine force of the KRN' he added 'was the PPR.'[22]

This version of the national front was too narrow for Moscow; the Polish Communists in the Soviet Union, whose views were of course the same as Stalin's, still hankered after an agreement with the London Poles and there was a considerable amount of party infighting in 1943 and 1944 over this issue, between the more radical communists of the homeland, led by Gomułka, and the Moscow Poles, led in effect by the Bulgarian, Dimitrov, former head of the Comintern. Dimitrov criticised the KRN's radical socio-economic programme, saying it was a 'popular front' rather than a 'national front' programme.[23] These points of course reflected the preoccupations of the Soviet Government: Stalin was trying to retain the option of an agreement with the London Poles, assuming that they might become 'more reasonable' with the obviously impending defeat of Germany by the Red Army.

Not until May 1944 was the KRN recognised by Stalin as the 'kernel of a new Polish Government'; Stalin also authorised the KRN to administer the liberated areas of Poland.[24] The tug of war between the indigenous Communists and the Moscow Poles continued even after this, with the home based Polish leaders standing considerably to the left of those in Moscow. The PPR slogan of a 'democratic national front', (the word 'democratic' functioning here as a code word for 'radical') was countered by the Moscow Poles' slogan of a 'national front'. The setting up of the Polish Committee of

National Liberation (PKWN) on 21 July 1944 represented a victory for the Moscow faction over the KRN and the PPR, because Moscow Poles predominated on the Committee (10 out of 15 members, and both deputy chairmen) and the PPR was rebuked for its 'sectarian positions on land reform, nationalisation, and the National Front'. The PKWN manifesto avoided all socialist phraseology; Former German factories were to be nationalised, but others were to be placed 'under provisional state management' with compensation for former owners. Small and medium enterprises would remain in private hands. Large landed estates would be confiscated and become a land 'fund' to be distributed later among the peasantry.[25]

This moderation did not have the expected result. The entry of splinter groups from the Socialist and People's parties into the PKWN did not prevent the polarisation of political life into pro- and anti-communist camps. In October 1944 Stalin finally lost patience and adopted a harder line ('there had not been enough arrests', he said), a line reflected by Gomułka in his speech of 10 October 1944: 'The world has crossed the threshold of people's democracy, a new type of democracy . . . This does not allow the activities of reactionaries . . . The democratic national front does not signify any kind of rotten class compromise. Quite the contrary, it excludes it.' [26] By October 1944, therefore, the national front in Poland had assumed the character of rule by the Communist party. 'The basic links in the apparatus of coercion (state security, citizens' militia, the political commissars of the Polish Army) were run from the start almost exclusively by the PPR . . . 80% of industry was nationalised, including all the key industries . . . A dictatorship of the proletariat was set up in Poland in the form of a people's democracy.'[27] This was the situation faced by the head of the Polish Government-in-exile, Stanisław Mikołajczyk, when he returned to Poland to join the Provisional Government of National Unity, established under the provisions of the Yalta agreement of February 1945.

Ultimately, then, despite promising beginnings, the national front in Poland was no more of a reality than the national front in Yugoslavia. I now want to consider the one country where it did seem to have some real content—Czechoslovakia. Only in Czechoslovakia were the Communists able to find appropriate coalition partners. As we have seen, the KSC, with remarkable prescience, had already gone some way towards a broad-based national front in its guidelines of May 1941. There were far fewer points of conflict between the London-based government of President Beneš and the Moscow-based KSC than in comparable cases. The argument between the 'passive waiting policy of the bourgeois resistance' and the communist line of immediate partisan warfare was common to most European countries. However, it was less of a stumbling-block to cooperation in Czechoslovakia, first because the extremely effective repressive measures of the German authorities had annihilated the Resistance in the Czech lands by 1942, and second because KSC activity was itself until 1944 organisational and non-violent in character (the setting up of National Committees and work in the legal trade unions).[28] The proposed 'National Committees' (a way of making sure the old pre-1939 structure of local administration was displaced) were a general wartime communist policy all over eastern Europe. In the negotiations of December 1943 Beneš temporised on this. The really thorny problem was Slovak autonomy. Beneš rejected this, but it was a point on which the KSC and the KSS (organisationally independent as early as May 1939) were adamant. Eventually Beneš had to give way. In fact the whole story of the wartime negotiations between Beneš and Gottwald is one of concessions by Beneš to each successive demand, after initial hesitation. The Government programme of liberated Czechoslovakia, the Košice Programme of March 1945, was, in form, an agreement between the London-based Government and the Czechs and Slovaks in Moscow. In fact it simply took over the 16 points presented by Gottwald, after consulting the Slovak National Council (SNR). The composition of the Košice Government also reflected communist views: the KSC was to have the Ministries of the Interior, Information, Agriculture, Education and Social Security. As Gottwald said on 8 April 1945, referring to his coalition partners: 'They need us more than we need them.'[29] Even in Czechoslovakia, the National Front coalition was not an equal partnership.

The character of the victorious national fronts

The national fronts set up originally to fight Hitler changed their character as the war drew to a close. Unity in the struggle against the Nazis was replaced by conflict, explicit or implicit, over the shape of the new Europe. This fact was independent of Stalin's overall foreign policy, which remained directed towards the maintenance of the alliance with the west. Stalin, and those who transmitted his views to the Communist parties of the world (for eastern Europe this was Georgi Dimitrov), continued to advocate as broad a national front as possible, but now the objectives were different: communist hegemony in the national front alliance; a guarantee of this by control of vital positions in the police; measures of social reform, particularly land reform and a certain amount of nationalisation of industry; grass roots participation in these processes through national committees, factory committees and citizens' militias—in short the replacement of the old administrative infra-structure.

All this required a narrowing of the basis of the original national front. Almost everywhere the period 1944–45 sees the setting up of narrower groupings led by the Communist parties, and implying a union of the workers in town and country, with the exclusion of the bourgeoisie and its political representatives. In Czechoslovakia a 'Socialist Bloc' was set up in 1945, comprising the KSC, the Social Democrats and the National Socialists.[30] In Poland the 'Democratic Bloc' excluded the Polish People's Party (PSL). Similar developments took place in Romania ('National Democratic Front') and Hungary ('Left Bloc'). In Yugoslavia the Communists did not need to set up an exclusively 'democratic' grouping since they already had the AVNOJ firmly under their control. When the National Front (or, perhaps more accurately, People's Front) of Yugoslavia was set up in August 1945 (long after this had happened elsewhere) its rubber stamp function was evident: 'It did not have the task of choosing one or another alternative; it just had to link up with the heritage of the war of liberation. Hence it was not a coalition of parties but an association of the working masses on the basis of a social order in which the interests of the working masses defined the political line of the whole activity of the state.'[31]

The new and more radical post-war programmes of the National Front did not imply a full-scale socialist transformation in the sense of moves towards the Soviet model of complete nationalisation, collectivisation, expropriation of the bourgeoisie and sole power for the Communist party. This was officially 'People's Democracy', not yet the dictatorship of the proletariat or socialism. Not until 1948 did the East European regimes redefine their character, arguing, as Dimitrov did in December 1948, that 'People's Democracy is a special form of the dictatorship of the proletariat.[32]

But in 1945 anyone who talked of establishing Soviet power in their country was sharply called to order. In Slovakia, for instance, where the Slovak National Council (SNR) had called for the distribution of land among the peasants, the introduction of workers' control, the nationalisation of key industries and the abolition of the old multi-party system,[33] Dimitrov stressed that 'the question of Sovietisation is not to be posed . . . [O]nly when the time is ripe. You people in Slovakia who are in far too much of a hurry as regards Soviet power must calm down . . . It will not be sufficient to rely on one class and one party alone after the war . . . The Communists need allies on a patriotic basis'.[34] The SNR programme was leftism 'from above'; there was also a danger of leftism 'from below', not necessarily Communist in inspiration. In 1945, both the Social Democrats (Bohumil Laušman in particular) and the works councils in Czechoslovakia were calling for the 'creation of a socialist order'. The Communist head of the trade unions (Antonín Zápotocký) rejected this as 'politically inopportune'.[35] 'The other, non-Socialist parties in the National Front must not be ignored', he said.

This insistence on the need for allies did not, however, affect the real power relationships. One could summarise the situation in 1945 by saying:

there will be no socialism, but the party will be in power. Gomułka put the position very frankly in June 1945, speaking at the Moscow Conference with Mikołajczyk which set up the Polish Provisional Government of National Unity: 'It is we who are in power. We sincerely wish to come to terms with you . . . But please do not think our existence depends on it. We will never surrender the power we have seized.'[36] Politically speaking the period 1945–48 in Poland was one of mopping up both an illegal armed opposition (the remnants of the Home Army) and a legal, unarmed opposition under the PSL leader Mikołajczyk. 'Moderation' is here a question of greater subtlety in attaining the goal, not a different goal. Gomułka's explicit refusal to share power is not in contradiction to his strictures in May 1945 on the way his colleague, Alexander Zawadzki, was interfering with the PSL: 'If the PSL is to be a real coalition party it cannot tolerate "plants" . . . There must be an end to sectarianism . . . Several party organisations have reduced the PSL to a simple appendage to us, a necessary evil, [and this must stop].'[37]

In Czechoslovakia the situation was less clear. There the hegemony of the Communist party was hidden behind the façade of an apparently voluntary cooperation with other parties. But the national front system in Czechoslovakia did not allow for an opposition—it was cooperation or nothing. The overwhelmingly powerful position of the KSC in the trade unions (they had the chairman, and an 8:5 majority in the managing board of the Central Council of Trade Unions) and in the police (12 out of 17 regional police commanders) and in the state security service is fully documented, thanks to Karel Kaplan.[38] Hidden communist control of the country had existed for 3 years before the Prague coup and the non-communist parties had closed their eyes to, or at least accepted, this fact—the Social Democrats because they approved of most of what the communists were doing, the National Socialists out of a sense of isolation, and also respect for President Beneš' foreign policy priorities. It was for Gottwald to define the political agenda, and his policy was one of gradual takeover, in which the government-behind-the-scenes would become the legitimate government by imperceptible transitional stages. This was a policy of gradual strangulation of the other parties, the stages in which were the non-controversial 'Construction Programme' of May 1946 and the 'absolute majority' slogan of January 1947.

This policy of drifting quietly towards sole power was superseded by events elsewhere, the final breach between the Soviet Union and the United States and the start of the cold war. The change was signalled in Europe by the unceremonious removal of the Communist Party from the French coalition government in May 1947; by the rejection of the Marshall Plan in July 1947 by the east European countries, and by the meeting of major communist parties which took place in September 1947 at Szklarska Poręba in Poland which set up the Cominform. It is hard to say which of these events was the most important. For Czechoslovakia, the turning-point came in July 1947, when Gottwald and the KSC leadership were called to Moscow and forced to abandon their policy of accepting the Marshall Plan. This explains why the KSC did not wait until September to put forward a new strategy. On 21 August 1947 the General Secretary of the party, Rudolf Slánský, advised the Central Committee that pro-communist groups should be organised and made use of within the existing non-communist parties, to enable alternative leaderships to be set up, and that the slogans of 'reactionaries set out of the national front' and 'renew the Socialist Bloc' should be proclaimed.[39] The first of these techniques mentioned was already in use all over eastern Europe for example the replacement of Imre Kóvacs by the more pliable Ferenc Erdei as head of the National Peasant Party in Hungary in February 1947. Now the KSC was catching up. Slánský's second proposal, for a narrower bloc within the national front, had little meaning unless an alternative, pro-communist leadership could be found for the National Socialists; until then its main practical effect would be to exclude the Democrats from the national front in Slovakia, where they were indeed dangerous rivals to the KSC.

The meeting at Szklarska Poręba on September 1947, apart from setting up the Cominform, seemed mainly directed at criticising the French and Italian Communist parties for their failure to engage in a revolutionary struggle against their governments, but the KSC was also attacked for failing to work out a real strategy for seizing power and for its alleged obsession with the parliamentary road. The session turned into an orgy of denunciation by the parties in sole power, directed against their weaker brethren who had not attained this position. Gomułka told the Czechoslovaks that they had left it too late to seize power.[40] Kardelj attacked the the national front policy as practised in Hungary and Czechoslovakia. 'The search for peaceful roads of development', he said, 'has led in some Communist parties to a kind of coalition fetishism.' [41]

Kardelj's accusation was hardly justified in the case of Hungary—the National Front was already an empty shell there by September 1947, but in Czechoslovakia it was still a functioning coalition of parties. Due warning had now been served by the other Communist parties that Czechoslovakia must cease to be an exception. The KSC did not ignore the warning. There were many techniques of pressure that could be applied without going beyond the formal framework of the national front, for example: building up or using left groups within other parties; calling on 'sleepers' within the other parties who were already communist by conviction but had been advised to stay in their old party for the moment; generating artificial conspiracies by other parties; calling the masses onto the scene to underline communist demands; progressively slicing off the furthest right elements of other parties (Rákosi's 'salami tactics', so effectively applied in Hungary). All these methods were now put into operation and, after a partial success in Slovakia (the October crisis), a full victory was secured over the opponents of communism within the other parties in February 1948. This meant the end in practice of the national front, although it has continued up to the present time to lead a shadow existence over most of eastern Europe. To conclude, the national front idea in eastern Europe was mostly an illusion fostered by the Communists for their own purposes. It came nearest to being realised in the later stages of the war. Once the war was over, membership of national fronts for non-communists merely meant acceptance of a situation in which they were powerless. Yet this situation is by no means permanent; both in Czechoslovakia in 1968 and in Hungary and Yugoslavia in the late 1980s, the surviving institutions of the National Front have been revitalised and allowed to assume a more independent position. The future may well hold some surprises in this respect.

Abbreviations

AVNOJ	Antifašističko vijeće narodnog oslobodjenja Jugoslavije
ECCI	Executive Committee of the Communist International
KI	Kommunisticheskii Internatsional (Russian edition), or Die Kommunistische Internationale (German edition)
KPJ	Komunistička partija Jugoslavije
KPP	Komunistyczna Partia Polski
KPS	Komunistička partija Slovenije
KRN	Krajowa Rada Narodowa
KSC	Komunistická strana Československa
KSS	Komunistická strana Slovenska
NF	National Front
PKWN	Polski Komitet Wyzwolenia Narodowego
PPR	Polska Partia Robotnicza
PS	Polscy Socjaliści
PSL	Polskie Stronnictwo Ludowe
RPPS	Robotnicza Partia Polskich Socjalistów
SL	Stronnictwo Ludowe
SNR	Slovenská Národní Rada

Notes

1. *Die Kommunistische Internationale* [hereinafter KI (German version], **2**, 25 February 1939, p. 123, editorial.

2. KI (German version), **1**, 20 January 1939, p. 84.
3. KI (Russian version), **3**, March 1939, p. 123.
4. *Za svoboda ceského a slovenského národa* (Prague, 1956) p. 99.
5. F. Janáček, 'KSC a politika národní fronty 1938–1945', p. 45, in *Národní fronta a komunisté* [hereinafter NFK] (Prague, Institut za izučavanje radničkog pokreta, 1968).
6. Printed in *Za svoboda českého a slovenského národa*, op. cit., (Prague, 1956) p. 157.
7. P. Morača, 'KSJ a vytvoření národní fronty v osvobozeneckém boji a revoluci 1941–1945', p. 159, in NFK.
8. E. Fischer, 'Ot narodnogo fronta k obshchenatsional'nomu frontu' ('From the popular front to the all-national front'), KI (Russian version), 8–9, 12 October 1942, p. 30; quoted in J.B. Urban, *Moscow and the Italian Communist Party* (London, Cornell University Press, 1986) p. 158.
9. It is sometimes suggested that Bulgaria is another case; but the cooperation between Nikola Petkov's Bulgarian Farming People's Union [BZNS] and the Fatherland Front only lasted from September 1943 to August 1945, when the party split and most of its members followed Petkov out of the Fatherland Front. (See V.V. Mar'ina, 'Vzaimo otnosheniya rabochikh i krest'yanskikh partiy v revolutsiaykh 40-kh godov v stranakh Tsentral'noy i Yugo-Vostochnoy Yevropy', *Voprosy Istorii*, **2**, (1975), p. 8.)
10. J. Marjanović, 'Forme borbe i rada KPJ u narodnoj revoluciji', *Komunist*, January 1951, p. 116.
11. P. Morača, op. cit., p. 165.
12. P. Morača, op. cit., p. 173, report of 11 September 1941 from Ranković to Tito.
13. M. Pijade, *About the Legend that the Yugoslav Uprising Owed its Existence to Soviet Assistance* (London, Yugoslav Embassy, 1950), p. 9.
14. *Zbornik Dokumenata i Podataka o Narodnooslobodilačkom Ratu Jugoslavenskih Naroda*, vol. VI, bk. 5 (Belgrade, 1956), doc. 70, pp. 187–188.
15. *Istorijski Arhiv Komunistički Partije Jugoslavije*, vol. 1, bk. 1 (Belgrade, KPJ, 1949), p. 140.
16. P. Auty, *Tito, A Biography* (London, Longmans, 1970), p. 231.
17. E. Kardelj, *Pot nove Jugoslavije* (Ljubljana, 1946), p. 94.
18. M. Malinowski's contribution to 'Boj Polské delnické strany o vytvoření národní fronty v letech druhé svetové války', in NFK, p. 239.
19. J. Pawłowicz, *Strategia frontu narodowego PPR* (Warsaw, Panstowe Wydawnictwo Naukowe, 1965), p. 292.
20. A. Przygoński, 'Dwie Koncepcje strategii frontu narodowego PPR', *Nowe Drogi*, 5, May 1974, p. 189.
21. *Kształtowanie sie podstaw programowych PPR w latach 1942–1945* (Warsaw, Partia Robotnicza, 1958), pp. 150–151.
22. W. Gomułka, in *Nowe Drogi*, September–October 1948, p. 45.
23. J. Pawłowicz's contribution to 'Boj . . .', in NFK, p. 309.
24. J. Pawłowicz, *Strategia frontu narodowego PPR*, op. cit., p. 170.
25. *Polska Partia Robotnicza. Dokumenty Programowe 1942–1948* (Warsaw, Partia Robotnicza, 1984), pp. 554–601.

26. W. Gomułka, *Artykuły i Przemówienia*, vol. 1 (Warsaw, Ksiaska i Wiedza, 1962), pp. 114–5.

27. J. Gołębiowski and W. Góra, 'Charakter i etapy revolucji ludowej w Polsce', *Z Pola Walki*, 3, (1975) pp. 151–3.

28. J. Hřibek's contribution to 'KSČ politika národní fronty 1938–1945', NFK, p. 86.

29. K. Gottwald, *Spisy*, (Prague, 1955) Vol. 12, p. 21.

30. More precisely, a 'National Bloc of Working People of Town and Country', set up on 8 June 1945 (See S. Schröder-Laskowski, *Der Kampf um die Macht in der Tschechoslowakei 1945–1948* (Berlin, Akademie-Verlag, 1978), pp. 176–179.

31. P. Morača, in NFK, p. 224.

32. F. Fejtö, *Histoire des démocraties populaires* (Paris, Editions du Seuil, 1952), p. 279.

33. *Cesta ke květnu* (Prague, KSS, 1965) Vol. 1, pt. 2, p. 487.

34. Dimitrov, speaking in Moscow to KSČ representatives on 6 December 1944, quoted in M. Bouček, M. Klimeš and M. Vartiková, *Program Revoluce* (Prague, 1975), p. 235.

35. J. Bloomfield, *Passive Revolution* (New York, St. Martin's Press, 1979), p. 80.

36. W. Gomułka, *Artikuły i Przemówiemia*, op. cit., Vol. 1, pp. 215–6.

37. Gomułka, speaking at the 20–21 May 1945 Plenum of the CC of the PPR, doc. 75 of A. Polonsky and B. Drukier, *The Beginnings of Communist Rule in Poland* (London, Owen, 1980), pp. 424–42.

38. K. Kaplan, *The Short March* (London, Hurst, 1987), pp. 43–44.

39. Ibid., p. 75.

40. Ibid., p. 76, quoting the report of Š. Baštovanský, one of the Czechoslovak representatives at the Szklarska Poręba meeting.

41. Y. Lahav, *Der Weg der kommunisticshen Partei Ungarns zur Macht* (Munich, Oldenbourg, 1985), Vol. 2, p. 263.

13 The American challenge and the origins of the politics of growth

David Ellwood

'The most unprecedented phenomenon in post-war Europe', wrote Michael Postan in 1967, 'was not so much the purely material record of her economy as the spirit which moved it. What was really remarkable . . . was that economic growth was so powerfully propelled by public sentiments and policies . . . In all European countries economic growth became a universal creed and a common expectation to which governments were expected to conform.' How could this have come about? What were the roots of such a powerful collective impulse? In Postan's view no contribution 'to the doctrine or actual process of European growth [was] nearly as decisive' as that made by the United States. Throughout the postwar period America had used its influence 'to foster all actions and attitudes serving the purposes of European economic expansion'.[1]

So economic growth contrived by public choice—as natural a part of contemporary life and aspirations as traffic or central heating—turns out to have a history, and in this history the United States appears to have had the starring role. Growth is both doctrine and process, suggests Postan; how else might it be identified conceptually and in history?

Its current meaning dates back to the Marshall Plan, as Charles Maier has demonstrated.[2] The New Deal economists who used it then were clearly referring to a special kind of managed expansion not only going beyond stability but also beyond the hitherto accepted definitions of good times, such as abundance and prosperity. The language they projected suggested a new dynamic of progress, potentially infinite, whose benefits would be assured to everyone. With the benefit of at least 25 years of growth and, just as important, the experience of seeing what happens when it stops, we can now suggest what, historically, the concept might embrace:

1. A specific phase after the Second World War with unprecedentedly and continuously high rates of increase in capital formation, gross national

product and living standards. From two World Wars and the 'intervening upheaval' to the years of the 'miracles', the passage was extraordinarily short. It enabled Europe to enter the 'age of high mass consumption' laid down in 1960 by W.W. Rostow as the highest expression of capitalism— the great model offered by America's pioneering experience.[3]

2. An economic fact, measurable with techniques developed before and during the Second World War, which transformed the degree of control governments possessed over macroeconomic processes. Together with the Keynesian revolution in demand management ideas and the Taylorite revolution in production management, economic objectives such as welfare, full employment and rising living standards were now within the reach of the governments of industrial nations.

3. A political strategy, ending the struggle over distribution, promoting change without conflict and promising the end of extremism—particularly of the Left—as *embourgeoisement* advanced. Whether as a cement for Atlanticism, the means for defeating the Soviet Union or the promise for Third World 'development', growth had no rival. It was conservative politicians, as well as consumers, who had 'never had it so good' in 1959.

4. An ideology or way of life, banishing thrift, austerity and savings as ethic, defining wants, needs, opportunities and aspirations. From the 'revolution of rising expectations' (the phrase invented by a Marshall planner) came a new stereotype: the affluent worker, with his constantly improving income at the root of a new mentality of consumption.

Once established and successful, growth became an object in itself, especially in the form of 'fast growth', which would be stable and non-inflationary. By the time the OECD was founded in the name of this ideal in 1960, growth had became a key basis of legitimacy of western ruling groups, a basic organising principle of contemporary societies which had redefined modernisation and progress in explicitly economic terms.

How had this happened? How did the growth idea catch on so successfully and quickly in Europe? Was it through Americanisation or some other hybrid of modernisation? What did the Europeans take and what did they refuse of the model the United States came to propose so vigorously. While none of these questions has a satisfactory answer of any kind at the moment— perhaps they never will—what follows is one proposal on where to start looking for them.

In 1948 a little-known classic of geopolitics was published entitled *The Mediterranean: Its Rôle in U.S. Foreign Policy*. In his chapter on 'Stability', the author, a Brookings Institution professor named William Reitzel, writes of the kind of direct influence economic power has on social relations: 'It makes immediate claims on the material interests of the masses, stands as a primary factor in the hopes and plans of individuals, and provides a leverage for securing compromises.'[4]

The Americans of the Roosevelt and Truman administrations were convinced that in the experience of the New Deal they had empirical confirmation of the determining role of economic ingredients in a strategy of social and political stabilisation. As Roosevelt told Stalin at Yalta:

> . . . in his [Roosevelt's] opinion any leader of a people must take care of their primary needs. He said he remembered when he first became President the United States was close to revolution because the people lacked food, clothing and shelter, but he had said, 'If you elect me President I will give you these things', and since then there was very little problem in regard to social disorder in the United States.[5]

By the summer of 1944, US State Department planners had developed a comprehensive analysis of the past, present and future situation of countries such as Italy. At its heart it stated that:

> American policy is based on the premise that the economic well-being of a country is a primary factor in its internal stability and its peaceful relations with other states.

For this reason Washington looked forward to:

> An economic reconstruction designed to create an expanding economy which will offer the Italian people genuine opportunities for their economic betterment.[6]

But the length and destructiveness of the war in Europe worked to split the concept of stabilisation into two distinct areas of concern: recovery and expansion. Inside America this was not the case. There the immediate problems were seen in terms of how to ensure a smooth transition to peacetime production and how to provide work for the 4.5 million.employed by the war, as well as markets for their products. But in Europe Keynes's famous lessons stood ready for application:

> To what a different future Europe might have looked forward if either Mr. Lloyd George or Mr. Wilson had apprehended that the most serious of the problems which claimed their attention were not political or territorial, but financial and economic, and that the perils of the future lay not in frontiers and in sovereignties, but in food, coal and transport . . . The fundamental economic problem of a Europe starving and disintegrating before their eyes was the one question on which it was impossible to arouse the interest of the four.[7]

Commenting on these issues and the new relationship he saw between self-determination and economic power. E.H. Carr pointed out in 1942 that the nineteenth century political rights accorded to minorities in 1919 did not extend to the right to work or 'the right not to starve . . .'

> In retrospect it is not difficult to see that the prudent course would have been—and the same would be equally true today—to attend first, as an immediate practical measure, to the urgent needs of economic recovery, and then to evolve, in the light of the experience gained, the necessary compromise between the claims of national independence and the imperative exigencies of economic interdependence.[8]

To tackle this task in the aftermath of the Second World War, the ruling classes and most of the populations in western Europe looked to Washington, as the flood of American troops, American equipment and American propaganda prompted them to do. However the US executive, while paying serious tribute (in the Atlantic Charter, the Lend-Lease Master Agreement and above all the Four Freedoms) to the lessons learned from the First World War and the Depression were decidedly much more interested in the second half of Carr's formulation, 'the exigencies of economic interdependence', than in his first, 'the claims of national independence'. Roosevelt himself defined his fourth freedom (freedom from want) in terms of 'economic understandings which will secure to every nation a healthy peacetime life for its inhabitants'. But State Department Secretary Hull's vision was much more expansive, according to a famous passage in his memoirs:

> To me, unhampered trade dovetailed with peace; high tariffs, trade barriers, and unfair economic competition with war. Though realising that many other factors were involved, I reasoned that if we could get a freer flow of trade—freer in the sense of fewer discriminations and obstructions—so that one country would not be deadly jealous of another and the living standards of all countries might rise, thereby eliminating the economic dissatisfaction that breeds war, we might have a reasonable chance for lasting peace.[9]

In Hull's State Department and at the Council of Foreign Relations, committees were at work throughout the war developing this line of thought, which can be traced consistently from the middle of the 1930s to the post-war period in the Department's public statements. It built on the thought of men like Walter Lippmann, whose 1934 essay, *The Method of Freedom* discussed the impact of mass democracy on economic demands. Lippmann insisted that 'the modern state cannot endure unless it insures to its people their standard of life', and contrasted the narrowness of national politics with the cosmopolitan trends in economic life.[10] Inside the Administration Vice President Wallace had by 1942 'established himself as the spokesman for a messianic liberalism of abundance', seeing the war as 'an act of millenial liberation that would usher in "the century of the common man" '.[11]

Roosevelt and his men believed that projecting abroad the American experience in general and the New Deal model in particular was the way to do this. Even before America's entry into the war, in September 1941, discussion of the future cultural relations programme of the United States in the State Department was looking to goals which were economic and social as well as intellectual and artistic, 'a common effort on the part of all to improve living conditions and to attain democratic participation'. This, according to the planners, meant that, in order to realise the major objectives of US foreign policy: 'world stability and economic advancement' would have to be secured.[12] Among the favourite Administration models for export was the Tennessee Valley Authority Scheme. Under-Secretary of State Sumner Welles pinpointed the Danube and the Balkans as the most suitable terrain for such a scheme, and in October 1944 he wrote:

> The poverty of the masses underlies every problem of the Balkan peoples. Only through a higher standard of living can they develop the social foundation upon which to construct stable national governments . . . The potentialities inherent in some vast power project which might be established in the Danube valley are almost unlimited. The electrical power derived from such an installation, cutting across all the national lines of Eastern Europe, could within twenty years create an entirely new industrial civilisation in the area . . .'

—on condition that barriers to trade were abolished, a regional customs union set up and all sorts of other methods were adopted for cooperative control of 'intra-regional development'.[13] Here then was one design explicitly linking regional economic unity to the general objective of raising living standards everywhere.

Although Welles had left the government by the time he set down the words just quoted, schemes such as this one were typical of the work being done in the network of State Department committees planning post-war policy. This planning effort has always attracted historical interest but has never been taken too seriously, partly because of the easily discernable distance between the planners and the policy-makers, and partly because of the well-known political feebleness of the State Department under Roosevelt. But the Department was not isolated in wartime Washington. In its research and speculation on post-war prospects it could count on the collaboration of eminent congressmen, journalists specialising in international affairs, and academic experts as well as the resources of the Council of Foreign Relations in New York.

Thus the contents of the 'Notter File' (the collection of post-war planning material collated by Under-Secretary Harley A. Notter[14]) are the product of an entire political culture: generally internationalist but not necessarily New Dealer, convinced of the rightness of Roosevelt's vision of collective security but anxious to know how to put it into practice, determined to make sure that America's public and her allies understood the dominant rôle the United States would naturally play in the post-war world. The highest expression of this culture was to be the Marshall Plan, a far more complex yet also more concrete design than anything thought up in wartime. The plans of the war years in fact all, more or less, failed by 1950: the UN, the IBRD, the ITO, the visions of the Hot Springs Agriculture Conference of March 1943, but the underlying historical, political and economic analyses persisted and the goals remained the same.

Of the evolving political and economic situation in the European countries this culture knew very little; rarely was any thought ever given by its members, sophisticated and worldly as they were, to the possibility that these countries might have evolved their own ideas on what should happen to them after the war was over.

In a 'Progress Report on Postwar Programs' of September 1944, the State Department experts specialising in economic and social policy spelled out their view of US objectives as follows:

1. An expansion of economic activity.
2. The maintenance of high and stable levels of employment.
3. Rising standards of living.[15]

How these objectives determined specific policy approaches in fields ranging from commodity policy to cartels, from reconstruction finance to reparations, was detailed in papers attached. Monetary stabilisation and international investment were assumed to have been taken care of by the Bretton Woods conference.

This dynamic view of the economic future of the world had prevailed, without too much effort, over a line of argument in the Department which preferred the apparently safer objective of stability. In a February 1943 discussion on Hungary about how to reform land holdings and bring about industrialisation, the Committee on Territorial Problems saw the basic choice in such cases to be between 'a free trade economy leading to a higher standard of living but less stability in times of world crises and . . . a balanced self-sufficiency with a lower standard of living but more continuous stability'. All agreed that 'conditions in the surrounding area were relevant to the degree of stability which any state could attain'.[16]

By October 1943 there was less caution and more detailed plans. 'A large measure of international cooperation in many directions' was expected by the US delegation to the Moscow Conference of Foreign Ministers. This meant activity to free trade, eliminate cartels, stabilise currencies and guarantee their convertibility, promote 'development', modernise communications, raise nutrition and consumption levels, improve labour standards and conditions: all in the name of '(improving) progressively . . . production, distribution, employment and living standards' in the world.[17]

By this time the Department had become aware that currents of thought were changing in Europe, looking forward to some form of closer association between the countries of the Old World after the war. Churchill's visit in May 1943 had introduced official Washington to his views on a European regional council, even a kind of 'United States of Europe'.[18] This was practically the only time during the war that the planners reacted to a proposal from outside. The challenge then was to find ways to reconcile this new geopolitical suggestion with recognised US economic priorities. In any event no one liked the idea of regional security plans. Hamilton Fish Armstrong, Chairman of the Council of Foreign Relations, told a high level meeting in the State Department, with the Secretary present, that ideas such as Churchill's would encourage isolationists to go for an exclusive American hemisphere council, would not deal with the risk of war which was broader in scope, and would weaken America's freedom of manoeuvre.[19]

The Department took the question sufficiently seriously to set up a special, new research and analysis committee on European regional organisation. Its remit was nothing if not wide-ranging. The 'Specific Groupings' covered included: Continental, Low Countries (with or without the Rhineland), Low Countries and France, Habsburg bloc, south Slav bloc, Czech-Polish confederation, east European confederation, Scandinavian bloc; religious groupings included were: Catholic bloc, Latin bloc, Communist, Orthodox, Slav and Peasant. At the Committee's first meeting the Chairman, Hamilton Fish Armstrong, insisted that the principal issues involved were security and the prevention of war and others agreed that these, rather than economic priorities, would dictate whether anything came of the impulse to integration.[20] By the end of the year, commentators in the Council on Foreign Relations had decided that gains from a loose regional organisation in Europe were 'likely to be of far more modest dimensions than their advocates appear to realise'.[21] But the economic prospects were being taken seriously and we find the first use of the language of free trade and expansion which would become so familiar under the Marshall Plan. Removing internal barriers to trade and forming a larger market, 'would lead to a higher degree of regional specialisation and hence to a higher level of real income in Europe, from which American trade with Europe would be likely to benefit'.[22]

At the same time opinions were expressed to the effect that America's attitude would necessarily depend on this European union's external commercial policy: it might turn out to be very damaging to US interests. For this reason, and on the basis of worries that any regional arrangement would detract from the world security organisation, 'extreme reserve' was chosen as the official posture on moves towards European unity.[23]

Of course it had always been understood that free trade meant closer economic collaboration and that sovereignty as it was traditionally understood was a fetishism or curse standing in the way of this process. As far back as 1942 the Council on Foreign Relations had asked how the Big Three could pool their sovereignty and how the 'popular association of sovereignty with national freedom and independence [could] be effectively broken'. At this stage the economic objectives were still being defined as 'economic security' and 'social welfare' (including full employment) on an international scale and the means proposed were almost exclusively functional and institutional.[24] By 1944–45 American experts were conjuring up the vision of the 'chain reaction' that might be set off by huge, planned capital inputs into countries such as Greece. Roosevelt was searching for a country which could be transformed by American capital and methods from virgin desert into a fully developed modern state. The country he was inclined to choose for the experiment was Iran. The planners in the State Department were now ready to propose 'a thoroughgoing reorientation of its economic and social life' for France, a revolution in its values which would 'place less emphasis on security and more emphasis on risk and enterprise', with the State providing 'direction, coherence and encouragement' in a 'general scheme of industrial and agricultural development',[25] but by this time (December 1944) reality on the ground was beginning to catch up with the visionaries in Washington.

In Greece, the British had been struggling since early 1943 with a situation of total financial and economic collapse. The afflictions of the local currency were particularly prominent: the cost of living, which had started from a base of 1.0 in 1941 had reached 1,572.7 by December 1943, 2,305,948,911.0 by October 1944 and increased 10 times more during the course of 1945.[26] The December insurrection of 1944 came shortly after the first attempt to substitute the currency and, in the aftermath of its repression, several more attempts were made under British direction. If, as Wray Candilis claims, Greece offered an important experience in teaching American planners the gravity of European conditions—and their possible consequences—the effect of this situation on the British was much more immediate. While Keynes and his colleagues regarded inflation and food shortages as the crucial economic problems to be faced before there could be any talk of free trade or expansion, Harold Macmillan—political overlord of both Greece and Italy— did not hesitate to warn in Allied Force Headquarters near Naples that trends left uncontrolled in Italy would produce consequences identical with those in Greece.[27]

Officially it was now the Americans who were in charge of economics in liberated Italy. Under the division of labour worked out in the Allied Control

Commission (the joint Anglo-American military regime overseeing co-belligerency and the passage from Fascism to democracy) its Economic Section was to be handled by a civilian nominee from Washington, but no one who got close to the desperate ruined condition of liberated Italy wanted anything to do with confronting the enormous tasks of reconstruction. When the State Department planners had initially tackled the question of Italy's economic future, in October 1942, they had been confronted by Roosevelt's travelling grandee, Myron Taylor, who had told them that all the Mediterranean leaders he had talked to on a recent trip had expressed fear of 'widespread communist uprisings in west and central Europe at the end of the war', which could only be prevented by getting in huge relief supplies to feed the starving millions, but he was not taken seriously, possibly because his interlocutors had been the Pope, Franco, Salazar and members of the Italian aristocracy.[28] Instead the Committee on Territorial Problems thought that 'consideration should be given to the possibility of a really considerable improvement in Italy's living standard in the post-war years'. Even if it remained low in real terms, said one of the participating experts, 'the very fact that it was improving would satisfy the demands of the people and thereby tend to maintain a stable government in the country'.[29]

The man who brought this mentality to Italy after the armistice was Henry F. Grady, an eminent businessman and politician, who was the first and only figure of significance to head the Allied Control Commission's (ACC) Economic Section.

> Our national contribution . . . (must) be made, so far as possible, the means of furthering our national policies in the international field, designed for the reconstruction of a world of expanding economic activity and peaceful development, unhampered by excessive trade restrictions special spheres of influence, and the other concomitants of the economic imperialism which must ultimately lead again to war.[30]

Just how these policies—which Grady termed the 'development of Italian initiative and responsibility'—could be applied there no one knew. Grady himself disappeared back to Washington within a matter of weeks, thereby establishing a pattern for the job which persisted until the United Nations Relief and Rehabilitation Agency (UNRRA) period. Most of the time the post was unfilled, partly because, as Robert Murphy, the American Political Adviser to the Supreme Allied Commander, told the State Department in June, 1944, 'I have never seen a concrete analysis or statement of our economic objectives'. Murphy was convinced that the British did have economic aims in Italy, but he did not say what he thought they were.[31]

In fact, by mid-1944 the British did have one economic aim in Italy: finding the means to stop communism. The inevitable corollary of inflation and a shattered economy took on a sharply focussed form in Italy after Togliatti's return from Moscow in March and his subsequent re-orientation of the Italian Communist Party (PCI) and entry into the government. With the armed Resistance, dominated by the Communist party, expanding in the north and the Red Army going from strength to strength to the east, communism in Italy, as elsewhere, seemed to have all the winning cards.

The rise of the communist question, challenging Italy's position in Europe and the Mediterranean and dominating the path to the political future, brought about a qualitative change first in British and eventually in American approaches to the problems of the 'liberated territories'. The British Foreign Office analysis of the situation foreshadowed much of American policy towards Italy, France, Greece and elsewhere in subsequent years with its premise that communism would gain influence rather than direct power, that the national state was not equipped to deal with the question at the roots and, above all, that economic causes, and hence economic remedies (which only America had the means to provide) were the key to the Communist parties' mass following. In the short term, said Sir Orme Sargent, Deputy Under-Secretary at the Foreign Office, there would have to be widespread and rigid control of the whole economy by the Allies; in the long-term it was necessary to restore Italian industry 'to comparative prosperity within as short a period of time as possible, and in the interval to provide consumers' goods'.[32] But the Allied military were quite incapable of controlling the economic situation and as for a reconstruction loan, when Italy sought one from London in the spring of 1945, members of both Treasury and Foreign Office declared themselves 'outraged' in personal terms and in the name of the British public.[33]

Only days after this judgement Macmillan was in London telling the Foreign Office that the only real hope for influence in Italy lay in economic means. Churchill and Macmillan agreed that nothing could be done without the Americans, 'but their desire to get out of Europe will make them take the easiest way out whether on Italy or on Russia', said a tired and gloomy Prime Minister.[34]

In spite of the apparent intimacy between the British and the Americans at the highest levels, there was of course little real institutional involvement. The British seemed to be unaware of the post-war planning effort going on in Washington and would have been surprised to read documents such as 'The Treatment of Italy', prepared at the end of August 1944. Here no mention is to be found of communism as a problem in Italian reality. Instead militarism is seen as enemy number one, understood as the tendency of small cliques to take control and use it to thrust Italy aggressively onto the international scene as a great power. To prevent this in future the experts looked not to a punitive peace treaty but to the 'political and economic recontruction of the nation', including:

... an expanding economy which will offer the Italian people genuine opportunities for their economic betterment . . . (by) the elimination of uneconomic activities, such as those which have grown out of concentration on production for war or out of the system of autarchy . . . (and the) return to a policy based on multilateral, non-discriminatory foreign trade.

The paper did begin to acknowledge that a period of transition might be necessary before the country could fully live up to this vision and that, since further disintegration would be 'disadvantageous', it might be necessary to 'undertake certain measures to meet emergency conditions . . . not in harmony with the long-term objectives'. Quite impractical proposals for relief, rehabilitation and reform followed.[35]

But the summer of 1944 saw the liberation of Rome and in its aftermath came the first journalistic descriptions of what was really happening in the country. 'Bankrupt Italy is capable of anything', declared a feature in the *Saturday Evening Post*, 'in which the American partner will put up four-fifths of the goods necessary to save the assets of the country, while the British partner will put up four-fifths of the brains and leadership'. All US policy consisted of, said the writer, was sending 2,000 calories per day per head and hoping there would not be a revolution. Italy was a 'test of the Allies' capacity to reorganise the Continent', asserted Anne McCormick in the *New York Times*, a test of 'the power of democracy to satisfy the elemental hungers of man for peace, work and bread'. No political or territorial settlement, no security organisation, meant anything while people were starving. The danger for Italy, as for all the other 'poor, broken nations of the Continent', was not that it would go Communist, 'not a violent but clearly directed shift from one system to another . . . [but] an uncontrolled breakdown of the whole social structure'. Both she and the State Department consultant emphasised at the end of September that confusion and resentment were spreading and everywhere people were asking 'what will America's policy be?'.[36]

The White House did announce a modest relief and reform package at the end of September 1944, just in time to catch Italian-American eyes before the November elections. The State Department talked of an investment in 'the development of democratic institutions and policies', while journals such as *Newsweek* spoke more explicitly about halting the 'drift towards communism' and concern over 'the mounting prestige of the USSR',[37] but observers were soon complaining that there was no change on the ground; that a gulf had opened up 'between visible American power and the purposes for which it was being used'. Typical was Herbert Matthews' late November protest in the *New York Times* that Allied rule was still that of the iron hand, while the British (who were assumed to be backing the Italian monarchy) as well as the

Americans were so afraid of revolution or civil strife that they would support the forces of conservatism against any supposed threat. Whatever Anglo-American wishes might be, Italy was inescapably a test case for the future of Europe.[38]

But it took a bruising row with the British over their intervention in a Rome cabinet crisis, a visit by Harry Hopkins to Rome and the prospect of the Yalta conference to make Washington develop a specific policy for Italian relief and rehabilitation. Yet American trade unionists on the spot were complaining that, as long as the Atlantic Charter lacked teeth, Italy was being handed over to the Communists; there was 'semblance of a concerted and constructive policy to cope with conditions' visible in practice, complained Sumner Welles in the *New York Herald Tribune*.[39] The controversial Congress representative from Connecticut, Mrs Clare Booth Luce, told a press conference early in the New Year that Italian people were 'literally dying of cold and starvation before your eyes by the thousand', to which the administration replied by stating that an expanded Allied supply programme to aid restoration of the Italian economy was now seen by all concerned to be 'advisable'.[40]

What this meant when liberation came was sending 2 million tons of wheat per month into western Europe for June, July and August, according to Henry Stimson. 'This', said the Secretary of War 'would be good psychology . . . We could turn the tide of communism in all those countries. Hoover stamped out communism in this way in central Europe.'[41] The United States did, of course, continue to provide relief supplies on a large if chaotic scale after the liberation, but there was no question of tackling communism in countries like Italy, France or Greece this way. A holding operation was all that could be tried while local political forces tried to assert some sort of control over the situation and until the Big Three could meet for a preliminary settling of accounts. The consequences of this hiatus were graphically described by Anne McCormick in mid-June in the *New York Times*:

> Italy has no ships, no material for reconstruction, no access to Lend-Lease, no assistance from UNRRA except to a limited number of children and displaced persons.
>
> The situation is so desperate that no party is willing to assume responsibility. It is very doubtful that any government could survive an election in present circumstances. And so far the occupying powers, Great Britain and the US, have apparently not decided on a policy towards Italy, beyond the elastic cover-all of 'military necessity'. They have not decided whether it is in their interests to help build up the country again or let 45m people, industrious, fundamentally peace-loving and friendly, sink to a level that will inevitably swing them away from the west towards the Balkans and into the Soviet orbit . . .[42]

But the army, the State Department and the Foreign Economic Administration (the agency nominally responsible for wartime economic operations overseas) were unable to formulate an effective policy on a joint basis or even agree on a name to lead US operations in Italy, so it was again left to the press to point to the next step forward for America in Italy. In a feature article entitled 'Italy Awaits Allied Help' which appeared in the *New York Herald Tribune* at the beginning of July, John Chabot Smith declared: 'Everyone said win the war first. Now no one knows what to do'. Smith's article is important as a signal of an important shift in thinking on economic problems in liberated Europe beginning to take place in US internationalist opinion at that time.

According to Smith, the objective circumstances were clear to all concerned: there was a general consensus that everything in Italy depended on US aid in economic and military terms, but the army had big plans to demobilise and/or send large contingents of its forces to the Pacific theatre. Those who had originally pressed for maintaining a strong US presence in Italy had been conservatives fearing mob rule and civil war, but now many high-level Americans were coming round to the same opinion. They were concerned, said Smith, that the forces of the Left sought totalitarian rule and might well provoke civil war to get it. As for the conservatives, who in the beginning had asked for nothing more than Allied charity, they were now more concerned with those conditions of poverty and civil war which fed Leftism: 'there is a growing disposition among some Italian and American officials to look deeper into the problems of economic reconstruction,' Smith reported, 'and into the possibilities of developing a permanently higher standard of living in Italy'. In Smith's opinion, instead of merely asking for large public loans, Italy might have done better to interest US businessmen in providing technical know-how and money, the essential resources necessary 'for rebuilding and developing Italy on a profit-making basis'. The essential political premises, of course, were stability and public order, so that the days of a 'hands-off' attitude on America's part were probably numbered. Many Italians and Americans, Smith concluded, 'would like to see the US take a more direct hand in Italian politics'.[43]

Looking deeper into the economics of reconstruction then, meant connecting up the long-standing plans for expansion everywhere with responses to the now generally recognised challenge of Leftism in Europe. Conceptually the shift was almost effortless, even too much so since the original distinctions made intuitively between stability (law, order, food and work), development (industrialisation) and expansion (raising living standards everywhere) disappeared as the cold war set in, not to be seen again until the late 1950s.[44] But politically and practically at least eighteen months would pass by before the United States was willing or able to take 'a more direct hand' in European politics—months of drama and confusion as America paid the price for 'putting off politics' till the end of the war. The Truman Doctrine and the Marshall Plan declared that the United States had now decided unequivocally to project its power abroad and had conceived a whole variety of means to do so, with short- and long-term applicability. The objectives were set out in a Marshall Plan propaganda booklet for the Italians in 1949 'A higher standard of living for the entire nation; maximum employment for workers and farmers; greater production', to be obtained by exploiting all their energies (increased productivity) and close economic collaboration (integration) between all the ERP countries.[45]

Notes

1. M.M. Postan, *An Economic History of Western Europe 1945–1967* (London, Methuen, 1967), pp. 22, 25, 48–49.
2. Charles S. Maier, 'The Two Postwar Eras and the Conditions for Stability in Twentieth Century Western Europe', *American Historical Review* Vol. 86 (1981), p. 346.
3. W.W. Rostow, *The Stages of Economic Growth* (Cambridge, Cambridge University Press, 1960), Chapter 6.
4. W. Reitzel, *The Mediterranean: Its Role in American Foreign Policy* (New York, Harcourt Brace, 1948), p. 150.
5. *Foreign Relations of the United States, 1945. The Conferences at Malta and Yalta* (Washington, U.S. Government Printing Office, 1955), p. 923.
6. State Dept. doc. n. CAC-248, 'The Treatment of Italy', 31 August 1944, in National Archives (NA), Record Group (RG) 59, Records of Harley A. Notter (Notter File).
7. In E.H. Carr, *Conditions of Peace* (New York, Macmillan, 1943), pp. 57–8.
8. Ibid.
9. Roosevelt and Hull cited in J.L. Gaddis (ed.), *The United States and the Origins of the Cold War 1941–1947* (New York, Columbia University Press, 1972), pp. 11, 19.
10. W. Lippmann, *The Method of Freedom* (New York, Macmillan, 1934), pp. 12–14, 36.
11. Charles S. Maier, 'The Politics of Productivity: Foundations of American International Economic Policy after World War II', in Peter J. Katzenstein (ed.), *Between Power and Plenty. Foreign Economic Policies of Advanced Industrial States* (Madison, University of Wisconsin Press, 1978), p. 28.
12. Precis of the Discussion of the General Advisory Committee on the Future Cultural Relations Program, 18 September 1941, in NA, RG 59, 'Notter File'.
13. Sumner Welles, *The Time for Decision* (New York, Harper, 1944), pp. 152–53.
14. A substantial selection of this material is available in Harley A. Notter, *Postwar Foreign Policy Preparation 1939–1945* (Washington, Department of State, 1949).

15. 'Progress Report on Postwar Programs', 1 September 1944, in NA, RG 59, 'Notter File'.
16. Committee on Territorial Problems, Minutes of Meeting of 12 February 1943, in NA, RG 59, op. cit.
17. 'Bases of Our Program for International Economic Cooperation', 22 October 1943, Memorandum of US Delegation to Moscow Conference, in NA, RG 59, op. cit.
18. See Sir Llewellyn Woodward, *British Foreign Policy in the Second World War* (London, HMSO, 1962), p. 446.
19. Advisory Committee on Postwar Foreign Policy, Political Subcommittee, Minutes of Meeting of 1 May 1943, in NA, RG 58, 'Notter File'.
20. Committee on European Regional Organisation, Minutes of Meeting of 4 June 1943, in NA, RG 50, op. cit.
21. Council on Foreign Relations: Studies of American Interests in the War and the Peace, Memorandum of Discussion, Political Group, P-B71, 'European Regionalism and Postwar World Organisation', 27 September 1943.
22. Committee on European Regional Organisation, Minutes of Meeting of 15 October 1943, in NA, RG 59, 'Notter File'.
23. Ibid., Also Regional Documents File, doc. R-62, 'How would a European full customs union affect the long-run economic interests of the US?' n.d., and R-63, 'How would the political unifications of Europe affect the interests of the US?', 13 October 1943, in NA, RG 59, op. cit.
24. Council on Foreign Relations, doc. P-B48, 'National Sovereignty and the International Tasks of the Postwar World', 31 August 1942, by Walter R. Sharp (a comprehensive paper anticipating many themes and objectives of postwar American foreign economic policy).
25. Greek case cited by Reitzel, *The Mediterranean*, op. cit., p. 145; Roosevelt quoted by Secretary of State Stettinius in Edward R. Stettinius, *Roosevelt and the Russians. The Yalta Conference* (New York, Doubleday, 1949), p. 180; French case discussed in State Department, Committee on Territorial Problems, doc. T-556, 'The Future Industrial Development of France: Problems and Prospects', 12 December 1944, in NA, RG 59, 'Notter File' (no reference exists in this document to the extensive discussions going on already in the French anti-Fascist movement on the country's postwar economic design).
26. Cited in Wray O. Candilis, *The Economy of Greece 1944–66. Efforts for Stability and Development* (New York, Praeger, 1968), p. 15.
27. See D.W. Ellwood, 'Al tramonto dell'Impero britannico: Italia e Balcani nella stragegia inglese, 1942–46', in *Italia Contemporanea*, n. 134 (1979); Ellwood, *Italy 1943–1945* (Leicester, Leicester University Press, 1985), p. 136.
28. State Department Committee on Territorial Problems, Subcommittee on Security Problems, Minutes of Meeting of 23 October 1942, in NA,RG 59, 'Notter File'. Part of the record of Taylor's travels at this time, including his written papers, is to be found in Ennio Di Nolfo (ed.), *Vaticano e Stati Uniti 1939–1952* (dalle carte di Myron C. Taylor), (Milan, Angeli, 1978), pp. 174–219.
29. State Department Committee on Territorial Problems, Minutes of Meeting of 18 December 1942, in NA, RG 59, 'Notter File'.

30. Report by Grady, 28 March 1944, in NA,RG 169; see Ellwood, *Italy 1943–1945*, op. cit., pp. 128–29.
31. Ibid., p. 129.
32. Ibid., Ch. 6, on particular pp. 127–28, 130.
33. Ibid., p. 224.
34. Ibid.; Minutes of meeting at Foreign Office—Macmillan, 30 May 1945, with comment by Churchill, 10 June 1945, in Public Record Office (PRO), Foreign Office General Correspondence (FOGC), ZM/3140/1/22.
35. See note 6; discussed also in Ellwood, *Italy 1943–1945*, op. cit., pp. 130–31.
36. *Saturday Evening Post*, 23 September 1944; *New York Times*, 7, 9 and 11 September 1944; cf. Ellwood, *Italy 1943–1945*, op. cit., pp. 112–13.
37. cit. in Reitzel, *The Mediterranean*, op. cit., pp. 32–33.
38. *New York Times*, 26 November 1944; cf. Ellwood, *Italy 1943–1945*, op. cit., p. 119.
39. *New York Times*, 31 January 1945; *New York Herald Tribune*, 31 January 1945; cf. Ellwood, *Italy 1943–1945*, op. cit., p. 170.
40. Ibid., p. 169.
41. Cited in G. Kolko, 'The Politics of War', in *The World and United States Foreign Policy 1943–1945* (New York, Random House, 1968), p. 498.
42. *New York Times*, 18 June 1945.
43. *New York Herald Tribune*, 8 July 1945; cf. Ellwood, *Italy 1943–1945*, op. cit., pp. 234–35.
44. Cf. Rostow, *Stages of Economic Growth*, op. cit., Ch. 9.
45. In D.W. Ellwood, 'From Re-Education to the Selling of the Marshall Plan in Italy' in N. Pronay and K. Wilson (eds), *The Political Re-education of Italy and her Allies after World War II* (London, Croom Helm, 1985), p. 231.

Index

Austria 89, 143, 146, 171

Belgium 13–14, 56–8, 71, 106,
112–32, 133–45, 146, 156, 159,
164, 165
Beneš, E. 167, 170, 176–7, 179, 180
Bottai, G. 30–1, 34–6, 41
Briand, A. 20–1, 23, 161
Brouckère, C. 114, 128–9, 136
Bulgaria 24, 96, 178, 182

Chamberlain, N. 23–4
Churchill, W. 15, 25, 157, 159, 160–6,
190
Coudenhove-Kalergi, R. 20, 161–2
Czechoslovakia 12, 87–97, 158–9,
160, 167, 170–2, 176–81, 190

Daitz, W. 88
Dimitrov, G. 172–3, 175, 177–8
Doriot, J. 58

Eden, A. 160–5

Finland 88–9
France 20–1, 50, 52, 56–60, 80,
89–90, 106, 126, 138, 143–50,
156–7, 164, 167, 179, 190
Funk, W. 27, 33, 35, 88

Gasperi, A. 148–9
Germany 4, 9–11, 16, 18–26, 31–9,
46–97, 102–4, 106, 124, 126,
143–9

Goebbels, J. 23, 67, 69, 80–1, 86
Gomułka, W. 175–80
Gottwald, K. 170–1, 177, 179
Greece 24, 35, 37, 158–9, 191
Gutt, C. 126, 136

Hitler, A. 10, 15, 21–4, 35, 38–9,
49–50, 67–9, 78, 156–8, 177
Hopkins, H. 159, 166, 195
Hull, C. 159–61, 187
Hungary 39, 46–7, 89, 95–6, 167,
180–1

Italy 27–45, 75, 89, 143, 145–50, 164,
191–6

Kleffens, B. 135–9

Leo XIII 144–5, 147

Maniulsky, I. 170, 173
Mikołajczyk, S. 176, 179
Molotov, V. 158–9
Mussert, A. 58
Mussolini, B. 11, 28, 34–8, 101, 145

Netherlands 12–13, 56–8, 81–2,
98–111, 133–41, 145–6, 156, 159,
164

Pierlot, H. 113, 126, 128, 135
Poland 90–1, 158, 160, 172, 174–6,
178–9, 190

Quisling, V. 58, 73

Rens, J. 113, 114, 125–6
Ribbentrop, J. 39, 85, 158
Riccardi, R. 32–4
Romania 39, 46–7, 87, 178
Roosevelt, F.D. 24, 69, 70, 74, 77, 81,
    157, 159–62, 182, 188, 191–2

Sauckel, F. 57, 65
Sikorski, W. 159, 174
Soviet Union 14–15, 24, 46–50,
    52–3, 66–7, 80–81, 156–67,
    169–81
Spaak, P.H. 113, 126, 135–9, 165
Speer, A. 57, 65
Stalin, J. 15, 24, 81, 158, 160, 162,
    165–6, 173–7, 188
Stresemann, G. 20–3

Sturzo, L. 145, 148

United Kingdom 14–15, 23–5, 89,
    106, 118, 123, 126, 135–6, 138,
    156–67, 191–3, 195
United States 15–16, 24–5, 66–86,
    115–16, 118–19, 123, 156–63,
    166–7, 184–99
Welles, S. 73, 161, 188, 195
Wirsing, G. 75–8

Yugoslavia 24, 35, 87, 91, 96, 158,
    170–4, 178

Zeeland, P. 112–15, 119, 121, 123,
    125–6
Zoretti, L. 59–60